MARION M

ALSO BY WILLIAM H. JOHNSON

Hal Trosky:
A Baseball Biography (McFarland, 2017)

MARION MOTLEY

A Life In and Beyond Football

WILLIAM H. JOHNSON

McFarland & Company, Inc., Publishers
Jefferson, North Carolina

ISBN (print) 978-1-4766-8912-8
ISBN (ebook) 978-1-4766-4716-6

LIBRARY OF CONGRESS AND BRITISH LIBRARY
CATALOGUING DATA ARE AVAILABLE

Library of Congress Control Number 2022047078

Front cover: Cleveland Browns fullback Marion Motley, 1948
(Cleveland State University)

Printed in the United States of America

*McFarland & Company, Inc., Publishers
Box 611, Jefferson, North Carolina 28640
www.mcfarlandpub.com*

To my family, immediate and extended,
and to those friends who might as well
be family (you know who you are).

Table of Contents

Acknowledgments

Capturing Marion Motley's entire story two decades after his death, since most of those who played with or against him have passed away, is a Sisyphean task at best and an impossible one at worst. This attempt has been imaginable only with the help of a number of individuals, along with access to repositories of news stories yet to be digitized.

From the outset, the most important contributors to this project have been Bianca Motley Bloom and Joe Dose, both children of Motley's youngest son Raymond, Aldreeta Kennedy, daughter of son George, and Marion's eldest living niece, Candice Washington. Their willingness to make themselves available, and to answer the random email or telephone question about the family, has been useful beyond words. Equally important has been their tacit approval of the project, of this attempt to tell the story of their famous family member. If this narrative meets their expectations, it will be a success.

Ted Bowersox and Dave Jingo were instrumental as well. They know the Canton McKinley football story verbatim, and their 2017 film *Timeless Rivals* is a terrific rendering of the entire, storied history of the story of professional football and the ongoing high school rivalry between the McKinley Bulldogs and the Massillon Tigers. The word "rivalry" is perhaps a bit soft as a descriptor, akin to calling Mt. Everest a "hill," but this film tells a story difficult to find anywhere else. Both men have been encouraging at every step.

Guy Clifton is quite possibly the most knowledgeable Nevada sports historian who ever lived, certainly that I have ever met. Not only did he provide a great deal of insight and chronology into Motley's college years, but he shared his primary source material without hesitation, much of which I have yet to find anywhere else.

Jon Kendle, Director of Archives and Information at the Pro Football Hall of Fame in Canton, Ohio, despite the burden of supporting two years of player inductions, a Hall of Fame game, and the 2021 NFL draft, all under the cloud of a global pandemic, was kind enough to share the entire Motley clippings file from the Ralph Wilson, Jr., Pro Football Research and Preservation Center. Recounting this story would have been impossible without the files and the audio recordings of Motley from 50 years ago.

In exploring the early days of Marion Motley's football life, the Stark County (Ohio) Public Library provided access to the microfilm history of the *Canton Repository*, the local newspaper, and Bailey Yoder, Curator of Football Heritage at the Massillon Museum, graciously took time out of her schedule to speak and to expand my knowledge of Paul Brown and his life. To understand Marion Motley's career and life is to understand the role Paul Brown played in both. The Museum is a terrific resource, and Yoder's work there is not just compelling, it makes the Massillon Museum well worth a day trip in northern Ohio.

Peter Elwell, at the Sports Research Center of the Cleveland Public Library, not only helped propel this project forward, but he connected me with the research staff in the library's Center for Local & Global History. Their holdings of the *Cleveland Plain Dealer* and the archives of the Black newspaper *The Cleveland Call and Post*, filled in many gaps in the story that could not have been filled elsewhere. This project would not have been possible without their assistance.

There are numerous books—all listed in the bibliography—that contained either nuggets of information about Motley's career, or reference lists that opened even more research avenues. Oral histories taken by Stuart Leuthner and Myron Cope are notable, but every one that I found added to the depth of this biography. The *Akron Beacon Journal* and the *Canton Repository* offered the most comprehensive body of reporting on Motley throughout football and beyond, but a number of periodicals contributed stories and insights to this book, and they are listed as well.

Mike Holt freely gave his time and attention to reading and discussing various drafts, and his direct, honest feedback is the difference between what I originally wrote and what you are reading. Any faults in the narrative are mine, but the degree to which Marion Motley's story has any coherence is largely due to his contribution.

My daughter, a blossoming writer and historian in her own right, set the performance bar for this narrative too high for me to jump, but I

Acknowledgments

hope this has at least come close. The encouragement from her and my son have been enormously important throughout.

Finally, my wife Chris kept the manuscript moving forward during those times when courage flagged in the face of the magnitude of the story to be told, of the need to treat Marion Motley's life with respect and equity, and of the effort necessary to cross the publishing finish line. Without her patience and support, the mere notion of writing Marion Motley's life story would have passed without a second thought.

Preface

Professional football is a game, a lucrative one to be sure, but a game that thrives at an intersection of commercial marketing, gambling, social interaction, and media. Over the second half of the 20th century, and now well into the 21st, it has transcended the status of mere sport and has become an integrated part of the figurative American way of life. This conquest was not a revolution per se, but rather a slow and steady takeover. Nineteen fifty-eight is generally acknowledged as the year that the NFL and national television entered a common law marriage, and from that point forward, the game has claimed an increasingly large slice of the American psyche. For more than a century, baseball has often been regarded as the National Pastime. Since the 1960s, though, football has become inextricably linked to America with such frequency that it has become, in truth, not a pastime but instead a National Obsession.

Under the figurative "big tent" of such a national sport, themes emerge and reveal themselves, and events unfold that transcend simple line scores and generic fandom. Sport and life outside the game merge. Race relations in the United States, as a theme, exist in another of those intersections of sport and culture. The game of baseball has rightly prided itself on the sport's collective history in correcting six decades of racial negligence. Between 1887 and 1946, no Black athletes were permitted in what was referred to as the organized, major leagues of the professional game. The Negro Leagues were a shining counterpoint to that imposed segregation, a testament to the importance of sport and the indefatigable nature of the human spirit, and they ultimately helped carve a path for Jackie Robinson to walk in 1947. Football offers no such analog for the segregated sports era.

Professional football, in the form recognizable today, was organized in 1920, when professional baseball was already 50 years old. In

1

1945, it too enforced a stringent racial exclusion on a national basis. While baseball began to famously desegregate in 1947 with Jackie Robinson, professional football had actively and effectively cracked that ceiling eight months earlier, in 1946. That year, Bill Willis, Kenny Washington, and Woody Strode stood at the vanguard of the cadre that began to re-integrate professional football. That fourth member, Marion Motley, perhaps even more than Jackie Robinson in baseball, went on to enjoy an athletic career that ranks among the greatest ever in the annals of his sport.

In researching Motley's story, it quickly became apparent that it would be difficult to keep any biography of Motley from morphing into a hagiography, a filmy, feel-good story about one of the greatest players in the history of the American game. The challenge in writing from the perspective of an observer, and not a fan, created a continuing conflict throughout the development process. In a 1988 book, *That Noble Dream: The "Objectivity Question" and the American Historical Profession*, Peter Novick argues that objective history has never existed, and that such a goal can never be reached. Facts, he argues, are beyond interpretation, but historical narrative, such as this story, emerges from a selective presentation of those facts. Choosing some facts and ignoring others is the essence of persuasion. Some facts are used, some are ignored, so true objectivity is impossible. That stipulated, this book's central argument, offered as objectively as possible, is that Motley's story is valuable and ought to be remembered.

In the figurative library of American history, there is an empty slot on the shelf where the biography of Marion Motley should sit. Motley's was a life that can still be instructive, in a historical sense, but can also inspire. It is a story worth remembering.

Introduction

Memory is the thread of personal identity, history of public identity. Men who have achieved any civic existence at all must, to sustain it, have some kind of history, though it may be history that is partly mythological or simply untrue. That the business of history always involves a subtle transaction with civic identity has long been understood, even in America where the sense of time is shallow.[1]

So wrote one of the giants of the profession of historian, Richard Hofstadter, in 1968. The scope of applicability of the words is wide, ranging from Hofstadter's personal political leanings all the way to the intersecting topics that include those of sport and racial equity in the United States. Marion Motley achieved his civic fame on the football fields of the 1930s, 1940s, and 1950s, and his public identity, that of a Hall of Fame athlete, is part of the story that follows. His private identity, the memory of him, is similarly fascinating and relevant, and in a real-world context is perhaps even more valuable than his football story. The intent of this book is to cobble together his history as can be documented, not exclusively limited to the age-edited memories of others, and to be as true and authentic and respectful of not only the athlete, but of the man as well.

Marion Motley was a sensational football player. After his on-field days were done, though, he lived a life in two separate worlds. One of those was the glorious sphere of an honored man. Motley became only the second Black player ever to be enshrined in the Pro Football Hall of Fame in his hometown of Canton, Ohio. He signed autographs, appeared at store openings and events, lent his name to fundraising efforts, and inspired awe in those who had watched him or heard the stories of his feats, especially when they finally had the chance to meet their hero in person, perhaps ask for a signature or even a picture. Over the succeeding years, newspaper stories often included short retrospectives of the "where are they now" variety, never letting Motley the Football Immortal stray too far from the public—perhaps mythological—history.

The other world in which Motley walked, a world more familiar to the rest of us modest mortals who only know football as outside observers, was one very much in keeping with his times. In 1960, five years after hanging up his cleats and taking off his helmet for the last time, Motley returned to life as just another man. He was a Black man at that, without a college degree, a man trying to keep a roof over his family and some food on the dinner table. He could be overlooked in that world, forgotten even, by the same troupe that held such sacred recollections of his football career. Hofstadter might have written that Motley's identity was, to onlookers, neither neatly bounded nor easily understood. After his glory days, Motley took a series of relatively menial jobs, in the era before money and sports memorabilia colluded in a profit-making construct, and he was glad to have them. Marion Motley was not afraid to work, and he refused to live solely in his honored past. In that dichotomy, simultaneous fame and obscurity, a profile barely recognizable in a more recent era of social media and the ubiquity of celebrity, he has become an even more fascinating story.

First, though, appreciating Motley as a football player is vital to understanding the rest of his story. There is a picture, published somewhere in 1948, of four Cleveland Browns football players, not uniformed and clearly having fun with a photographer before practice, sprinting in a row toward the camera. On the left is Edgar Jones, the talented running back from Missouri and a star on the early Browns. Next to him is a lithe, normal-sized human being, hamming it up for the camera with an open-mouthed, wild-eyed expression of contrived fury as a caricature for the photo. That is Otto Graham, a Hall of Fame quarterback and longtime teammate of Motley's. Next to Graham is the most intimidating image in the frame, 6'2", 238-pound Marion Motley, wearing a white tee-shirt and carrying a football with a sober mien that suggests more "impersonal businessman" than elite game-changing athlete. The shoulders appear unnaturally wide in contrast to the other players, certainly so in that era before regular weightlifting took hold in football, and they are squared to the camera. To the viewer, it is the same, naturally intimidating look, minus the jersey, the shoulder pads, and the helmet, that a linebacker might have seen when confronting, and contemplating tackling, the ball carrier. He appears to be one of the biggest, most athletic men imaginable, and in the camera eye he is charging directly at you.

For perspective, watch a sprinter on a track from up close, from the front. As they approach, you begin to feel the uncomfortable sense of the impending collision, of speed and bulk charging toward someone attacking from the opposite direction. The idea of jumping in front of a human being—of any size—running at full speed, certainly one capable of covering 100 yards in ten seconds flat, instantly seems like a bad one, like trying to catch a cannonball that had been fired from hundreds of yards away. Imagine not only putting your face, your knees, your entire core, into that runner, but charging at him yourself, at whatever velocity you might generate. Easier from a distant and relatively benign observer's perch, but as the milliseconds tick by, the idea of trying to physically impose your will on that runner, the one coming at you, becomes reality, and beyond daunting. There will be damage. Pain for sure. Maybe blood. Now, imagine that sprinter and you are on a football field, and he is one of the four or five largest people on that field. He is bigger than you, as well as most of the slower linemen that clog the middle of the various formations, but he is also as fast, or faster, than all but the quickest defensive backs on your side. And he has a football and an unquenchable, instinctive need to score. And he's coming directly at you. At full gallop. Just jump in there and just try to slow him down, much less tackle him. That was the problem that Marion Motley created every time he took the field, on almost every play, at least before the undefeated tandem of injury and age eventually won out and slowed Motley the way no human ever could. Yet before that moment, before the clock struck midnight, Motley had many days that were all his.

On several occasions, *Sports Illustrated* writer Paul Zimmerman called Motley the greatest football player in the history of the game. Not the greatest running back, he stipulated, but the greatest player, period.[2] Marion Motley also played defense whenever called upon, and Paul Brown wrote in his autobiography, "I've always believed that Motley could have gone into the Hall of Fame solely as a linebacker if we had used him only at that position. He was as good as our great ones."[3] Beyond those skills, he was also a tremendous blocker,[4] and an even better runner, averaging 5.7 yards per carry over a nine-season professional career.[5] The latter mark has twice been surpassed in the entire history of professional football, by Michael Vick and Randall Cunningham, rushing quarterbacks who were often able to exploit defensive lapses and unique in-game situations. ESPN named Motley #74 on their All-Century football team, despite the limited access to films of his play. So stunning are some of his on-field performances that his contributions simply cannot be ignored. He is, much like baseball's Oscar Charleston, one of the greatest players in the history of the sport, yet virtually anonymous to an overwhelming number of fans of the game.

Appreciating Motley's football career, his relevance in the game's collective history, is a challenge. In addition to the ESPN honor, he was named to the NFL's all-time roster of the 100 greatest players in professional football's history.[6] During the telecast introducing the team, Bill Belichick spoke well about the player and the man, but Motley's segment was brief. His summary on the NFL's website is similarly abbreviated and focuses almost exclusively on Motley's running achievements. There is a figurative hat tip to his abilities as a "deadly pass blocker," and an acknowledgment that he "played linebacker early in career," but the NFL clearly places him on the list almost entirely due to his running skills.

Sports data analyst and well-respected historian Sean Lahman, in his *Pro Football Historical Abstract*, noted that Motley is tough to judge comparatively since he did not start playing as a professional until he was 25 years old, and because his first four years were spent in a rival league. Lahman cites a sampling of quotes by Motley's contemporaries as testament to his abilities, including one by Hall of Fame receiver Dante Lavelli: "Motley really built the passing attack for the Browns because of his blocking."[7] As Lahman concludes, "Motley basically invented the modern fullback position, the idea of a versatile power back that also caught passes." Finally, he circled back to Paul Zimmerman and his belief that Marion Motley was the greatest football player ever: "The more I think about it, the more I think that Zimmerman might just be right about Motley."[8]

Marion Motley led both the All-America Football Conference (AAFC) and the National Football League (NFL) in rushing yards in different seasons, helped lead the Cleveland Browns to four AAFC titles and one NFL championship, yet perhaps most importantly, he was one of four professional football players that ended the sport's 12-year de facto ban on Black players in the game in 1946, the year before Jackie Robinson did the same in major league baseball.

Introduction

Although the sport had not been exempt from collectively segregationist attitudes in the early 20th century, for a time football was a more inclusive game than professional baseball. Iowa's Duke Slater, a 2020 Pro Football Hall of Fame inductee, and Fritz Pollard (HoF, 2005) were the first Black players signed after the American Pro Football Association was established in 1920. By 1926, there were just five African Americans on the field, and each year or two the number shrank until Oregon's Joe Lillard arrived in 1932. Lillard became the 12th Black player in the league, but by the next season he and Pittsburgh lineman Ray Kemp were the last two remaining Black players on the professional grid. For reasons neither clear nor defensible, Lillard was arbitrarily accused of being a poor teammate by his team's ownership, and simply released. After that 1933 season, due in large part to the efforts of Boston (then Washington) Redskins owner George Preston Marshall, the NFL was populated exclusively by Caucasian athletes. For the next 13 years, professional football in the United States was a White-only game. In 1946, Marion Motley and three others broke that exclusionary barrier, this time forever.

Following his playing career, though, and despite the magnitude of his achievements, Motley returned to a non-football life in America. In a sort of reversed rags to riches story, Motley transitioned from being a nationally known superstar to a living embodiment of Ralph Ellison's *Invisible Man.* Over time, though, the collective perspective cleared, and a degree of Motley's celebrity returned. It was an extraordinary life, albeit one lived—by his own admission—by an ordinary man. As in many such stories the hero emerges from the humblest of origins and relative anonymity.

Marion Motley's life story is no exception.

Early Years

Motley's Great Northern Migration

Marion Motley's biography, his contributions, can neither be understood nor fully appreciated without first considering the social and physical contexts in which he lived. Motley's story began in Georgia in 1920, fewer than 60 years removed from the U.S. Civil War, and on the heels of the great influenza epidemic of 1918–1920. The nation had retreated from war in Europe and was embarking on a decade of stability and prosperity, the "Roaring '20s" as they have come to be known. As for many Americans, the Motley family lived precariously from day to day, but on the cusp of vast change that evolved throughout the decade. Their family values were shaped by a world in which hard work was expected, even essential, and in which opportunity for success was not equally spread across the population.

The first thing nearly everyone seems to notice or, more accurately, cannot escape when venturing outdoors in the summertime in southern Georgia, even those born and raised in the region, is the heat. It's not the gentle, Spanish-moss-swaying-in-the-live-oak-trees type of summer heat that one might imagine from the pages of Faulkner or Tennessee Williams, warm and moist, inviting romance and contemplation. Instead, this heat immediatcly soaks into the bones. Though it is not malevolent by design, it is still evil and everywhere, almost instantly sapping strength, the will to move, sending everyone it touches in search of shade and a fan or an air conditioner and a cold drink.

The summer heat in the area that includes southeast Alabama, the Florida panhandle, and southwest Georgia is different from that in the desert. That region in Georgia, of which the city of Albany remains the largest town, has always been the least populated section of the state. The land is flat and fertile, nurturing cotton and peanuts and lumber into tidy profits for the shrewder farmers, even if achieving that end entails brutal work in the wind-less fields. The heat and humidity linger, inescapable for months at a time. Stand outside for more than a couple of minutes, and the sweat becomes palpable, starting in the normal places on the body, but soon covering the forehead and face, dripping down the back, then even lower, and soaking every fiber of clothing. That perpetual dead calm in the summer, even close to the nearby Flint River, affords no respite from both the soaking, soul-sucking temperatures, or from the seemingly infinite waves of gnats and other tiny pests that ride the muggy air into mouths, eyes, ears, even nostrils. This is home to the "Georgia Wave," a physical demonstration in which shaking an open hand in front of your face isn't necessarily a friendly greeting to a passerby, but a survival mechanism to clear the tiny bugs from the immediate proximity and to briefly fan the sweat from the eyes.

The town of Albany is about 80 miles from Columbus, 150 from Atlanta, 90 from both Macon and Tallahassee, Florida, and 85 miles from Dothan, Alabama. It is, in short, the biggest little city in a yawning, empty plot of sun-soaked farmland. This was the province in which John Henry Motley, and his wife, Ada, lived in 1899. Motley, a mulatto sharecropper, farmed rented land nearby, and Ada worked a small, private garden farm for vegetables, nuts, and other essential staples of life.[1] The Motleys had given birth to a total of eight children, but only two survived beyond adolescence, Shakvol (also written as Shakeville and Shakeful in various census documents and records), who was born in late 1899, and Annettie, in 1909. Shakvol was raised to support the family, as were all boys of that station and in those times, and after the fourth grade, worked exclusively with his father on their rented farm on the outskirts of Albany.[2] Sometime around 1919, the younger Motley married Blanche Jones, a local girl, and they soon gave birth to their first son.

Marion Motley (no middle name) was born on either June 5, or June 10, 1920, in a home in or adjacent to Albany.[3] In various sources his place of birth is listed either as Albany (draft registration) or Leesburg (death certificate), Georgia, and while the two towns are just under ten miles apart, they are in different counties. As no specific birth record exists in either Dougherty (Albany) or Lee (Leesburg) county archives, the residence of Marion's father is the more likely birthplace. Marion was not the only child that Shakvol and Blanche greeted, though, as

1. Early Years

they would also later have a daughter, Dorothy (1924), along with sons William Countee—later known to much of the family as Uncle Bill—(1926) and Clarence (1928).

Jackie Robinson, baseball's future racial barrier buster, was born in Cairo, Georgia, a town roughly 50 miles south of Albany. The Robinsons were sharecroppers as well, and a year after Jack was born, the entire family packed up and moved to California. In 1923, in the heyday of post–World War I America, after the 1918 influenza epidemic but before the economy shattered in the Great Depression, Shakvol and Blanche joined what is now referred to as the Great Northern Migration. Rather than go west like the Robinsons, though, the Motleys packed up young Marion and moved, along with some other, extended family members, to Canton, Ohio, where Shakvol took a job in a steel mill.

The rationale for the move, for why the Motleys left southwest Georgia for northeastern Ohio, are not documented, but there are some relatively obvious possibilities. One was for the money. Agricultural work in the South involved long days and seasons, out in that relentless and often unforgiving sun, while relying on the ground, the weather, and all the other potential farm maladies to cooperate to produce enough to barely get by. Every blistering summer was followed by a winter of uncertainty, and that by the prospect of repeating the cycle the next spring. When the first wave of the migration started, around 1916, the average salary in the industrial jobs in the northern part of the nation was two to three times what a man could earn working the land in the South.[4]

Shakvol Motley's new job in the Ohio steel mill was typical of those available to Black men of the time in that it was low paying and low status. In his case Motley was hired as an unskilled molder, pouring molten metal into various containers, skimming flux metal, and breathing clouds of silica dust and the array of other, more toxic fumes. It was brutally hot and often deadly work, but in contrast to farming, there was occasional respite from the heat, and the pay was much better than he had as a sharecropper. In Ohio, in the mill, a man also did not have to worry about weather and bugs and rain to feed his growing family or keep a roof over their heads. "While economic causes are very important," George Haynes wrote in 1917, "let us not blink at the fact that there are other powerful influences that are moving the Negroes from the rural districts to southern cities and from the South to the North. In the cities the Negro feels greater protection for his life and for his hard

11

earned although limited property; in the northern city he has a feeling of greater security than in the southern city."[5]

The other reason for the Motley's northern migration may well have been rooted in the virulent racism that oozed throughout the southern region. It was inescapable, it was omnipresent, and it was almost impossible to overcome. Overtly racist attitudes were not necessarily inculcated throughout the national culture, but in that time, there was an undeniable and palpable level of irrational bigotry against other races, most of it targeted at the Negro race. There were social structures that arguably made racism a natural, default attitude for Caucasians in that time. This biography is not, and never was, intended to serve as any sort of exploration of the legacy effects of the institution of slavery in the United States, nor of the definition or application of the term racism and the larger influence of that word in the nation's history. Marion Motley, before and after his football career, was a Black man in America, and the events in his life are matters of record. To reduce his life story to mere evidence in any aspect of the ongoing (likely pre-dating recorded history) discussion of the role of race in a particular society is to presume that national culture can be reduced in the same manner. That is a naïve and useless, perhaps even harmful, presumption, one that diminishes all humans, so it is not part of this biography. That acknowledged, the presence of some level undefined racial discord in the history of the United States is undeniable, even if few agree on a definition of the word or the relative ubiquity of inequality based on skin pigmentation.

At the end of the United States' civil war in 1865, the country enjoyed a brief moment of opportunity to change course, to reject the old thinking, and in places like Beaufort, South Carolina, to embrace a more egalitarian society free of racial division. That moment passed, and some communities began to enact repressive laws like the Black Codes, rules specifically intended to restrict the new-found liberty of the freed slaves, but which resonated across the entire Negro race. The post–Reconstruction "Jim Crow" laws, the social boundaries that kept White people in a collective position of presumptive superiority, were actually born in the northeastern part of the United States,[6] but like a virus, those rules found the warm Southern states a much better place to thrive.

In the mid–1870s, still close to the end of the American Civil War, Blacks and Whites in the reunited South were often equally poor, and there are numerous examples of racial parity at local levels. Black elected representatives and legislators, and White constituents, were not unheard of in the Southern states, but such was abolished with the arrival of Jim Crow in the region. By 1896, the U.S. Supreme Court ruling in *Plessy v. Ferguson* instituted a doctrine that separate but equal facilities and opportunities among Whites and Blacks were not only acceptable, but legally mandated. Such was the culture throughout America at the end of the 19th century.

By 1910, "Jim Crow" and all the associated perniciousness was alive and well in the South, as was the omnipresent specter of lynch mobs. In 1916, for example, in Albany, 17-year-old Shakvol Motley had suffered, along with his predominantly Black community, through the lynching of six Black men who had been accused (not convicted) of killing a sheriff. A local, White resident had tricked the jail house guard into opening the door to the building where the suspects were incarcerated one evening, and the mob burst through and dragged the men off in a 15-car convoy. The Black men were recovered the next morning, hanging from trees just across a river.[7] There were so many examples of that sort of behavior, like another 1922 lynching in Hot Springs, Arkansas, in which citizens brazenly broke into the local jail, took a man, and hung him in the center of town. The newspaper report was almost dismissive, written as if such actions were not just legal but warranted.[8]

The net effect of the tactic was that the White majority exercised a sort of consistent repression of many, if not most, Black families. There are images of parades of Ku Klux Klan members in hoods and robes, parading by torchlight through Southern communities, unmistakable warnings of the consequences of simply being a Negro in the South. Collectively, these types of events amalgamated into a visual and visceral slice of that American South, writ large, in 1922.

Roosevelt "Rosey" Grier's story corroborates the existence of such attitudes. The famous L.A. Ram, from their "Fearsome Foursome" defensive line of the 1960s, and a three-time All-Pro before in injury forced his retirement into television, was born just over a decade after Motley, in Cuthbert, Georgia. Cuthbert is 45 miles directly west of Motley's birthplace in Albany, and Grier's stories from his youth provide some context about the world the Motleys left behind, and the rationale for Shakvol and Blanche's risky move. Grier's memoir is a relevant generalization of life for Black families in Georgia in the first half of the 20th century. "Poppa was a farmer, and life was hard.... Most black farmers were sharecroppers ... the sharecropper paid the landowner at least half and often all the crops he could grow. It was a system that perpetuated many of the patterns that had prevailed during the slavery days."⁹

Grier described his own perceptions of the time, a time and place in which Blacks deferred on the sidewalk to Whites, and endured the reality of segregated drinking fountains, restrooms, restaurants, and schools. It was a time almost beyond the imagination of those born after 1970 or so, but it was daily life for the Motleys and their neighbors. For Shakvol and Blanche, and their family, the unknown of Ohio was safer than the known of the Deep South. He may well have simply decided that working right next to liquid steel in a foundry five or six days a week was at least safer than grinding out a life of farming by day and fearing by night, and was an acceptable price to pay for escaping that cloud of oppression.

In terms of the physical environment that shaped Marion Motley's infancy and early life, the move from the Deep South to the industrial North critically influenced both his development and his perception of the world. Once the Motley family was safely ensconced in Ohio, they settled into a desegregated neighborhood near the steel mill in Canton. Their house, on Eighth Street and Madison SE (they moved a few years later to 10th and Lafayette SE), was certainly not opulent, but it was comfortable. Motley later said, "I was raised in a good family, and I was raised around whites. We never had any problems. Most of the neighborhood was Italian. We all played together, ran around together. If you were at someone's house and it was time to eat, they fed all of the kids. It didn't matter if you were black or white."¹⁰

By the early 1930s, swirling in the auger of the Great Depression, as Ohio's unemployment rate approached 40 percent and many families struggled simply to feed themselves, amid all of that associated turmoil, the Motley family survived.¹¹ Shakvol Motley's decision to move north a decade before, to the harsh but stable job in the steel mills, proved prescient. Their relative security also allowed Marion's athletic gifts to blossom during those school years.

Even as a young boy, Marion was physically larger and stronger than most his age. It is an article of faith for just about any athletic coach, in any sport, that size and natural athleticism are two qualities that exist beyond the coach's power. Speed cannot be taught, but it can be improved. Strength training can add muscle. Flexibility and balance both increase over time with enough effort. But size and the intangibles of athletic genius are innate. Marion Motley possessed both in wonderful excess.

"When I started playing football in Canton, Ohio, there weren't that many black kids playing, and you had to be three times better than the white kids to make the team," Motley told Stuart Leuthner, in the latter's fabulous collection of oral histories of early football stars. "I was the only one in my family who played sports, and I almost didn't get to do it either. When I went out for junior high football, they didn't give me a suit, so I stood around for two weeks in a pair of World War I khaki pants my uncle gave me, waiting for a chance to play. Three days before our first game the coach asked, 'Who hasn't been in yet?' I said, 'Me,' and they put me in on defense."[12]

Without pads, the coaches did not feel any obligation to give the big, Black teenager an opportunity, but once he got his chance, he made the most of it. "I was playing tackle, and they were really going to use me for fodder because I didn't even have any pads on. Well, nobody could block me. I was knocking everybody down and broke up every play they tried." After wreaking havoc on the other players as a defender, the coach asked him where he'd been. "I said," Motley told Leuthner, "I've been standing right here." He told the manager to make sure I got some equipment the next day.[13]

Motley excelled on the track and on the basketball court as well, but it was his football prowess that dazzled teammates, opponents, and spectators. His school teams were integrated, or at least desegregated, but that could not free him from the burden of the occasionally overt racism whenever he took the field. He felt like he needed to be better than the White players, and when they travelled to away games, often ran into opponents that could not get past the skin pigmentation.[14] As a rule, that sort of behavior tended to lead to extra physical contact between Motley and the offender(s), none of which fazed the big running back in the slightest. "If you weren't hurting somebody, they wouldn't let you play and it made you so mad you ended up taking it out on somebody. I had a friend ahead of me in high school, and he was a very light skinned guy. They were playing some team in southern Ohio, and the guy he was playing against said, 'Hey, I hear you got a n***** on this team. Where is he? When is that n***** coming in the game?' My friend didn't say anything, but he sure beat that guy's ass during the game."[15]

15

The Motley family was closely knit, and enthusiastically supported Marion's sports accomplishments. Blanche, the loving, but strict, matriarch marched Shakvol and the boys to the Shiloh Baptist church in Canton every Sunday. She was tough, but full of love for her entire, extended family. Motley's niece Candice Washington (Clarence's daughter) remembers that, even in later years, Blanche could still be stern with her boys even though the latter were fully grown men with families of their own.

Clarence, the youngest Motley brother, was not yet a teenager when Marion played at McKinley. Since he was not a student, he was not allowed to ride the school's bus to the elder brother's football games, even though he enjoyed just watching his brother play and hearing the crowds cheer Marion's name. This did not stop the enterprising Motley boys. On more than one occasion, Clarence described how he would stand outside the bus, near the back, as the team boarded to go to away games. With the coaches distracted, ensuring all the players were present, Marion and a couple of the other boys would pull Clarence through a rear window, and then he'd hide under a bus seat for the trip. Getting off the bus was easy once the team had headed to the field, and they'd simply reverse the process going home.

Canton McKinley High School played a schedule comprising local rivals, but also included the occasional cross-state trip to take on the better schools from the southern part of Ohio. Along with Massillon, they routinely competed against Erie East, Washington High School, Steubenville High, Alliance, Wellsville and Warren. Motley

Marion Motley as a senior at Canton-McKinley High School, 1938.

16

and quarterback Jack Barthel led Canton McKinley high school to a 13–0 win over Erie Academy in 1937, an achievement that led to one of the first mentions of his name in the sporting press (referring to the junior, Motley): "Canton McKinley kept its slate clean, but was given a hard battle by Erie Academy. The Bulldogs won 13–0, but were unable to score their touchdowns until the last five minutes. Two sustained marches produced the points, Marion Motley and Jack Barthel going over the goal."[16]

A month later against Steubenville, Motley scored on an 83-yard run near the end of the first half, and then threw the game-clinching, 15-yard touchdown pass in the last minute of the 13–0 win.[17] That capped an undefeated season, with only archrival Massillon (coached by Paul Brown) remaining for Motley's junior season. Now standing 6'1" and weighing 183 pounds, one of the largest players on the field in just about every contest, Motley was ready for the challenge.

The annual McKinley–Massillon game, for the uninitiated, is one of the longest running, and most prolific, high school rivalries in American football history. The series began in 1894, not among school teams but between nearby communities. In 1912, the towns agreed to excise the "ringers," the quasi-professionals and talented imports that often competed on both sides, and became an annual high school game. It was merely two Stark County schools just eight miles apart facing each other for bragging rights. Today, as Massillon claims on their website, "no high school football rivalry in the nation can claim the extraordinary tradition of Massillon vs. Canton ... it's bigger than a family feud and it's more intense than a street fight. In fact, it's almost akin to going to war."[18]

So significant is the rivalry that, in 2017, Dave Jingo and Ted Bowersox assembled a local all-star team of writers, cinematographers, historians and filmmakers to produce *Timeless Rivals*, a two-hour film on the history of the rivalry, the alumni, and the coaches.[19] The reach of this particular game is wide, and the producers were able to capture film interviews with NFL luminaries like Bill Belichick, Bengals owner (and son of legendary coach Paul Brown) Mike Brown, Minnesota Vikings general manager Rick Spielman, his brother and College Football Hall of Famer and NFL Pro Bowler Chris, along with Ohio State head coaches Jim Tressel and Earle Bruce, as well as many other football legends who had brushed up against this annual contest. The influence of the participants in the game continues to echo throughout the generations of college and professional football in the United States, but in 1937 it was the single hurdle to be cleared for a Canton McKinley perfect season.

On Friday, November 19, 1937, under "overcast skies and an inch and a half of snow" at Lehman Field,[20] and with Coach Reed taking a risk and starting the versatile but enormous Motley at right guard, instead of ball carrier, the Bulldogs lost 19–6. That 1937 game was carried locally on radio station WHBC and played (as always) in front of a capacity crowd of 14,000 fans. Throughout Motley's three-year varsity

Football mural depicting "A Century of Heroes" in downtown Massillon, Ohio. Football is the common thread among citizens and generations in northeastern Ohio.

football career at Canton, his teams lost only three games, all of them to Massillon's Tigers.

One of the interesting footnotes to the game was an exchange between Motley and his Massillon counterpart, Gus Peters, one that made the papers. Massillon Tiger coach Paul Brown related, "At one point in the game, Gus put a hard block on Motley. 'Nice block, Peters,'" said Motley, extending his hand after regaining his feet. But Motley watched his chance to get even with a beauty that sent the 215-pound Massillon tackle somersaulting backwards. "Nice block," said Peters, shaking Motley's hand.[21] With Motley, football collisions were never personal, unless someone else made them so.

That series of games against Massillon changed Marion Motley's life in a way no one could have predicted at the time. While Canton McKinley was losing to Massillon over those years, the latter's coach, the young, smart and ambitious Paul Brown, was taking it all in, and storing relevant information in case it would be useful later. Brown left Massillon within a year of Motley graduating Canton McKinley, but the paths of player and coach would soon cross, and both would benefit.

Throughout high school, Motley's role in running the ball was erratic. His performances, when he was given the opportunity, were uniformly brilliant, but his coaches could never agree on the best place for him on the field. On occasion, he was used as a lineman, a decision favoring his size and agility as a blunt force instrument, instead of focusing on opportunities to gain yardage. As a junior, in 1937, Motley carried the ball a mere 58 times, but gained an amazing 950 yards, resulting in ten touchdowns. That worked out to just under 16.4 yards per carry. He also completed six passes (nine attempts) for more than 200 yards and four more touchdowns.

Motley later told an interviewer:

> Well, when I went to high school, it was about seven or eight of us Blacks on the team, but I was the main stay. The only thing is back in those days it was hard for Blacks to get anywhere. I never made the Ohio All-State team in three years. Originally, I was a lineman and in those days they didn't want the Black students to get ahead of the White boys, so they put me on the line, although I was about the second fastest, well maybe the fastest. For example, when I pulled out, I'd go around and hit somebody. That guy I knocked down, well, that sucker had time to get up and still make the tackle. Afterwards, my junior year, one of the fellows in the backfield— he was big and lumbering—got hurt. One day coach said, "Motley, you get back here." And I went to fullback. Well, I led everything coming out of

there in ground game and touchdowns. So my senior year which was 1938 they kept me at fullback.[22]

This ongoing indecision as to where to best play Motley became a running joke of sorts on the football banquet circuit in later years. Paul Brown, Massillon coach and later Motley's coach in both the Navy and with the Cleveland Browns, wrote the following in his autobiography: "I spoke at an affair in Canton at which Motley was being honored, and among the guests was his former Canton-McKinley High School coach, Johnny Reed. When John spoke, he recalled how he had played Marion as a guard before moving him to fullback. John had been fired after Canton had lost for the sixth straight time to Massillon, and when I got up to speak, I kidded him about it. 'You know, John,' I said, 'anyone who would play Motley at guard should be fired.'"[23]

Motley played basketball on the Bulldog team over the 1937–38 winter but was forced to withdraw—and denied another varsity letter—due to ineligibility over the latter half (second school semester) of the season. Prior to the 1938 football campaign, the Ohio High School Athletic Association (OHSAA) finally cleared the rising senior for school sports.

The confusion arose over an OHSAA rule that prohibited an athlete from competing after six semesters of high school (in a grade 10 to 12 program). Motley played at Central Junior High School in 1934–35, but he lacked the final half credit necessary for promotion to 10th grade by the time school started. He played football in the fall of 1935 but was not technically classified as a sophomore until January 1936, making his 1935 freshman year "not count-able" for the six-semester accounting requirement. Once the OHSAA approved Motley's petition to play, based on that underlying rationale, he was reinstated for the 1938 football season.[24]

The player's senior year in high school, 1938, was even more spectacular than his junior campaign. In the season opener Canton defeated Lehman 48–6 on four Motley touchdown runs, complementing his receiving, kicking, kick returning, and defensive abilities. Although statistics are incomplete, the *Akron Beacon Journal* observed, "Motley also does most of the Canton passing."[25] In a brief, early season promotional blurb in the *Mansfield News-Journal*, a reporter wrote: "Marion Motley is a name Mansfield football fans should remember. Much will be heard from this young boy during the current football season ...

[last] Saturday this halfback made about 85 percent of McKinley's gains, scored four touchdowns, threw passes all over the lot and distinguished himself defensively, too."[26]

The McKinley Bulldogs of the late 1930s were almost a dynasty and earned the school a spot on the national stage every year. Canton's 1938 season, Motley's senior season, produced the following results.

Canton McKinley	48	Canton Lehman	6
Canton McKinley	32	Akron South	0
Canton McKinley	7	Erie Academy	6
Canton McKinley	19	Huntington (WV)	6
Canton McKinley	52	Elmira (NY)	6
Canton McKinley	33	Alliance	26
Canton McKinley	37	Steubenville	0
Canton McKinley	37	Mansfield	6
Canton McKinley	265	All Opponents (less Massillon)	56

In the *Beacon Journal*, as part of the relentless pregame analysis before the Massillon–McKinley game in 1938, Bob Elliott concluded, "On the basis of offense and defense, McKinley rates one-tenth of one point superior to the Tigers—whatever that means."[27] The teams, in other words, were deadlocked, at least on paper. Motley, for his part, had averaged more than 17 yards per carry during his senior season, and he knew what to do in the open field. Against Elmira, he scored 27 points on touchdown runs of 72, 30, 18, and seven yards, respectively, and kicked three extra points as well. During the 37–6 romp over Mansfield, Motley ran for two touchdowns, passed for another, and booted an extra point. In Canton McKinley's toughest game of the stretch, against Alliance High, he repeated his four-touchdown performance from the opener,[28] which included scoring runs of 54 and 34 yards (although he also threw an interception which Alliance returned for a touchdown), so—again—the end of the season battle between Canton McKinley and Massillon evolved into a high stakes showdown of undefeated schools.[29] The latter, under Paul Brown, had won the state title each of the last three years, but the 1938 edition afforded Canton McKinley its best chance in Motley's school years to defrock the figurative kings. The local press provided the context and injected a bit of drama into the build-up: "How long Massillon could stay up there was problematical for the Tigers run into Canton McKinley Saturday afternoon. The

Bulldogs, who have scored 256 points and allowed 50 in winning eight in a row, and boasting in big Marion Motley one of the state's finest triple-threat stars, are rated even with Massillon's well balanced crew.[30]

To appreciate the McKinley–Massillon game, it is necessary to appreciate the role of football in Massillon, Ohio. The town fewer than ten miles from Canton. It had attracted people with its thriving economy rooted in auto manufacturing and steel, so in the years between 1910 and 1940, the population rose from 10,000 to more than 25,000. In addition, it had contributed one of the very first professional football teams in the country. Massillon and Canton played each other as professionals up until 1919, when the American Professional Football Association was launched in Canton (two years later, renamed the National Football League). Abandoned by the new league, the high school adopted the moniker and took up scholastic football, and over the next 100 years has remained one of the most successful high school programs in America.[31]

A football ethos, if such a thing can really exist, dominates the area. At one of the largest road intersections in Massillon, a mural covers the entire wall of a three-story building.

The quotation below the game depiction reads: "In the beginning, when the Great Creator was drawing plan for this world of ours, He decided there should be something for everyone. He gave us mountains that reach to the sky, deep blue seas, green forests, dry deserts, gorgeous flowers, and gigantic trees. Then He decided there should be football, and He gave us Massillon. He created only one Massillon; He knew that would be enough."

Football is more than sport in Massillon. It is identity. The town hosts a wonderful museum, one dedicated to capturing all the aspects of Massillon's history, but there is a special part of the second floor dedicated to Massillon's first son, Paul Brown, and to the community's football heritage. There is even a billet at the museum—a dream job for so many—called the "Curator of Football Heritage" that is tasked with preserving and enlightening the past as prologue to the seasons yet to be played. In short, Massillon takes their football seriously, and has done so for decades. Their annual successes in the 1930s were no surprise to anyone in the region.

After the 1938 game was over, the game to end all games between McKinley and Massillon, the headlines summed up the harsh and unexpected end to Canton's storybook season: "Tigers Beat Bulldogs 12–0 to Win State Championship," with the subtitle "Crowd of 18,000 Gets Thrill at Massillon Defense on Goal Line."[32] It was Canton's fourth consecutive loss to the Tigers, and had been Motley's last shot at a win in the series.

In the game, the first Canton drive started at midfield, and Motley gained 28 yards on the ground, drilling into Massillon's superb defense, but—in the first quarter and in what can only be described as ironic—Massillon Tiger and future Cleveland Browns teammate of Motley, Lin Houston, "tackled him so viciously on the 10-yard line that Motley left the ball game, never to come back again."[33] The rest of the Bulldog squad rushed for only 56 yards for the remainder of the afternoon.

With their star offensive weapon knocked out of the game, Canton was unable to generate any sort of sustained scoring momentum. That same news story noted that "Canton had three opportunities to score, all in the second half, but failed each time, because it could not penetrate a Tiger line that summoned super-human courage when forced back to its goal."[34] Canton McKinley's offensive juggernaut, one that had averaged over 30 points per game over the rest of the season, suffered its sole shutout of the year, against their biggest rival, on an enormous stage. There is no doubt, however, that a healthy Motley could have created a quite different outcome.

The game raised a few eyebrows in the community and was so controversial that Motley and Houston were still talking about that game in 1994. Houston told the Canton Repository, "I asked Marion one day how much he got paid." There was some speculation that the McKinley star had been bribed to take a fall and not return to the game. "He told me, 'A big fat zero. I didn't throw that game. Hell, I couldn't run.'" Houston added, "I know because I hit you and it was a hard hit."[35] Houston later went on to achieve a unique trifecta. He was the only person to play for Paul Brown in high school, at Massillon, in college at Ohio State, and as a Cleveland Brown. He was one of many graduates of Canton McKinley and Massillon that later starred at the highest levels of amateur and professional football.

By the end of that 1938 season, Marion Motley was regarded as one of the state's finest triple-threat stars (he kicked as well), and he garnered the attention of (South Carolina's) Clemson University.[36] Motley later told Stuart Leuthner, "[S]hortly before I graduated I got a letter from Clemson University asking me if I'd like to come and play football for them. I wrote back and told them, I think you might have made a mistake because I'm a black player. I never heard another word from them, and I went down to South Carolina State College, which was an all-black school."[37] Evidently, once Clemson administrators had discovered that their prized recruit was Black, communication abruptly stopped.[38] Nevertheless, with economic effects of the Great Depression easing, Marion Motley took the best opportunity available. He packed his suitcase and headed back south. This time, though, it was in pursuit of an education, the chance to play a game for which he was so well suited, and the opportunity for a life beyond the steel mills of northern Ohio.

The College Years

South Carolina and Nevada

Nineteen-year-old Marion Motley arrived in Orangeburg, South Carolina, amid no fanfare, joining a football team that received very little media attention outside the immediate campus community. South Carolina State A & M College (since rechristened South Carolina State University) had been around for over four decades by the time Motley arrived. Founded in 1896, and at the time it was the only public college accessible to, and built for, Black students in that part of the state, it originally focused on agricultural and mechanical curricula. Over the years it has produced teachers, scientists, humanists, and scholars.[1] At the time, few schools could boast any sort of viable football tradition, and South Carolina A & M was no different. A few years later, Motley would become the first "Bulldog" football player to ultimately ascend to the Pro Football Hall of Fame, and he was later followed by Deacon Jones and Harry Carson. In 1967, John Gilliam became the first South Carolina State player drafted into the NFL.

In September 1939, though, optimism for the football team and the upcoming season ran high in the few local and regional newspapers that reported Black college sports. Starting at fullback for the home team in the September 29 opener against the Elizabeth City, North Carolina, Teachers College (also referred to as North Carolina Normal, Elizabeth City) was one of the new in a crop of prized freshmen, Marion Motley. The Bulldogs prevailed 47–0,[2] and the *Knoxville Journal* began hyping the Southern Intercollegiate Athletic Conference opener between South Carolina and Knoxville scheduled for October 7. While few statistics were reported in the various newspapers that covered South Carolina State's games, there are clues about player performances in the narrative snippets of the various weekly papers throughout the region. Motley

25

must have run well in the opener, since the *Knoxville Journal* wrote in a game-day article that "Orangeburg dope has it that the man for K.C. [Knoxville College] to stop is big 200 pounder Motley at fullback."[3]

By the end of October, with South Carolina State preparing to travel to Atlanta to take on Clark University, the *Atlanta Constitution* was calling the Bulldogs a "rough and rugged South Carolina State football aggregation" and noting that "among the players of prominence making the trip will be [halfback] Nat Harney [and] Marion Motley."[4] Another article observed that (Clark) coach Robinson "is working hard with his defense in order to put a stop to Motley's crushing attack."[5] South Carolina State won the Clark game, 7–6, with all the scoring accomplished in the first quarter, and not by Motley.[6]

It is possible, even likely, that Motley was injured during the afternoon tilt against Knoxville, although that was not reported in any game accounts. In a report about the subsequent South Carolina State athletic banquet, much later in the year, there is a curious observation that "Nathaniel Harney [of South Carolina State] was the outstanding broken field runner of the team after.... Motley, a newcomer and 200 lb. fullback, received a serious ankle injury in the first conference game that kept him out of the remainder of the season."[7] That opener would have been the Knoxville College game, which ended in a 7–7 tie and which listed Motley as the starting fullback.[8] Motley must have tried to play through the injury, as he was still reportedly a focus for opposing squads weeks later.

Regarding Motley, it is likely, at least from a cursory review of the existing records, that he was injured in Knoxville, although the extent of the trauma was not reported in the papers. None of the intervening narratives surrounding the reporting of South Carolina State's schedule or results mention any special achievements by the freshman fullback, and after the Clark pre-game article, there is no mention of Motley at all until December. Probably due to his later enshrinement in the Pro Football Hall of Fame, and not for the half season in Orangeburg, South Carolina State posthumously inducted Motley into their athletic hall of fame in 2000.[9] In 2019, the Historically Black Colleges and Universities released their list of the 100 greatest HBCU players from their (then) 127-year football history. Marion Motley was ranked #7, after Jerry Rice, Walter Payton, Deacon Jones, Willie Lanier, Buck Buchanan, and Mel Blount.[10] Given that degree of success, regardless of his short tenure in the South, it was surprising that Motley even considered leaving the college. But just like his father's family's move from Albany to Canton, Marion Motley looked for relief from local harassment.

In 1997, Motley told the newspaper *Black Voice News* about the details of his transfer to Nevada: "Originally when I went away to college, I went to Orangeburg, South Carolina, at South Carolina State College, and, in those days it was very ... well, they didn't like Blacks too well and I got disgusted my first year down there. It so happened the coach that preceded me in high school got the job at the University of Nevada. The head coach at South Carolina College called me and told me that I had a letter from the University of Nevada. And he said, 'Do you want me to open it and read it,' and I said, 'Yea, open it and read it.' I kind of knew who it was, where it was from."[11]

After a somewhat disappointing year of relative football anonymity in Orangeburg, Motley was ready to move on. That opportunity to move west had come in the form of an invitation from the University of Nevada at Reno, and their legendary coach Jimmy Aiken. "Aiken," Motley told Stuart Leuthner, "told me that he had left Akron and was now at the University of Nevada, in Reno, so I changed schools.... I didn't like being down in Orangeburg, South Carolina.... I didn't like that at all."[12]

Coach Aiken

Jim Aiken is one of those football names many may be reading about here for the first time, yet his legacy, his effect on Motley's career as well as on the game of football, grows with each generation. In the figurative gallery of genuinely great football coaches, there are the famous, like Lombardi and Paul Brown and Bill Walsh; the polarizing, like Bill Belichick and Jimmy Johnson and "Bear" Bryant; and, along with those luminaries, a slew of the relatively anonymous. That last category, obviously, is the largest in the taxonomy, as so many great coaches and their careers have lapsed into the obscurity conferred by the past. In that latter group, however, are written the names of coaches whose long-lasting influences are etched on the game every week, yet whose identities are consigned to a misty, fading memory.

For illustration, one such example of generational influence is embodied today in Bill Belichick. Almost all football fans are aware of the coach, and few are ambivalent in their feelings toward him and their perceptions of him. His success, however, is undeniable, and his football "genetic" legacy is clear. Beginning back in 1935, coach Bill Edwards took positions as the head coach at the college level at Western Reserve, Vanderbilt, and Wittenberg, and mixed his college stops in with a stint with the Detroit Lions of the NFL. Edwards also spent time as an assistant to Paul Brown, and in 1986 his career was finally and appropriately recognized when he was inducted into the College Football Hall of Fame. That catalog of jobs that filled much of his illustrious 37-year coaching career brought him into contact with a number of aspiring, younger coaches as well.

One of Edward's many assistants, coach Steve Belichick, not only went on to write a comprehensive book about football scouting, but also played a year in the NFL, and then coached for 43 years before retiring in 1989. Belichick's son, and Bill Edwards' godson, Bill, still prowls the NFL sidelines as of 2021, and has been head coach of six Super Bowl champions, named AP NFL Coach of the Year three times, and was afforded a coaching spot on the NFL's official All-Time Team. Bill Edwards' legacy, from Bill Belichick to all who will subsequently spring from that coaching lineage, is remarkable for a man that continues to exist in the mire of such a degree of anonymity.

Edwards' story is but one of many case studies in how coaching greatness is passed through generations. Jimmy Aiken, Motley's new coach in Nevada, was part of a similar football genealogy story. Born in 1899 in Wheeling, West Virginia, Aiken attended Washington and Jefferson College in Pennsylvania. At the start of his coaching life, he was part of the team that, led by head coach Greasy Neale, tied the much larger University of California in the 1922 Rose Bowl. After college, Aiken took up coaching full-time and won an Ohio state championship with Findlay High School in 1925. From there he moved to Scott High in Toledo, and then to Canton McKinley in 1932. Over the four years there, he and Paul Brown squared off each year in series of epic season finales. In 1932, McKinley won 19–0, but the team finished with a record of 6–3. The next season, 1933, McKinley lost to Springfield 6–0, but beat Massillon 21–0 to claim the Ohio State "runner up" spot.

In 1934 McKinley went undefeated, including a 21–6 win over Massillon, and allowed just 18 points all year in claiming not only the state title but the national championship as well. In 1935, the year before Motley joined the Bulldog varsity, McKinley went 6–3–1, but Aiken lost his only game to Brown, 6–0, and watched Massillon claim the state championship and the national title as well.[13]

From McKinley, Aiken took the head coaching position at the University of Akron, and after three years there and a 20–6 record, he was hired by the University of Nevada at Reno.[14] In 1947, and this is where the legacy begins to take root, he moved to the same position with the University of Oregon. Not only did he pick Norm Van Brocklin (future head coach of the Minnesota Vikings) to quarterback his T formation offense, but he also actively mentored a young John McKay. After the latter's playing career ended in 1949, Aiken hired him as a backfield coach, which ultimately led to the head coaching job at USC. In that seat, McKay coached four national titles, won five Rose Bowls, and nine conference championships. His final coaching job was with as the expansion Tampa Bay Buccaneers head man in 1976 and 1977. The coaching tree, the legacy lineage, that can be traced to McKay and thus to Aiken, includes John Robinson along with the slew of influential assistant coaches and players at all levels of the game.

Off to Nevada

Aiken, until the year before Motley arrived on the high school varsity, had been the head coach at Canton McKinley, and during his time at the University of Akron the coach enjoyed the opportunity to observe the entire three years of Motley's high school tenure. Once Aiken moved to Reno to accept the Nevada head coaching opportunity, he reached out to the football prodigy he'd watched play in northeast Ohio, a potential star languishing in South Carolina.

Motley accepted Aiken's offer. After his first spring game, an intrasquad scrimmage, local writer Ty Cobb wrote, "Motley was hit hard and often but it usually took three tacklers to drag him down after he plowed, side-stepped and sprinted to long gains."[15] One paper called Motley "a herculean young Negro ... 6 feet 2 inches tall, and weighs 225 pounds, runs the 100-yard dash in 10 seconds and can hit a basket from 50 yards with a pass. He blocks and tackles with the finesse of an All-American already and experts who have seen him perform most sensationally as a prep, predict that he will be a riot on the gridiron."[16]

The latter article's comparison of Motley with Kenny Washington was apt. The UCLA star had graduated the year prior, in 1939, after rushing for more than 9,000 yards in his college career and with a terrific reputation on the West Coast, and would—along with Motley, Bill

Willis and Woody Strode in 1946—become one of the four Black players that ended the informal NFL's 12-year racial barrier that permanently desegregated the league.

In moving west, though, Motley appeared to simply be relocating from one bastion of racism to another. An attorney named Michael Green later wrote in the *Nevada Law Journal* that "throughout the state of Nevada [in the first half of the 20th century] ... African Americans faced discrimination politically, economically, and socially in ways that seared the soul."[17] As late as 1954, author Roger Kahn described a casino visit by Willie Mays, already a national superstar. Kahn described one of the casino employees telling others to "get that n----r away from the white guests."[18]

Still, Marion Motley fit in well despite his status as a racial oddity. In a late-life interview, Motley spoke about his impressions of life on campus and on the football field while at the university, remembering, "San Jose had some [black players]; San Francisco had one or two, and I think College of the Pacific had one or two. I was the only black player [at Nevada–Reno] in first year. I was treated very well. No one gave me no flak, no one called me any names.... I think that Jim [Aiken] being from the east, he had coached a lot of black players ... he paved the way for me."[19]

The sophomore decided to major in physical education, but nothing could change the reality that he was the Black player on the team and, at the time, the only Black student at the university. It would have been understandable if he had become restless, but Motley took it all in comparative stride, and persistently made the best of his situation. Of campus social life, he told an interviewer, "It was rather, uhhh ... it was dull.... I lived at Lincoln Hall ... didn't have a roommate. I was comfortable ... it was a dull life."[20] He remembered, "I was the only black on the football team.... I never had too many altercations there ... they treated me right and I stayed in the dorms with the white fellas. But I knew the distance where I could go and what I could do."[21]

Despite Nevada's wider reputation as the "Mississippi of the West," Motley was embraced by the university community.[22] This feeling became palpable after the player was involved in a fatal car accident in California. The incident occurred on March 25, 1940, along US-40 in California (a four-lane artery subsequently replaced by I-80 during President Eisenhower's transportation infrastructure boom in the 1950s), between San Francisco and Sacramento. Motley was driving from the

Bay area toward Reno on the pre-interstate highway, with three passengers and, while trying to pass another car, crashed into an oncoming vehicle. Berkeley resident Tom Nobori and his wife were in the other car at the time, but only the 60-year-old Mr. Nobori was seriously injured, suffering a fractured skull.[23] Nobori later died from his injury.

Sadly, the Nobori death was not the only automobile fatality in Motley's life that year. On Saturday, August 31, Marion's father Shakvol was driving the rest of the Motley family up to Detroit. In the car was Blanche, along with Motley's sister Dorothy and younger brother Clarence, as well as passengers Reuben Bell and Arnella Matthews. On a curve on Ohio State Highway 120, at the outskirts of tiny Elmore, Ohio, Shakvol was driving too fast for the turn and lost control of the vehicle. It crashed into a tree, instantly killing him. He was 39. Blanche suffered cuts to her arms and legs, and Dorothy a few bruises, but Clarence and Arnella were unharmed.[24] The tragedy echoed for the remainder of Blanche's life. Even after her remarriage, 25 years later, her niece Candice Washington recalls that her aunt would harp on her husband if he began to speed in the car. The decision took an instant, disastrous turn for the Motley family, and almost certainly weighed heavily on Marion, now far away at college, recovering emotionally from his own collision, and simultaneously getting ready for the upcoming football season.

In October, following the Nobori's death, the California Highway Patrol finally upgraded Motley's reckless driving charge to negligent homicide. On October 29, he was convicted and jailed in Fairfield, California. Unable to pay the $1,000 penalty, Motley faced a year in jail.[25] Back on campus, though, the university community joined together and raised the entire $1,000 to take care of the fine. Six private Nevada residents made the trip to the Bay Area as character witnesses for Motley. Even today, the community involvement was spectacular, more that might have been reasonably expected given Nevada's collective reputation for racial intolerance. Included among the emissaries that travelled to defend their student and favorite son were Reno's chief of police Andy M. Welliver, local business representatives Tate Williams, and Ed Walker, Ray Garamendi, who was president of the university student body, along with assistant football coach C.B. Schuchardt, and an English professor, Paul A. Harwood.[26]

Along with the university's formal, community support, a local Reno attorney travelled to Fairfield and ensured the player's release and return to school. "I cannot tell you in words," Motley wrote in a statement to the Reno media once he was back on campus, "how grateful I am for what you have done for me."[27]

As the calendar turned to 1941, Motley's life continued to spiral toward the complicated when, on February 13, Mrs. Violet Nobori filed a $26,543.99 damage suit in the superior court against Motley.[28] While this proved to be the last public entry concerning that incident, it remains unclear as to how the suit was resolved. The bottom line was that Motley finally put the accident into past tense, and proceeded forward with his college career, but the incident was not the last time Motley would get into trouble in a car.

Back to Football

On the football field, Motley's star was brighter than ever, but the issue of race, of simple skin pigmentation, seemed to always loom in the background. Local sportswriter Ty Cobb (again, not the baseball player of the same name) interviewed one of his trusted, anonymous fan sources and critics of Nevada football, and wrote, "you know every time I see Marion Motley in action, I like him better. All along we have contended that he is all–American timber.... That boy is not only a champion but a true sportsman."[29] This was clearly an opinion and not rooted in any specific action, but the approval of a writer like Cobb marked an important turn in how Motley would be perceived in the future. After one game later that year, against Eastern New Mexico, the same source told Cobb:

> Yesterday I heard certain remarks from the New Mexico players that were a direct insult to a man of Motley's race. Yes, they were shouted so loudly that I heard them in my seat. I was furious myself and I watched Marion closely to see his reaction, and he seemed absolutely unconcerned. I noticed intentional piling up on the big fellow. The officials doled out one penalty for that offense, but they should have called many more. The only noticeable effect on Motley was that he played a little harder, and instead of side-stepping players, he bowled them over and when he tackled a ball carrier he hit ferociously.[30]

Nevada won that game 40–6, and 20-year-old Motley carried the ball just nine times but netted 125 yards, a 14 yards per carry clip. The incident, though, was not Motley's only brush with public racism over the course of the season. Some institutions and teams seemed to have no problem with Nevada's Black superstar runner, but others did. On occasion, that racism was masked by a superficial attempt by opponents to enforce arbitrary conference eligibility rules.

One of the more egregious ones occurred in November, in Moscow, Idaho, in a pregame meeting before the universities of Idaho and Nevada kicked off. According to Motley, Idaho's head coach

> called Jim [head coach Aiken] over and said, "Marion can't play the first half, he can't play" … I couldn't play because I was a freshman. Jim got very aggravated and called me over and I went over and was standing there talking to him, when he told Jim I couldn't play. I had to grab Jim and pick him up around his waist and hold him off the ground, you know, get his feet up, 'cause he was gonna punch him in the mouth. I said, "There's no need for that Jim. You go ahead and play the game" … but he said, before the game started … you know, the stands was roarin', "get that nigger, kill that nigger, kill that alligator bait…" and all that kind of stuff. It didn't bother me … you know. In those days, you were used to it … when you were in Rome, you did like the Romans did….
>
> But Jim and [the Idaho coach] were discussin' it and Jim said to me, "Motley, go on over there and tell all the football players come on, we're going home." And he looked at [the coach] and said, "You wait right till the game time to tell me that…. And he said wait a minute … the stands were full … they were supposed to beat us 30–0 … then they compromised, said Marion can't play the first half but he can play the second half.
>
> Well, Jim thought about it, … well that sounds reasonable. So, uh, I didn't play the first half. When the game started the second half, the first time I put my hand on the ball I went to the goal line. And when I [scored, I] dropped the ball, as a touchdown, looked back and the referee was beckoning me to bring the ball back. About 50–55 yards. About three plays later I went to about the six yard line, they brought the ball back … they only beat us 6–0. That was one of the incidents I had during my college career.[31]

The game reports in the papers noted that "the Wolf Pack bogged down until late in the second period when Marion Motley, big Negro halfback, began throwing storybook passes. One, travelling 70 yards, bounced out of the fingers of Left End Wes Goodner. Motley once got away for what appeared to be a certain touchdown. He was hauled down from behind on the Vandal 24 after covering 25 yards."[32] Once allowed to play, Marion Motley continued to be unstoppable, except by the officials.

The other race-related incident that Motley often recounted when discussing his college football experiences, occurred in 1941 in Utah, when Nevada travelled to play Brigham Young University. "When I went to Brigham Young, Utah, the kids were ... following us around ... you know, we were out walkin' before the game, and they [little kids] was askin' me 'Where's your tail? I thought you had a tail ... you're supposed to have a tail....'"[33] Rather than create an incident before the important game, Motley just returned to his room. Still, that sort of incident dogged him throughout much of his public life in football. It was, in retrospect, a horrifying illustration of ignorance in parts of the country, but Motley—as was his wont—took it in stride.

Maryland football coach Jim Tatum later recounted a story that he'd heard from coach Aiken's wife. Evidently the young student-athlete, the core of the football program, occasionally needed a bit of financial help. On this particular afternoon, Motley stopped by the Aiken residence, and Mrs. Aiken told the player that the coach had been called out of town and wasn't available. Motley told her he'd come for his "allowance" and she gave him the regular $2.80.

When the coach returned, his wife told him about the payment. "But what I can't figure," she said, "is why it's $2.80." She'd reasoned that since Motley had no regular job, and did not perform any chores around the Aiken home, the amount was a bit unusual. Tatum repeated Aiken's words: "It isn't. It's just a little pin money; something for toothpaste and the movies." But why not a round figure like $3? Aiken replied with direct honesty: "As soon as I brought Marion to Reno I went down to the bus depot and learned the fare to the nearest big city with a college is $3.00. I aim to do right by that boy, but I just want to be sure he never has $3.00 in his pocket."[34]

On balance, Motley embraced Reno and college life. In yet another display of his broad athleticism, Motley departed his figurative comfort zone, boxing in a local Gold Gloves tournament (eventually losing to Johnny Ebarb, who went on to a three-year professional boxing stint in the mid–1940s).[35] This was a high-level competition, even for an athlete as talented at physical contact as Motley, and he acquitted himself quite well in the bouts he fought.

Baseball

Motley's college life, despite the social tedium, was a full one. In addition to football, varsity basketball, and classwork, the gifted athlete also occasionally pitched on two of Reno's local, semi-pro baseball teams. One of those teams was the Black Dixie Club, and one of his mentors on that team was a former professional player named Jimmy Claxton.[36]

Claxton's place in baseball history is underappreciated by both fans and even most baseball historians. He was born in 1892, the son of a Black (a growing number of baseball scholars think it more likely that he was Native American, even though that distinction was lost on the sporting world of the day) Virginia coal miner and his 18-year-old, and quite White, bride, in British Columbia, Canada.[37] The family moved to Tacoma, Washington, when Claxton was only a few months old, and he grew up excelling at baseball for several town teams in the area.

In 1916, the young lefthander, a man with a very light complexion due to his actual ancestry yet regarded as a Negro for baseball's purposes, managed to work his way onto the roster of the pitching-desperate Oakland Oaks of the Pacific Coast League (PCL). The Coast League, at that time, was considered by many a near-peer level of competition for the eastern Major leagues, and more than a few talented players chose the PCL in lieu of the National or American leagues. The money was comparable, the travel easier, and the baseball nearly as good as the established "big leagues," but the pressure was less. Still, as a part of what was a loosely organized baseball universe, the PCL honored the standing de facto exclusion of Black players from their games.

Believed to be Caucasian, Claxton was signed and almost immediately inserted into a game against the Los Angeles Angels, pitching two innings in his debut before being pulled for a reliever. A few days later, however, and having recorded no other appearances, a friend let it slip that Claxton had African American ancestry.[38] No club bothered to sign the pitcher, and he spent the rest of his baseball days on smaller teams, well into his 50s, before hanging up his spikes in 1956.[39] Until Jackie Robinson, Claxton was the last Black man to play in organized White baseball.

In 1940, though, Claxton was the pitcher and leader of the Dixie club in Reno, and Marion Motley enjoyed the opportunity to play with, and learn from, a Black athlete who had played in both the gritty, authentic Negro leagues (with Pollock's Cuban Stars of the old East West League) and the segregated world of "organized" baseball.[40]

In the pre-war summer of 1941, Motley returned to the baseball diamond with some regularity. The other teams for which Motley competed, in addition to Jimmy Claxton's Dixie Club, were the mostly–White Reno Larks, who played a variety of exhibitions against both local and regional towns and against the higher profile professional barnstorming teams from the east, and the Reno Colored Giants. In the summer of 1941, the Kansas City Monarchs' barnstorming team (a few of the regulars of the legendary Negro American League team, supplemented by a roster of talented Black players who filled out the positions and were able to earn a few dollars by barnstorming baseball) came to town for games with the Larks, along with the Palmer House Stars (another Black travelling squad from Chicago).

The Reno Larks played both squads at various points in July, but Motley played a role in a three-game, mid–July series with the Kansas City Monarchs. The Monarchs are one of the most successful organizations in the history of Negro League baseball, and were a year from the cusp of a 1942 season in which they dominated the Negro American League before serving up a four-game sweep of the Homestead Grays in the Negro World Series. That 1942 Grays team that fell to Kansas City was no slouch either, their roster stocked with immortals like Josh Gibson, Buck Leonard, Ray Brown, and Jud "Boojum" Wilson.

Often, in such series like the three-game set with the Larks, the Monarchs would pick up a local player or two to join them for the final contest to drum up more local interest and paid admissions, and in July 1941, they allowed Motley to pitch a game for Kansas City and against the Larks. "The Larks entered into the local player-lending spirit, and Marion Motley of Reno, University of Nevada footballer, pitched the first six innings for the visiting team."[41]

Motley walked three and struck out four that afternoon with Kansas City, and went 0–2 at the plate, but only allowed one run in six innings. It was another unnecessary, but enjoyable, display of the young man's superb athleticism regardless of the sport.

The Monarch's box summary from that afternoon (Threlkel Park, Reno).

Monarchs

	AB	R	H
Cyrus 3B	4	0	0
McDaniel, CF	4	0	1
Marshall, SS	4	2	2
Wave, 1B	3	0	2

2. The College Years

	AB	R	H
Young, RF	4	0	2
Servel, LF	2	1	1
Sneed, 2B	4	0	1
MOTLEY, P	2	0	0
Tyson, C	3	0	1
Carter, P-1B	1	0	0
Bratford, LF	2	0	0
TOTALS	33	3	10

Bases on balls by Motley—3; Strikeouts by Motley—4

It was the barnstorming version of the Monarchs, but Motley still had the chance to suit up and play alongside "real" Monarchs like Sylvester Snead and Tom Young. Jack Marshall, the shortstop, had played for nine years in the Negro National and American leagues, and hit .388 with the Chicago American Giants in 1936 (at age 27); Cap Tyson was a 38-year-old catcher who'd just spent three years with the Birmingham Black Barons; pitcher Earnest C. "Spoon" Carter was a 38-year-old also just trying to squeeze out a living in baseball, and ended up playing for a bit in Mexico that year. Sylvester Snead and Tom Young were loaners from the big-league Monarchs, the latter having enjoyed a long and successful career with Kansas City.[42] In all, it was lofty athletic company for the young student.

In the fall the football team returned to action in winning their opener against California Polytechnic (Cal Poly) at San Luis Obispo, 32–0. They then proceeded to squander that start by losing three straight, to San Francisco, the University of Arizona, and Fresno State, before squeaking by Santa Barbara State (now University of California, Santa Barbara), 7–0. Motley spent much of the season, a campaign that ended with a 3–5–1 record, moving between fullback, linebacker, and passer, but not gathering any attention beyond the regional newspapers.[43] Against San Jose State, however, Motley captured his first, substantial national press. The Associated Press story, with a New York byline, begins: "You may not have heard of Marion Motley. You shall right now. He is the star Negro halfback of the University of Nevada's football team, who according to an annual Associated Press survey, made perhaps the longest run of the entire 1941 [college] campaign."[44]

The year ended on a losing note, to Loyola in Los Angeles. The Wolf

Pack had scheduled a New Year's Day game against the University of Hawaii in Honolulu, but that was—understandably—cancelled after the attack on Pearl Harbor on December 7.[45]

Motley had injured his hip earlier in the year, and followed that later in the season by suffering hits to both an ankle and a knee, but despite the array of aches and pains he still managed to carry the team. The great Ernie Nevers, later elected to both the college and professional football halls of fame, was very familiar with football in the western United States. He had starred at Stanford University, and later returned to coach there and at the University of Iowa before entering military service during World War II, and was well aware of Motley's ability. Nevers said, "I'd like to see that fellow with two good legs under him. Motley is the fastest big man we've ever seen, even on one leg. And he really levels off when he's finally trapped." After the San Francisco game, Nevers told the writer that "his one hand catch of a forward pass near the close of the game was a masterpiece. The [San Francisco] Dons should have protested against illegal equipment—baskets on the ends of his arms."[46]

It was during this time that Motley's personal life took decided turn for the better. He had become quite close to a young woman, albeit one four years older, named Eula Coleman. "She had a sister there [Reno] that was working in one of the families on a ranch, and we got married ... we [then] lived in the city, place to place."[47] Coleman was, by all accounts, a beautiful woman, and she and Marion wasted little time in marrying.[48]

The blissful union spurred Motley into a strong start for the 1942 season. Motley and the team rolled to an 18–0 win over Cal Poly, but in spite of a 95-yard touchdown run off an interception (and a kicked extra point) by the big senior, Nevada the fell to the University of San Francisco 27–7.[49] The following week, against St. Mary's at Emeryville Ball Park in Oakland, Nevada, lost 20–6. This time, however, it was Motley's defensive ability that was highlighted by the writers. "Although the Gaels were ever pressing, they couldn't crack the Nevadans defense wherein Don Talcott, a 230-pound tackle, and Marion Motley, the Wolves big Negro back, were the stalwarts again."[50]

A spate of fumbles negated another great effort by Motley against the University of New Mexico. The Lobos "played throughout in a six-man line designed to stop Motley, but the big halfback overpowered his opponents through sheer strength on off-tackle smashes."[51] After a

33–0 drubbing by Fresno State, Nevada, closed out the season at home against (what is now) the University of California at Davis. While the final score was a pedestrian 14–0 in favor of the hosts, Motley evidently contributed well beyond agate type and line scores (although that afternoon he ran for 125 yards in the win).[52]

In 1994, in a letter to the editor of a paper in Santa Rosa, California, one of the Aggies' starters on that Davis team, John H. Woolsey (at the time retired and living in northern California), recounted his impression of Motley that afternoon:

> I was the second-string end for the UC Davis Aggies in the fall of 1942, and we played Nevada-Reno on a frozen field in Reno. In the second quarter, our coach sent me in to stop this Motley fellow and put the fear of God into him. DO I KNOW SOMETHING ABOUT THIS MAN? Let me tell you. He ran around us, he ran through us and he ran over us. We bounced off him like BB pellets hitting a Sherman tank. The point I'm trying to make is that he needed no one to open holes for him. He was the essence of "Gimme the ball and get outta my way." He did me a great service that day, for I never played another game of football and sought my livelihood in gentler pursuit.[53]

It would not be the only time that Motley's play changed the course of another player's career, and it provided a fitting closeout to the man's stellar college career. Motley's college career, if it had occurred in the 21st century, instead of the 1940s, would have garnered reams of press, national television, Heisman Trophy considerations, and seemingly eternal fame. As it was, he labored in relative anonymity, remembered mostly by those against whom he played.

From 1940 through 1942, Marion Motley played fullback and linebacker at the level of one of the best "that has ever been seen on the university gridiron."[54] In 2005, the sports network ESPN produced a comprehensive encyclopedia of the history of football as played among the 300 or so largest colleges and universities in the United States. Each school is profiled in the volume, and a few relevant historical snippets are added to tell an encapsulated story of football at the respective institutions. The editorial team named Marion Motley as the finest player in the University of Nevada's history, an era dating back to 1896, and an unintentional trailblazer as well. "Motley," the editors noted, "scored 129 points in [his career, and] ... was one of the few black players in college football at the time. When Mississippi State said it would not play against the Wolf Pack because of Motley, the rest of the Nevada team voted to not make the trip, and the game was cancelled."[55] Motley was named as one of the running backs, along with Tommy Kalamanir (1946–1948), to the University of Nevada's All-Centennial Team in 1998. The encyclopedia closes with one final quote from Motley: "If I don't get you now, I'll get you later."[56]

Perhaps even more significantly, as he and Eula wed on February 1, 1942, they had learned that they would have a son, Ronald. They would also have sons Phillip (1943) and Raymond (1944). For his part, Motley also sired a fourth son, named George Kennedy, with a different woman, Minnie Kennedy. Motley and George were often absent from each other's lives.[57] In later years, however, "Grandpa Motley" remained active and engaged with George's children, especially granddaughter Aldreeta. If she needed money for, say, a school field trip, she remembers, he'd send a letter along with the money so she could participate. She and her brothers also shared in Motley's annual trips to the Hall of Fame during annual inductions, even sitting with him as he signed autographs and greeted fans. Aldreeta Kennedy still remembers meeting Bill Willis, among others, but mostly she harbors incredibly warm memories of her famous grandfather, a man who not only did

Marion Motley, wearing number 41, running the football during a game for the University of Nevada, 1941.

not shy away from his fourth son, but who embraced that branch of the family with love.[58]

But back in Nevada, at the end of the following year, 1943, Motley withdrew from the university, and brought new wife and new baby to Ohio to take a wartime job in a steel mill. The next phase of Motley's life, the adult phase, was just beginning.

Post College
and Navy Football

The burdens accompanying Motley's new status as a husband and father, along with the effects of all those brutal hits on both of his knees, effectively drove him to leave the university and return to a mill job in Canton in 1943 in order to support his new family. "I spent three years at Nevada," he told Stuart Leuthner, "and hurt my knee, so I came home to Canton and got a job with Republic Steel."[1] He told Leuthner that the knee was "pretty bad," a reasonable lay diagnosis in the age before the collective obsession with sports medicine, a time when pitching arms "went dead" and legs "gave out," but that the new job had offered some therapeutic benefit. Motley was using a torch to burn up scrap iron, and the ambient heat, he believed, had caused the knee to rebuild and heal. Of course, not getting battered by opposing defenses likely did not hurt the process either.

There may have been more to Motley's decision to leave school before completing his eligibility than he initially shared with the press. Later in 1943, he told the *Reno Gazette-Journal* that he desired to return to the university, but the story noted that "while it is unlikely he will be eligible to play football, he would be eligible for basketball next season—if his grades were sufficiently high to meet standards for athletic competition."[2] He was caught in both academic and regulatory seams. In the former case, Motley's studies as a physical education major were likely a means to maintaining a grade point average high enough to keep him on the field. Even contemporary athletes, sometimes star players, often joke about majoring in "eligibility" rather than enduring a more rigorous course of study.

As to the associated regulatory issues, while the rules were beginning to adapt to allow freshmen to play on all varsity teams, there was no clear guidance about the disposition of athletes who had played as freshmen elsewhere, specifically whether they would be allowed to finish a fifth year of football or basketball. The article concluded, "Being married and the father of an infant son, Motley, for the present at least, has a deferred draft rating," meaning that since he was not obligated to immediate military service, he could make decisions about work versus school entirely based on his immediate circumstances.[3]

Still, regardless of the circumstances that drove Motley's relocation back to Ohio, the player did find a job, and began a new phase of his life as a working man and husband. With son Phillip arriving in 1943, and Raymond in 1944, Marion and Eula Motley were on the cusp of settling into a more conventional life in Canton, albeit a life without football.

World War II changed all of that.

Military Football During Wartime

By August 1942, more than 50 major colleges had dropped football.[4] Given the national circumstances, with rationed fuel, food and an

Marion Motley's military draft registration, filed while a student at the University of Nevada.

array of other commodities, coupled with the service demands of a military engaged in a global conflict, the idea of reducing college athletics should not have been unexpected. Despite the national trend toward scaling back major sports, though, there remained a significant number of institutions that planned to carry on with a semblance of normalcy despite the logistical adversity.

In the place of those colleges that had abandoned the gridiron, and in consonance with the war effort, service teams re-emerged from places like the Naval Station at Great Lakes, just north of Chicago, as well as Iowa Pre-Flight on the University of Iowa campus, along with bases in North Carolina and Georgia, among others. These were not service academies like the U.S. Military Academy at West Point or the U.S. Naval Academy at Annapolis, but instead were based at actual military training facilities scattered across the nation. College football, needing teams to fill out the array of schedules, and acknowledging that a great many college students were already assigned to those service sites, allowed the creation of such college-level (college-ish) teams to play the Michigans and Purdues and Ohio States of the world.

The players were employed by the United States government, so their individual availability—season to season, or even week to week— was limited by the dictates of their respective military services. The Navy, for example, was concerned with their sailors fitting onto ships and into aircraft more than they were about winning football games, so it did not allow new sailors to be over 6'3" tall or heavier than 200 pounds. Individuals outside those specifications were sent along to the Army. For the aspiring soldiers and sailors who were also playing football, each also had his primary military training responsibilities to attend to throughout each day.

In this loophole construct for creating football teams, eligibility rules relaxed a bit. Not everyone who played for the military teams was a college-eligible player. Some of the training sites used high school-aged boys, and a few were rumored to have used former professional players. Similarly, the academic standards for entering military service were a bit lower than for an athlete entering, say, the University of Notre Dame.

This model for fielding football teams was not without precedent, as it had been used during the First World War as well. In 1918 the Navy training station team at Great Lakes had defeated the Mare Island (California) Marine camp, 17–0, in the "Granddaddy of them all," the Rose

Bowl. Perhaps presumptuously, but no doubt seeking even greater grid-iron glory, the Navy retained that Great Lakes team for the 1919 season. The service soon disbanded the squad though, since, with the war over, there were not enough players to man a team that could still compete at the collegiate level. The 1918 team included football luminaries like George Halas and Paddy Driscoll. The 1919 team did not. Still, in 1942 and possibly remembering past glories, the Navy resurrected the Great Lakes team.

The 1943 *Street and Smith's Football Yearbook* opened with a note: "Football is being played under conditions which would have killed less hardy pastimes."[5] Major league baseball had continued on with Franklin D. Roosevelt's presidential endorsement, and college football was eager to do the same. "The closest thing to war in time of peace is football!" said Admiral Jonas Ingram, referring to the game's value in training and honing a martial ethos. Naval Academy coach Tom Hamilton declared in a Naval Aviation Physical Training manual: "Football! Navy! War! At no time in history have these words been more entwined and intermeshed than they are now."[6] That same manual outlined some of the traits shared by football players and aviators, including aggressiveness, physical fitness, discipline, coordination, teamwork, alertness, and toughness.[7] Iowa Pre-Flight's director of athletics, Bernie Bierman, "insisted that every cadet participate in football training 'climaxed by a full scrimmage session.'"[8]

With that level of top-down endorsement, football continued. College athletics' sanctioning bodies allowed the service teams to play a full schedule against a slate of teams that included the biggest university programs. The drawback for the service teams was that a particular squad or player could be transferred at a moment's notice should the war dictate such a move. Into that arena, the Navy commissioned one Paul Brown, head coach of the Ohio State University, to come to the Great Lakes naval station and take the helm of their football team.

Paul Brown and the T Formation

There is an oft-rehashed sports talk radio meme, or game, loosely termed "who is on your Mount Rushmore" of … whatever. Baseball. Football. Jockeys. Actors. The potential topic list is endless and without any formal criteria, and there are never universally accepted (i.e., unarguable) solutions. Not only does this sort of question tend to elicit lots of response, which is good for call-in radio shows and internet surveys (to wit: "Which 1920s sports star are you? Take this quiz and find out"), but it can stimulate some actual thought in revealing what individuals value in their "top four of anything" list.

Under the subject of "football coaches," there is similar debate over who is worthy of having their face chiseled into the side of a hill. As alluded to earlier, there are so many from which to choose, including the many more that few outside football know much about, so this tends to be a moot question from the start. It would be difficult, though, to convince any historian or knowledgeable enthusiast of the game of football that Paul Eugene Brown's face shouldn't be one of those carved into the granite. It is useless to try to understand Marion Motley's life without some awareness of the enormous influence of this coach.

Brown was born in 1908, in Norwalk, a town in the center of the bucolic Western Reserve, the northern swath of Ohio that runs roughly from Toledo in the west to Cleveland in the east. His father, Lester, was a railroad man, one driven by the unceasing, constant metronome of the clock. Time, punctuality, was everything to the railmen, and the younger Brown was raised in an environment that valued precision as one of the most useful virtues one could possess. In 1917, the railroad moved the Browns to Massillon, and Paul abruptly transitioned from a quasi-rural lifestyle in a quiet countryside to one in a steel town, a town in which football was the one point of intersection throughout the community. Rich, poor, executive, laborer, clerk, priest, homemaker ... and so on ... it did not matter. Football, specifically Massillon football, was the hub, the one egalitarian exchange in which class and social status did not matter, perhaps even facilitated social interaction. Brown took to the game naturally, which was fortunate for him, but likely as not he had no choice in the matter. Football was, and is, a condition of living in northeastern Ohio.

After playing for Massillon in high school and graduating from Miami University (in southwest Ohio), where he played quarterback well enough to make the AP's All-Ohio small college second team in 1928, Brown eschewed law school to take a coaching position in Maryland.[9] From there he moved to the head job at Ohio State, and with the outbreak of the war, to Great Lakes and the United States Navy. Brown

46

was ever and always the son of a railroad man, punctual and precise to a fault, and his natural inclinations meshed well with both the military ethos and the demands of high-level football.

A profile of Coach Brown, after two years on the job with Cleveland, in the 1948 edition of *Pro Football Illustrated* was illuminating:

> First and foremost, Brown is a perfectionist and as such is a taskmaster, a disciple of thoroughness and a fanatical worshiper of the god of discipline. He is self-confident, articulate, and cocky to a degree that positively infuriates his rivals.
>
> As a coach, he definitely knows what he wants in football talent and definitely goes after it, speed being a definite prerequisite.... His demands for thoroughness frequently are a strain on the family tie. His scouting reports, probably, are the most voluminous of all time and the same is true of the book of plays he prepares for the players.... The fact that he is a martinet of sorts and rules with an iron hand, doesn't endear him to the players, but they, like everybody else, admire and respect him—and come close to loving him when, in the off season, he hustles around getting them jobs and living quarters.[10]

Brown's successes, at Ohio State and beyond, were in part built on his innovative use of the T formation. Understanding a bit about how Brown implemented an offense based on the T, about the opportunities it gave his team, helps to explain how and why Marion Motley was such a critical node, and why he was so successful running out of the formation.

The T itself was nothing new, and in fact had been in football's arsenal since before the turn of the 20th century. According to most sources, none less than the "father of American football," Walter Camp, devised the formation as early as the 1880s. Originally constructed to create a sort of human wall of linemen in front of a ball carrier, and the two or three backs behind the ball, the concept was to form a figurative bulldozer and just force the football forward. The line would charge ahead with brute force, and the trailing backs would literally push—or even throw—the ball carrier forward into the breach. Just as with the flying wedge and similar formations of the day, the injury (even death) toll was high. The tight T formation tended to force a full-speed collision of 22 unarmored men on every play.

In the first decade of the 20th century, with some in the media calling for the end of football due to the extraordinary risk posed to the players, a series of rule changes were instituted to save the sport.

In 1904 and 1905, nearly 20 players died each season from football injuries like severed spines, internal bleeding, and concussive blows to the heads. President Theodore Roosevelt convened a meeting of the head coaches of Harvard, Princeton, and Yale universities on October 9, 1905, and asked the leaders to change the game in order to save it.[11]

With the attendant rule changes, notably that players could not push the ball carrier forward into the scrum, the tactic's popularity faded. Pop Warner instead improved on the concept with his single- and double-wing formations, as well as pre-snap motion that put additional receivers down field more quickly. In the single wing, there is no one, quarterback or other back, directly behind the center. The ball is snapped to either an offset quarterback or tailback, who then spins, fakes, and either throws or runs, using deception in lieu of the brunt force of the old T and flying wedge types of formation. The elimination of the constraints on forward passing, as well as slightly reshaping the ball itself into something that could be thrown further and with greater accuracy, reshaped the game of football into a version much closer to the one played today.

There are mist-shrouded myths about who "invented" the pass, but once the play was legalized, and could be thrown anywhere behind the line of scrimmage, it drove coaches to the collective drawing board, seeking ways to maximize the value. In 1933, as passing became legal from anywhere behind the line of scrimmage, a modified version of the T began to climb back into favor with some coaches, most notably Clark Shaughnessy of Stanford, Texas' Dana Bible, and the legendary Frank Leahy at Notre Dame.

The essence of the formation is that the offense remains balanced on both sides of the ball, preventing the defense from overloading one side or the other, and uses deception and quick hitting running backs, abetted by pre-snap motion, to disguise a play's direction. The single wing thrived on such athletic deceptions, but the unbalanced nature of the formation made it more likely that the ball would go to the stronger side of the line, the side on which more blockers and potential runners were available, while the newer T variant gave away nothing. Every back was a potential ball carrier, passer, or receiver, and every lineman a potential lead blocker. Properly applied, at least before coaches had the time to dissect and counter the playbook, it was lethal.

The T Formation (Generic Version)

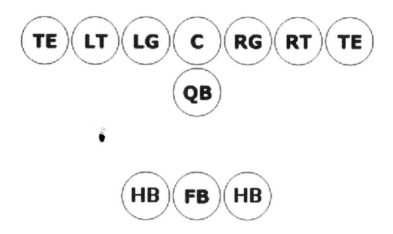

From this set, halfbacks (HBs) could be off and running, parallel to the scrimmage line in either or both directions, before the snap, and the fullback (FB) could either block, take the ball, or serve as a decoy. If left alone, the fullback could also work his way toward either sideline, ready to catch a quick pass from the quarterback (QB) if other receivers were covered. According to Otto Graham, the T gave the offense a choice among handoff, fake, lateral, or pass on every play, and with the uniform presentation of the formation and the pre-snap motion, defenses required uncommon athleticism in order to react in an appropriate manner.[12]

Brown had been largely a single wing coach until his Ohio State team faced Don Faurot's Missouri Tigers in the 1941 season opener. The Buckeyes would end up ranked 13th overall in the final AP poll that year, but the Tigers finished seventh, and only lost 12–7 in that matchup. The T presented Brown with a different tool with which to confront his opponents, but he soon realized that the athletic characteristics for some of the positions were different than those of the more conventional (at the time) offenses.

Frank Leahy, in his coaching guidance about how he succeeded with the T formation at Notre Dame, observed that "the greatest advantage of the T is that your center becomes 100 percent a blocker. He is actually into the play before any other lineman because he knows exactly where the ball is going ... [and] the T center gives no tip-off to the opponent, since he does not have to look through his legs to see where his target [the quarterback] is. He can feel him."[13] Beyond Leahy's observations, there is general agreement that there are two critical positions in the "T." Every coach from Shaughnessy to Faurot to Leahy to Bible to Brown lived or died with the quality of their quarterback (QB), and the speed and versatility of their fullback (FB). The T was, and is, an explosive formation, and when properly coached and with the right players at the key positions, almost unstoppable at the time. With Motley onboard, Brown's wartime experiences at Great Lakes with the T would provide the next step in the development of his playbook and would result in the most dominant five-year run by any team in professional football history. There will be a deeper examination of Brown's T later.

Great Lakes and the Navy

Back at Great Lakes, however, Brown's 1945 challenge was obvious. In his first year, 1944, Brown had guided his team to a 9–2–1 record and a final ranking at #17 in the Associated Press poll. Of note, on that final list, the U.S. Military Academy finished first, the Air Corps' Randolph Field third, Annapolis fourth, Bainbridge Naval Training Station fifth, and Iowa Pre-Flight sixth. They were followed by USC, Michigan, and Notre Dame. March Field rounded out the top ten. There were five additional service teams in that top 20, and Brown undoubtedly felt confident about an even better showing by his Navy squad in 1945.

Then, abruptly but not unexpectedly, the Navy shipped most of those players to California, where they'd be closer to the war in the Pacific. This forced Brown to deal with the reality of rebuilding his team on the figurative fly, an action somewhat analogous to the idea of trying to change the tire on a car while speeding down the highway. Fortunately, the coach had a mind for football and an unfailing memory. According to *The Sporting News*, "Brown always kept Motley in mind. When the coach went into the Navy and was given the Great Lakes team, he had the fullback with him. Brown had a great squad. 'But they took it away from me one day,'" recalled Brown, "and shipped it out to California. All they left was Motley because nobody thought he could play football."[14]

3. Post College and Navy Football

The war mobilization effort was on a level beyond anything experienced by any country in history. Businesses that had produced peacetime parts were instead churning out military support equipment, and every person and family were living with the restrictions of ration coupons for staples like gasoline, coffee, and even meat. It was a collective sacrifice, albeit one that contributed to unifying the country and elevated the desire to serve beyond anything possible through simple propaganda and posters. The steel mills were vital, but the lower-skilled laborers were poised to contribute even more by serving in uniform. Marion Motley readily accepted his civic responsibility to volunteer, regardless of where that service might take him.

Motley enlisted in the Navy on Christmas Day, 1944, and showed up at the Great Lakes naval training facility soon thereafter. Immediately, his planned wartime service changed from the Pacific theater to the football fields of the Midwest. "Paul Brown found out I was there and asked me to come over so he could see what size I was. He thought I'd be out of shape like some of the other guys, but I was a mean, 225 pounds at that time. He was elated over the fact that I hadn't gotten fat, and he put me in what they call the ship's company. That meant I could stay at Great Lakes, and I played football for Paul during the war."[15] It was a boon for the Great Lakes team, especially after most of that terrific 1944 squad had been shipped west. Brown later wrote that "the only player we got to keep was Marion Motley because he was unknown and had not been at the University of Nevada long enough to build up a great reputation. He became the cornerstone on which we built the 1945 team."[16]

There are several versions of how Brown finagled Motley out of the war and onto his team. The end result, however, was that Brown figuratively snagged Motley at the 11th hour. According to Mark Craig, interviewing Motley years later:

Paul said to me, "Hang up the phone, but stay right there," Motley said. About five or ten minutes later, the phone rings and a boatswain answers and says, "Hey Motley, some fool on the telephone says he's the commandant of Great Lakes." I picked up the phone and the voice says, "Seaman First Class Motley, this is the Commandant of Great Lakes."
Paul had talked to him.
"My bags were on the train heading out. I went down to get them and, wouldn't you know it, they were at the bottom of a big stack of bags." [After ripping apart the stack to get his bags, Motley got out of there before the

train pulled out.] "I said, 'I got them,' and I was gone. The guys who showed me where my bags were said, 'Hey Motley, you're not going to help us stack these other bags up again?' I waved over my shoulder and said, 'Go call the Commandant.'"[17]

There was another, at the time unknown, benefit from Motley's assignment to Brown's football team: a young second-class petty officer had become one of Brown's assistant coaches. Blanton Collier would prove to be one of Motley's greatest advocates over the next two decades, his support all the more credentialed by Collier's later success. After signing on as an assistant on Brown's Cleveland coaching staff, he then struck out on his own, earning SEC Coach of the Year honors as Kentucky's head man in 1954, and then leading the Cleveland Browns to an NFL title as head coach in 1964. He knew football, and he thought Motley one of the very best ever.

Blanton Collier

Collier is an interesting figure in the Marion Motley story, the Paul Brown story, and in the history of the entire Cleveland Browns franchise. He was a second-class petty officer in the Navy, stationed at Great Lakes in 1943, and he would often go to Brown's practice sessions and just take notes. Before the Navy, Collier had been a school coach, and he was jumping at the chance to study Ohio State's Paul Brown as he prepared his team and installed his schemes. At first, Petty Officer Collier would spend afternoons anonymously watching Brown's team practice from the stands, taking notes on the T formation and diagramming the plays that Brown had his team run. Brown, already hired by Art McBride to coach the new Cleveland All-America Football Conference at war's end, was suspicious that the man was a spy for another team, maybe even an NFL organization. Brown had the Master at Arms (the Navy's police force) apprehend the young coach and bring him to Brown. After some conversation and a bit of a trial period, Brown invited the man to help him with the team. Collier ended up volunteering to help Brown as an assistant coach, and after the war, Brown hired him into the new Cleveland Browns organization.

The relationship was a close one, and after Collier took the head job at the University of Kentucky, replacing one Paul "Bear" Bryant, they still talked often about football.[18] Collier's Wildcats posted a 41–36–3 record, but that was not enough success to save the coach's job. Brown re-hired Collier in 1962, as a few years later Browns owner Art Modell replaced Brown with the protégé, creating a long rift between the two football engineers. But in 1944, Collier was an eager acolyte and assistant to the older Brown.

1945

The Great Lakes season opener, at Wolverine stadium against the University of Michigan, occurred on September 15, 1945, in front of more than 25,000 maize-and-blue-clad fans. Likely lost on him at the time, there is some small irony that, after dominating football at Nevada in relative anonymity, Motley had finally reached the national stage not as a student-athlete at a major university, but as an enlisted member of the United States Navy.

In the first quarter of the game, after a quick Michigan touchdown, the fullback announced his arrival with all the authority of an explosion. Great Lakes managed two points in the first half, on a safety after a Wolverine fumble, but opened the second half with the ball. "First play after the Michigan kickoff, George Terlep, former Notre Dame reserve back now playing for the sailors, lateralled to Marion Motley, giant Negro fullback from Nevada university, who dashed 52 yards to a foot from pay dirt."[19] Michigan stopped the Great Lakes team without scoring and then scored twice more in the fourth quarter for the final margin. Motley, though, was pulled in the third quarter after he suffered a cut heel during a collision with one of his own teammates.[20]

As a rhetorical aside, sportswriters of the day appear to have been a bit awed by Motley the player, but like so many of their ilk, could not seem to ignore his race. The *Chicago Tribune* referred to him as a "giant Negro," while *Detroit Free Press* writer Lyall Smith took it up a notch and called him a "gigantic Negro fullback" in reporting the same game.[21] There were seemingly countless riffs on this theme throughout Motley's career, almost all focusing on the player's physical size and his race. It was as if such a characterization comforted the intended reading audience by diminishing Motley's football skills and attributing his ability to mutation, implying to the audience that Motley was a freak of nature of sorts. Rather than just embracing his outstanding production, the implicit argument was that he was an outlier, and that his accomplishments weren't so impressive, given his physical advantage(s).

The Michigan loss was not, perhaps, the most auspicious start to a football season, but the new Great Lakes team had performed well enough to avoid total embarrassment.[22] The following week, against Wisconsin, Motley again did not play. He was, likely, still recovering from the heel injury sustained against Michigan, and the Bluejackets tied the Badgers 0–0 in their home opener at Ross Field. The weather did not cooperate as, in a way normal to every cynical sailor who ever went to sea, the winds gusted to 40 miles per hour and rain fell throughout the entire, miserable afternoon.

After bottoming out with a 20–6 loss to Purdue, and then falling to the Fort Benning (GA) team, this time 21–12, Brown's team began to show signs of life. Against Purdue, Motley had finally been able to suit up and play, and the loss to the Army team was partly mitigated by the reality that Fort Benning was talented and had two former University of Alabama stars on the roster: running back Russ Craft, who had also been a fine receiver, and kicker George Hecht. "Both men had been sparks on the Crimson Tide's 1941 and 1942 teams that won the Cotton Bowl and Orange Bowl games, respectively, with Hecht registering crucial field goals in both games."[23] Motley scored one of the Great Lakes touchdowns against Benning, but missed on two extra-point kicks.

After all the early season frustration two weeks later on October 20, the figurative tide finally turned. Great Lakes beat Marquette 37–27, then defeated Western Michigan 39–0. A week later, against Illinois, Motley returned the opening kickoff 77 yards, leading to a difference-making touchdown in a 12–6 Bluejacket victory. After smiting Michigan State 27–7, and pummeling Fort Warren (WY) 47–14, Great Lakes used the Thanksgiving break to prepare for their biggest challenge of the season. On December 1, at their home stadium at Ross Field in Chicago, they welcomed the fifth-ranked University of Notre Dame for the 1945 season finale.

Before the game even began, though, there was internal crisis in Coach Brown's professional life. The Great Lakes Bluejackets were, first and foremost, U.S. Navy sailors, government employees, if you will, and not scholarship athletes. In other words, the Department of the Navy exerted control over the players and the team that not even Brown could contain. "Motley and Klemmer were eligible for discharge a couple of weeks before the game, so I called them aside before practice and said,

'I've been notified that you men have finished your tour and may leave. Or I can arrange to delay your discharge until after we play Notre Dame. Which will it be?'"[24]

Grover Klemmer, the other player eligible for discharge, had been a world class runner at the University of California in the early 1940s, and for a time owned the world record in the quarter mile. After the war, he would return to the Bay area and become a football coach, developing future Pro Football Hall of Famer Ollie Matson while at the City College of San Francisco, and also worked as an NFL referee between 1955 and 1986.[25] But in 1945, he was almost as valuable to the Bluejackets as was Motley. Both players agreed to suspend their discharges until after the game, moves that proved to be the first of many good tidings for the Navy that day.

The Fighting Irish of Notre Dame entered that game with a 7–1–1 record, and coach Huge Devore fielded a squad that included starting quarterback Frank Dancewicz, who became the first overall pick in the 1946 NFL draft, and backup George Ratterman, who went on to a ten-year NFL career and two All-Pro selections. Starting halfback Elmer Angsman went on to an eight-year NFL career with the Chicago Cardinals, including a championship in 1947, and was selected to a Pro Bowl along the way. The Irish's sole loss had come at the hands of the U.S. Military Academy (Army), but that team was led by two college football immortals, Glenn Davis and Doc Blanchard, and the loss was understandable. The bottom line was that the Great Lakes Bluejackets were facing what was, easily, the toughest team on their schedule.

From the kickoff, however, the sailors took control. Coming out of the locker room, the "Bluejackets put the ball in play on Notre Dame's 29-yard line after the initial kickoff, and went all the way in eight plays."[26] Future Pittsburgh Steeler draftee Frank Aschenbrenner returned the kick 54 yards and the drive culminated in a three-yard touchdown dive by the quarterback. Another touchdown in the second quarter made the halftime score 13–7, with the lone Notre Dame score coming after their defense recovered a Great Lakes fumble, by Motley, on the Navy 21-yard line. For Paul Brown's one-season team, the offensive and defensive lines established superiority and held it for the entire game. Behind that line, "Grover Klemmer, the fastest man in either backfield, Marion Motley, and Frank Aschenbrenner [all] advanced practically at will."[27]

The second half began with Great Lakes marching the ball 63 yards in ten plays. Klemmer and Motley, the two players that stayed to play, along with Aschbrenner and Terlep, battered Notre Dame's defense all afternoon. In the third quarter, Motley galloped for 18 yards, setting up another Great Lakes touchdown, and in the fourth he raced 44 yards for a touchdown that foreshadowed Bo Jackson and Brian Bosworth on a Monday night in 1987.

Paul Brown retold the tale in his autobiography:

> Notre Dame simply could not handle Motley that day and even had trouble knocking him down as he ran several trap plays that became his specialty over the years. We had particularly told Marion in practice, "If you come clear on the trap play, don't get fancy. If there is someone in front of you, just run in one end of them and out the other." That's exactly what he did. When he broke lose on his 44-yard touchdown run, there was only one man between Marion and the goal line; Motley never broke stride and simply ran over him en route to the end zone.[28]

In the *Chicago Tribune* the next day, "Motley ran 44 yards thru the line and pulled away from the secondary with speed comparable to Klemmer's best." Again, as a reminder, just three years earlier Grover Klemmer had held the world record in the 440-yard sprint, the fastest recorded quarter-mile run in history. Motley, though he was enormous for a running back, was as fast as the situation needed him to be, even if that meant motoring at a world-class clip.

The game ended with Great Lakes conquering Notre Dame, 39–7. The Bluejackets outrushed the Fighting Irish 263–87, and the four touchdowns scored against the Irish in the fourth quarter were the most anyone could remember being allowed by Notre Dame in a single period. The loss dropped them to ninth in the final Associated Press poll. Navy Shore Patrol denied the 23,000 fans in attendance the joy of rushing the field and tearing down the goal posts after the final gun, but it mattered little. The following day, at the end of the war, Ross Field was dismantled and consigned to memory.

The Notre Dame game was, in short, the most glorious exit imaginable for Motley's college and Navy football career, as it was for Grover Klemmer and coach Paul Brown as well. World War II had ended with the bombing of Japan in August, and by December the nation was already embarking on the transition from the wartime footing and back into the rhythms of relative peace. With the war over, Motley separated from the Navy soon after that game, and returned to the Republic Steel mill, once again resuming life as a foundry worker.

Fortunately for Motley, though, opportunity had already appeared on the horizon. The All-America Football Conference (AAFC) was in the process of being born, and local magnate Arthur "Mickey" McBride had purchased the Cleveland franchise rights a year earlier, in 1944. One of McBride's first tasks had been to find a head coach and general manager for his team. After being turned down by Frank Leahy, who intended to return to Notre Dame after his wartime naval service, McBride offered the job to the returning Ohio State University head coach and now-naval veteran Paul Brown. Brown accepted, and even as he was working with Blanton Collier and coaching Marion Motley, he began assembling his new, professional organization.

In the *Reno Evening Gazette* a few days after the Great Lakes win over Notre Dame, Frank McCulloch wrote, "Don't be surprised if big Marion Motley turns up on the roster of the Cleveland entry in the professional All-America football conference next year." Since Motley had been one of Coach Paul Brown's greatest stars, the most impressive college performer on a military team during his Great Lakes navy 1945 season, and had enjoyed such a tremendous afternoon with his performance against Notre Dame, "Brown, who will take over the pro coaching job when the navy releases him, has admitted for publication he would like to have Motley and several others from the sailor team go with him to Cleveland. The astute Brown has another reason for liking Motley, too, he saw the big colored boy perform as a high school star when he—Brown—was coaching Massillon."[29]

As it turned out, McCulloch was right.

4

Welcome to Pro Football
(1946)

The headlines, and the accompanying stories in the New Year's Day papers, tried to capture the euphoria and the feelings of not only the nation but most of the world as 1946 began. "Emotions were loosed into high-pitched revelry last night during a New Year's Eve celebration which probably was unprecedented ... [people] broke forth into a veritable bedlam at the stroke of midnight. Bells, whistles, sirens and horns added to the din of shrieking voices, vibrant with the thrill of victory, which heralded the first peacetime January 1 in five years."[1] That was merely one of so many examples of the rollicking expressions of American relief that the war was over and that the soldiers and sailors were returning home. No longer would there be gas or food rationing, or family members deploying for years at a time to lands where life and death too often collided, or even sports populated with athletes who were otherwise unfit to fight but could carry a ball or swing a bat.

Baseball was depleted to a point that it had employed a one-armed outfielder in St. Louis, and football had survived four years of constriction at many of the nation's colleges and universities. Now, at the start of the new year, the new normal, people seemed to gradually but collectively allow themselves to start to think again about lighter pursuits, about who could challenge the Gas House Gang Cardinals on the baseball diamond, or even if anyone could knock off Sid Luckman and the Chicago Bears in the rowdy NFL. In such anticipation of some version of the new mix of opportunity and enthusiasm, the All-America Football Conference had formed in 1944 to capitalize on the excitement of professional football and the money that might be made bringing the game to un- or under-served cities.

4. Welcome to Pro Football (1946)

At least one historian of sports and economics, in his outline of the primary reasons for the modern success of the National Football League, observed the creation of the AAFC presented a challenge to the NFL owners that ultimately resulted in the merger that created a unified, national game.[2] Combining a sports league that could be shared across the country, especially with the advent of televised games and a one-game, winner-take-all championship, eventually led to the national obsession alluded to earlier. There are several excellent histories of the AAFC, so what follows is a summary and not a deep dive into the league's birth.

James Crowley was hired as the first commissioner of the AAFC. Crowley had been one of the infamous "Four Horsemen" at Notre Dame, and his NFL counterpart in the front office was Elmer Layden, a fellow Horseman from the 1923 and 1924 seasons. Crowley's selection was almost certainly more than a coincidence. Commissioner Layden, when asked by a reporter about the potential for a World Series of football, a game between the best of the NFL and the best of the new conference, had dismissed the idea a year before. "Let them get a ball," his statement said, "draw a schedule, and play a game. Then I will talk to them."[3] AAFC founding father Arch Ward and his ownership recruits, all successes in their respective fields and industries, perhaps sought a commissioner who Layden had to respect.

The upstart league was well funded. As a group, the AAFC owners had money to invest, likely exceeding the capacity of their NFL counterparts. Mickey McBride of Cleveland, a real estate (and taxi) magnate, Tony Morabito, a lumber baron in San Francisco, and the Hollywood consortium of Benjamin Lindheimer (racetracks), actor Don Ameche, and producer Louis B. Mayer were the financial backbone of the Los Angeles franchise.

In the mid–1940s, just after World War II, Cleveland was still a city—if not one on the ascent, then one still relevant on a national scale—that demanded attention. It had been home to luminaries like John D. Rockefeller, hosted a vital port industry on Lake Erie, and was, in many ways, a midwestern rival to New York City in terms of economic contribution. Establishing a team in Cleveland was an easy decision for the AAFC in 1945, and that event facilitated the Rams' decision to accelerate their relocation to Los Angeles.

That move appeared somewhat surprising to the general public when it was announced, just a month after the team won the NFL championship in a 15–14 decision over Washington, but the possibility of moving the team had been in discussion for a while. Dan Reeves, the Rams' owner, claimed the team lost more than $40,000 in 1945, despite the title, and the city of Los Angeles was offering a significant financial incentive to attract the team.[4] In putting a head-to-head competitor for the Rams in southern California, the Los Angeles Dons, along with a natural geographic rival in San Francisco, the 49ers, all while holding on to the Cleveland market, the AAFC profitably presaged major league baseball's westward expansion a decade later.

In Cleveland, and throughout northeast Ohio, Mickey McBride conducted a team naming contest in the local papers, even offering a $1,000 war bond to whomever suggested the best name for the new organization. The winning name, the Panthers, lasted for mere weeks before McBride discovered that a semi-pro team from the 1920s had co-opted the name Cleveland Panthers, and that the name was still owned by George T. Jones, one of the former owners of the Panthers. Jones wanted compensation in order to give up his claim.[5] The old Panthers, starting in 1919 and before the enfranchisement of the NFL, booked games wherever and whenever they could find a paying opponent. Playing in baseball parks, on football fields, and even in pastures, against teams like the Buffalo Prospects and other teams in northern New York, the 1921 iteration was a winning team. In 1925, and overshadowed by the NFL's Cleveland Bulldogs, the Panthers began to fade. After one season in the original AFL (American Football League), the team de-affiliated and, by 1933, had folded.

Arthur McBride was, first and foremost, a businessman, and a wily one at that. Part of his success stemmed from his ability to not simply fritter away money on needless expenses, yet he was evidently willing to pay Jones' fee in order to keep the name Panthers. Of all people involved, though, Paul Brown was rumored to be the one to push McBride to reject the name buyout. Brown, an Ohioan through and through, had been coaching high school football in Canton during the demise of the Panthers 12 years earlier, and was well aware of the reputation associated with the failed team. A master of every detail, Brown did not want his new franchise burdened with the name of anything related to losing. Since it was just over a decade since the Panthers' failure, Brown and McBride may have also feared some degree of public association between the old, failed team and the new contenders. Rather than hold another contest, McBride persuaded Brown to lend his name to the team. Of note, not a single entry in the naming contest had suggested "Cleveland Browns."[6]

Motley, then back in Canton after his time at Great Lakes, was working at a local steel mill in early 1946. This time, though, his knee was working well. Evidently the University of Nevada had offered Motley a place on the team for his senior season. It would have afforded the player a chance to finish his degree, but once Paul Brown floated the idea of playing for him in the AAFC, the return trip to Reno fell off the figurative table. Motley later remembered, "I was set to come back to Reno for that last season [1946] until the Browns talked to me. [I had] a family to support and couldn't turn down the offer."[7] There are variations in the account of how Brown signed Motley to play for his team in 1946, but the consistent elements are that the coach, aware that Motley may have not fallen to him in a draft, had an intermediary bring the player to the Cleveland practice field for a "tryout."

In an oral history recording from the Pro Football Hall of Fame, Motley talked about his signing from his perspective:

> Paul later was coaching the Cleveland Browns in 1946, and I got invited to camp for a tryout. A cousin of mine drove me from Canton over to the camp in Bowling Green, Ohio, and I made it there in time to go straight out to the afternoon practice. That first day, we ran wind sprints and I was out in front of everybody. I beat all those guys—the fullbacks, anyway. So the next day Paul put me all the way up on the second team and I immediately saw resentment from the players.
>
> As Bill Willis and I were going to our room after practice, I said, "Gee, I sure hate Paul putting me on that second team today, 'cause some of those backs was just acting awful snotty." They hadn't said anything, but I could feel the tense-ness around me. I said to Bill, "I just wish Paul would put me back somewhere and let me work my way back up. Then I'll straighten some of them out up there."
>
> I think Paul saw the resentment, because the next day he threw me back on the fourth team. But it didn't take me long to move back up. They had a scrimmage and I played mostly on defense, at linebacker, and I had 'em standing on their ears. After the scrimmage was over, one of the guys asked Willis, "What the heck was eating Motley today? Was he trying to kill somebody?" Willis told him, "No, he's just trying to make the ball club." From then on, there seemed to be a change of feeling toward me. I had the best times in the sprints, I ran the ball as well as any of the others, and after they saw that I had the ability, their attitude toward me changed.[8]

That version differed slightly from what Motley had told Stuart Leuthner in the latter's book. "When I got out of the service," Motley said to Leuthner, "I wrote Paul and asked for a job. He turned me down and wrote back that he had enough backs." Later, Motley recalled in 1987, "Bob Voigts, one of the Browns' assistant coaches, called me and asked me if I'd like to try out. A few days later and he would have missed me because I was all set to go back to the University of Nevada. I told him yes, and one of my cousins drove me up to the Browns' training camp at Bowling Green University."[9]

Brown's version of the signing and introduction of Motley was a bit more nuanced. He felt that Motley "was all too available for a man of his talent."[10] Motley was a 27-year-old father and husband, content but not happy to be back in the steel mill. "I called Oscar Barkley," Brown wrote, "a friend from Canton, and asked him to drive Marion out to our training camp and have him ask for a tryout. I felt that was the best way to handle the situation, again in light of the potential publicity, because there was nothing unusual in a player's coming to his former coach and asking him for a chance to play."[11] "No other professional football team was interested in him [Motley] at the time because he had not played enough in college or in the service to attract an attention. That was their loss."[12]

The seeming cloak and dagger was important to Brown, in that he did not want any other team (or league) accusing him of exerting undue influence on Motley outside the legal framework. Ten years earlier, the commissioner of baseball had voided several contracts of young players, including Cleveland's Bob Feller, due to what he regarded as tampering. By getting Motley to show up at Bowling Green without a contract, and then signing him after a "workout," Brown gave all concerned a plausible deniability should anyone accuse the team of contractual funny business. Whether Motley asked for the job or Brown simply manipulated the system to sign the back, the outcome was the same. Not only had the team signed Bill Willis, a scary-fast defensive lineman from Ohio State (and a future Pro Football Hall of Famer, as well), but they also had snared Marion Motley.

Bill Willis

He was in large part the reason that Marion Motley was ever offered a contract with the Cleveland Browns in the first place, so no examination of Motley's life would be complete without an introduction to Bill Willis. If his athletic career had no other significance, Willis would still be a vital tile in the mosaic of Cleveland's football history. In truth, Bill Willis' contributions on and beyond the gridiron deserve a book-length biography of their own. His college football career at Ohio State, playing for Paul Brown, so impressed the latter that Brown signed Willis to the new Cleveland Browns squad before the teams had set foot on the practice field in their inaugural 1946 season. Brown signed Willis, a Black athlete, before Branch Rickey signed Jackie Robinson to play baseball with the Brooklyn Dodgers in 1947, and mere days after the Los Angeles Rams' signings of Kenny Washington (March 21, 1946) and Woody Strode (May 7). Bill Willis was a spectacular athlete, and Brown wanted his star defender wreaking havoc for the Browns the same way the former had done in college. Of course, Willis needed a roommate, a Black roommate, and with the arrival of Motley the two were joined forever in sports and social history.

Marion Motley (left) and Bill Willis in the locker room, 1947. Motley and Willis were roommates in every training camp and road trip throughout their time together in Cleveland. Willis later presented Motley at the latter's Hall of Fame induction in Canton, Ohio (*Cleveland Press* collection, Michael Schwartz library, Cleveland State University).

As with Motley, Willis had never intended to play the role of racial pioneer. He was born William Karnet Willis on October 5, 1921, to Clement and Williana Willis, a sharecropping family in Gordy, Georgia, after elder brother Claude and sister Georgia. Gordy is a small farming community in southwest Georgia just under 20 miles from Motley's birthplace in Albany, making the two future Hall of Famers near neighbors, but the Willis family preceded the Motleys in the Great Northern Migration by a year. Clem moved the extended family to central Ohio in 1922, but contracted pneumonia and died in April 1923, at the age of 32,[13] leaving his widow and her father to raise the family.[14]

Willis thrived in Columbus. He was a gifted athlete, but his intelligence and willingness to work elevated him to an elite level rarely seen in any sport. He was fast enough to star in the sprint events on the Columbus (East) high school track team, but also perform as one of the best shot putters in the school. Outside the decathlon, those events are traditionally incompatible, but for Willis they were simply manifestations of his athletic genius. His older brother, Claude, was an all-state fullback for Columbus East before Bill's arrival, and the latter's reluctance to be compared with his brother drove the younger player to the line. As a tackle and end, Willis made all state (honorable mention) as a senior, and in 1941 he enrolled at Ohio State University to run track, but primarily to play football for Paul Brown. Gene Fekete, future Willis teammate on the Browns and also an Ohio State linebacker who was drafted by the Detroit Lions in 1945, told David Campbell about the first time he encountered Willis when they were opponents in a high school game in Columbus. "The only recollection I have of that game," Fekete recalled, "is that we had a fifth man in our backfield—and it was him [Willis]."[15]

At 202 pounds, fast as well as quick, Willis was a surprise on the Buckeye defensive line. He was one of the very few Black students at the university, and he managed to succeed in the classroom despite having to live so far from the campus that he often hitchhiked to both class and practice. Lining up at what was then referred to as "middle guard," today more of a "nose tackle," Willis was normally positioned across from the offensive center, yet he was able to control the gap on both sides of that center. He was a key member of the Buckeyes' 1942 national championship and was named an All-American in both 1943 and 1944. He had been classified "4F," unsuitable for military service, due to varicose veins, but the college football community did not care as much, and Willis was named the Outstanding Player in the 1944 College All-Star game. After graduating from Ohio State, he was named head football coach at historically Black Kentucky State University in 1945. Though he only coached that one year in Frankfort, the team lost but two games, and Willis was elected to the school's Athletic Hall of Fame in 2007.[16]

Willis also underwent knee surgery late that year, so when Paul Brown called on his old star, recruiting him to the new Cleveland Browns in the All-American Football Conference for the 1946 season, Willis was ready. "This was no social idea," Brown told a newspaper writer in 1977. "I was looking for guys who could play football, men among men. He was the most popular guy on our team. He was the quickest down lineman in football history."[17] Once in camp, he soon impressed his new teammates. "Everybody got knocked down [in training camp]," remembered teammate Mike Scarry. "We used to just line up over the ball and snap it. With Willis, though, you had to put the ball as far as you could out in front of you, to get as far away from him as you could. He changed the whole way we snapped the ball."[18]

Paul Brown's signing of Willis was historic, in that the latter was the first Black player in the AAFC. Since even Brown was not willing to further challenge the racial mores of the time, he sought out Marion Motley to join the Browns and provide a roommate for Willis. Of all the terrific personnel decisions with which Brown is credited, and of all the innovations the coach brought to the game, signing Willis and Motley may have been the move that made the others possible. The two, quite literally, propelled the Browns to apex of professional football.

The two stars leaned on each other in enduring the racial challenges inherent to breaking through the racial wall in professional sports, and dominated their respective positions on the field. According to his Professional Football Hall of Fame biography, Willis' charge off the line "was so quick that coaches felt he had to be offside."[19] Willis took that talent to eight consecutive championship games between 1946 and 1953. His single most notable play may have come in the 1950 rematch with the New York Giants in the playoffs, when he caught the Giants' Gene Roberts from behind, after a fourth quarter reception, that prevented a touchdown and preserved the 8–3 Cleveland win.

In his Hall of Fame induction speech, Willis observed, "Motley and I became fast friends because we had to be fast friends. We had to go through a lot together and we had to depend upon each other."[20] Both were named to the NFL's 1940s All-Decade team, and both are enshrined in Canton in the Hall of Fame. Willis was also elected to the College Football Hall of Fame in 1971. In 2007, Willis' jersey, and his number 99, were retired by Ohio State University, and in 2010 he was among the first 16 players inducted into the Cleveland Browns' Ring of Honor.

Willis retired from professional football after the 1953 season. He had been married since 1947 to Odessa Porter, and they raised three successful sons, William, Clement, and Daniel. Willis took a position working in the Cleveland's recreation department after he retired, but in 1963 the family settled in Columbus where he worked for the Ohio Department of Youth Services. Willis retired from the working world for good in 1983.

He suffered a stroke in 1989, but endured an even greater challenge when Odessa passed away in 2003. They had been married for 53 years. It was devastating for the aging star. In his Hall of Fame speech, he had waited to thank his teammates until he had thanked his wife. "This is a great, great day for me. I am very thankful I have been blessed in many, many ways for the love of my dear wife, Odessa. She has given me inspiration and encouragement in her very strong love through the years. We have been blessed with three very fine sons. We are extremely proud of them. We are proud also of the beautiful daughters-in-law we have, and it makes me feel great to be able to have my entire family here with me and share in this most momentous occasion."[21]

Given his contributions to the world after football, working for and with some of Ohio's most troubled youth, the Touchdown Club of Columbus created the Bill Willis trophy, annually awarded to one of the nation's most talented defensive linemen, but who also embodies Willis' commitment to his fellow humans.

Willis' health gradually declined until he suffered another stroke and died on November 27, 2007, at a long-term care facility in Columbus. He was 86 years old. According to his obituary, he died in his sleep with his sons, their wives, and his four grandchildren at his side.[22] Son Clement said, "My father had a wonderful life, did a lot of great things and helped a lot of people." His contributions to the world merely began on the football field. They still echo today.

Back in Camp

There is a 1946 video review of the first year of the Browns that begins with footage from Cleveland's training camp in Bowling Green.[23] Into that bucolic college setting, a school nestled in a smaller town just south of Toledo and amid miles and miles of farmland, the team began the path toward coming together into a single entity. The most notable characteristic, universal among all the players who are shown checking in to the facilities, is the pigmentation of their skin. They are all Caucasian. Just like the AAFC. Just like the NFL, since 1933. Just like "organized" baseball, including the Major leagues. The players were supremely skilled behemoths with amazing physical gifts, yet all White. Paul Brown, though, needed to improve wherever he could, and the market for talented White football players had no inefficiencies left. The normal pool of good players was empty.

Brown was only motivated by winning, and certainly did not limit himself by race. At Ohio State, he'd coached Willis in 1942 and 1943. In 1942, Bill Willis helped the team to a 9–1 record, a Big Ten conference championship, and selection as national champions by the Associated Press. At 6'2", Willis was fast enough, even at his size, to compete in the 100-yard dash at the Penn Relays, and in 1943 he became Ohio State's first Black All-American in football. In 1944 he'd again been named to the All-American roster and his Buckeye team finished second in the final AP poll. He was, by every measure, an extraordinary athlete, and clearly an upgrade over the best on the Browns before his arrival.

The problem was that, as a Black man, Willis needed a Black roommate. All players were quartered in double rooms, in training camp and road trips, but not even Brown was willing to poke the societal taboo of Black and White rooming together. In Motley, not only had Brown found the Black roommate he had sought for his young defensive lineman, but also a fullback who could make his T formation go.

Local Cleveland papers like the *Press*, the *News*, and the *Plain-Dealer* did not spend much space talking about the two Black rookies in the otherwise all-Caucasian league, but the African American reporters certainly gave it some ink. Al Dunmore, of the *Pittsburgh Courier*, wrote a lengthy piece detailing the arrival of both Willis and Motley to the Browns' training camp.

On a sidenote, the African American press included some

substantial newspapers, dailies like the *Chicago Defender*, the *Afro-American*, the *Baltimore Afro-American*, and the *Pittsburg Courier*. The *Courier* rostered a staff of terrific sportswriters, and it is in their words that the enthusiasm around Motley, Willis and others remains visible.

> Marion Motley, former University of Nevada and Great Lakes star fullback, and Bill Willis, former Ohio State University All-American tackle, were both given try-outs last week by Paul Brown here at the camp of the Cleveland Browns.... Brown suggested he felt both boys would make the grade.... Motley brings both power and speed to the fullback spot ... [he] demonstrated that he had plenty speed [*sic*] when he finished several strides in front of the quarterbacks and fullbacks in the sprints.[24]

Presciently, Dunmore also observed that "Motley is also a brilliant defensive fullback [today, a linebacker]." Several members of the College All-Star squad of last year who scrimmaged against the Great Lakes team recalled that Motley made three-fourths of the tackles. "We just didn't seem to get by him," said former University of Missouri and Illinois halfback Don Greenwood.[25] Since coaches were limited to substituting players one at a time, one per play, Motley had no choice but to find a defensive home as well. "When Marion came to us in 1946, players had to go both ways," recalled Blanton Collier.[26]

Returning to the T formation and the ingredients necessary for success, the particulars of making the formation work, Frank Leahy had written, "look to your quarterback, for he is the heart and soul of the T formation ... offense is no better than its quarterback." Leahy believed that the optimum quarterback must "be an excellent ball handler—if he played basketball, all the better."[27] As Brown discovered later, when he signed Northwestern quarterback and professional basketball player Otto Graham to quarterback his team, his T formation became even more lethal.

The relationship between Marion Motley and Otto Graham, among all the teammate interactions on the football team, was perhaps the most critical to the phenomenal success of the Cleveland Browns in their first ten years of existence. Graham's appreciation of his fullback resonated throughout their lives. In his book about how to play quarterback within the T formation, he specifically states, "Marion Motley is as great a fullback as there has ever been in football. What makes him great is the ability to run and block equally well. There have been many devastating running fullbacks, and many others who were damaging blockers ... never have I seen a fullback who performed both functions so well."[28]

Otto Graham

Otto Everett Graham, Junior, was seemingly born to play football. He weighed almost 15 pounds when he arrived on December 6, 1921, and while he was raised by musicians to be a musician, it was in athletics that his gifts emerged. At Waukegan High School (Illinois) he made All-State teams in both basketball and football, and he actually accepted a basketball scholarship at Northwestern rather than play football at Dartmouth.

Technically, Graham chose Northwestern University because he could participate as both a music major and basketball player. Music was one of his passions, but he was talented enough to play with the varsity basketball team as a freshman. He was nicknamed "Automatic Otto" due to his reliable basketball shooting. Football was relegated to intramural recreation in Graham's early college tenure. In fact, Graham did not set foot on a collegiate football field until his sophomore year. As the story goes, Northwestern's football coach, future College Hall of Famer Pappy Waldorf, happened to see Graham throwing in an intramural game, and invited him to practice with the team. In his first college football game in 1941, against Kansas State, Graham returned a punt 90 yards for a touchdown. He also ran for another score and passed for a third while leading Northwestern to a 51–3 romp. Later that year, he gained Paul Brown's attention when he tossed two touchdown passes in a 14–7 win over Ohio State. It was the single loss of the entire year for the Buckeyes.[29] Graham not only paced the Big 10 conference at quarterback, but finished third in the 1943 Heisman Trophy balloting.

Right after graduating, Graham joined the Navy and entered the V-5 program. The V-5 and V-12 programs had been created to streamline aviator accessions, to build a pilot inventory should the war continue and exhaust the existing inventory of pilots. Graham was assigned to the North Carolina Pre-Flight unit, and again achieved All-American status in 1945, this time playing for Paul "Bear" Bryant.

The NFL's Detroit Lions drafted Graham in 1944, but the quarterback held out and signed with Paul Brown in 1945. In the interim, he exercised his basketball skills in playing with future Basketball Hall of Fame stars Red Holzman and Al Cervi with the Rochester Royals in their first season in the National Basketball League (NBL). The league was one of the predecessors of the modern National Basketball Association, and today the Rochester Royals are known as the Sacramento Kings. In that first post-war season, Graham and the Royals won the NBL championship, eventually making him one of the few to win a professional championship in two major sports.

Graham's AAFC time saw Cleveland win four titles in four years, and he quarterbacked the Browns to championship games in ten consecutive seasons. His teams won seven, making him the early antecedent of Tom Brady. In 1953, Graham became the first NFL player, quarterback or otherwise, to wear a facemask on his helmet. After retirement from active football, Graham picked up a whistle and found a home as a head coach. He led the College All-Stars each year between 1958 and 1965, and led them to two victories over NFL teams in 1962 and 1963 (Detroit and Green Bay, respectively). He worked for a time as the athletic director at the Coast Guard Academy, but in 1966 accepted the head job with the Washington Redskins. Despite having several future Hall of Fame caliber players, the team never won more than seven games during Graham's time, and he was replaced by Vince Lombardi after the 1968 season. Graham returned to the Coast Guard Academy and remained there until he retired in 1985.

Otto Graham was elected to the Professional Football Hall of Fame in 1965, was named to the NFL's 1950s All-Decade Team and the 75th Anniversary Team, and had his NFL jersey number, 14, retired by the Browns.[30] He died in 2003, and is buried in the Palms Memorial Park in Sarasota, Florida.[31] To call Graham a gifted athlete was to understate his abilities. He was probably the finest fusion of quarterback and system ever fielded. Better than Lombardi and Starr, Walsh and Montana, or even Belichick and Brady, Otto Graham was the ideal T formation quarterback.

Graham even wrote his own book on the T formation in 1953.[32] The book plumbs the technical depths of quarterback play, minute details that covered everything from the quarterback's toe position while lined up under the center to the flexion of his hips and knees, and even which hand should be "on top," or pushing on the center's backside. Should it be the throwing hand, to make the release a bit quicker, or the off hand, to protect the ball? The Browns subscribed to the former, and the debate underscores the level of detail with which Paul Brown, Blanton Collier, and the whole organization approached the game.[33]

Graham devoted an entire section of the book to quarterback spins. Because the formation, with its even spacing between players and balanced deployment of running backs and ends, afforded the offense the entire gamut of play options on every snap, there were few boundaries limiting the plays that the offense could run. On almost every play, the quarterback would either execute a reverse spin, a straight-away spin, or a double spin, depending on where the play was going and who would ultimately handle the ball.[34]

Such fakes and deceptions were fundamental to the formation's success. If the play was a hand-off to a running back, Graham wrote, the quarterback should always fake a setup for a pass. After the hand-off the quarterback should always continue the fake if only to freeze the occasional safety. As a corollary, on passes there should always be a faked hand-off. Play action on every play was essential to keeping the defense from guessing where to attack the ball. The quarterback's ability to conceal the ball while spinning often froze linebackers and defensive backs, and that moment of defensive indecision often allowed a disciplined offense to attack as planned.

The T Formation and the First Victories

The second key to the T was the fullback. An ideal T fullback would be strong enough to block for the quarterback or lead a halfback into an interior line hole, big enough to take the ball up the middle himself, and fast enough to make yardage if he found himself in the open field with the ball. As well suited to the T quarterback role as Otto Graham was, Marion Motley was equally ideal as a fullback. In a generic T formation playbook, the heavier, usually slower, fullback would either block while the quarterback passed, or lead a runner into the line, or attack the line himself. In Marion Motley's case, though, the power of a gifted athlete at the fullback position truly unleashed the full potential of the formation. Faster than even most running backs, he rarely went in motion, and when he took the ball, he was deep enough in the backfield to see which hole was open, quick enough to get there before the defense reacted, and strong enough to plow through even if there were a few defenders in his path. In Motley's case, he was also one of the best blockers on the field and could move to an advantageous position between Graham and the pass rushers in order to confront them head on.

Graham paid Motley's array of skills sincere homage in his book and used his fullback as the exemplar of one particular nuance of offensive play. Running backs, Graham wrote, might receive hand-offs differently, and this created an additional challenge for the quarterback. "One of the best examples of the different way backs receive the ball is Marion Motley. Marion is hard to give the ball to because he bends so low when he runs it is tough to get the ball into his stomach."[35] That deep, straight-ahead blast type of run demanded ball protection, and the taller Motley kept the ball under control by running low and fast.

Of course, and coach Blanton Collier was one of many to point this out, "he [Motley] was the greatest all-around football player I ever saw," in describing how Motley's defense was unfairly obscured by his offensive brilliance. "This man was a great, great linebacker. Believe me, he could do everything. He had no equal as a blocker; yes, he could do it all ... he was big ... yet he could run with anybody for 30 yards or so."[36] Brown had signed Motley for $4,500 a year, made him Bill Willis' roommate, and then set about dominating the AAFC for the four-year life of the league.[37]

That dominance began on September 6, 1946, against the Miami Seahawks.

Breaking Barriers

Throughout baseball, throughout the United States, it is part of cultural canon that April 15, 1947, was one of the most significant milestones in 20th-century race relations in America. That was the day that Jackie Robinson, a Black man, suited up and started a baseball game for the Brooklyn Dodgers. In playing that game, and throughout his ensuing Hall of Fame career, he is recognized as the first Black athlete to punch a hole in the wall separating the races, at least in the locker room, in professional sports. Robinson's feat is remarkable beyond words, though many have tried to capture it, and his appearance, his play, and his demeanor in nation's most popular sport made it unarguable that baseball was being played at the highest levels by both Black and White.

That fame, that echoing applause for Robinson and everything he gave to baseball and to his nation, is richly deserved. Professional football, though, was a sport on the rise with America. These post-war years were a time without a television in every living room, but the sport, and the games, drew considerable fan attention and sporting press. It wasn't pro football ca. 2020, but it was definitely a visible sport, and one about which fans cared. On September 6, 1946, a full six months before Robinson stood tall on the diamond at Ebbets Field and started a major league baseball game, Marion Motley and Bill Willis did so on a football field in Cleveland, in a game against the Miami Seahawks. Notably, a few hours later, on the West Coast, two of Robinson's Black college teammates from UCLA, Kenny Washington and Woody Strode, also took the field in an NFL regular season contest.

"Jackie's signing got a lot more [notoriety] because baseball was much bigger than pro football in the '40s." remembered Motley 50 years later. "What we did in football helped get Jackie into the major leagues. There was a quote from [Dodgers general manager] Branch Rickey, who said, 'If these men can play a contact sport like football, then Jackie Robinson can play baseball.' So we really opened the door in two sports."[38] The key within Motley's words, though, is that Branch Rickey of the Brooklyn baseball Dodgers was also Branch Rickey of the Brooklyn football Dodgers of the AAFC (the team played between 1946 and 1948). Before he brought Robinson to the majors, as he toiled in Montreal, Rickey was able to watch the football games, see the reality of more paying Black fans in seats for Browns games than for any other team's schedule, and see how Motley and Willis could withstand the epithets and abuse—from players and fans—triggered by their race.[39]

One interesting sidenote on breaking those racial barriers: the two Black players signed by the NFL's Rams, Kenny Washington and Woody Strode, were both teammates of Jackie Robinson on the UCLA Bruins football team in the late 1930s. In an almost unbelievable excess, a UCLA track runner named Tom Bradley later became the first Black politician ever elected as the mayor of Los Angeles. If there has ever been a group of more athletically distinguished alumni, it would be a challenge to identify the members.

Strode and Washington were both past their prime when they signed, their contracts offered because a group of Black writers from various California newspapers had waged a pressure campaign on the city to only allow the Rams to move into the Coliseum if owner Dan Reeves promised to sign Black players.[40] Reeves was no social justice warrior, though, and later one of his assistants said that the Rams would not have had any real interest in either player were the team still based in Cleveland.[41] Unlike Paul Brown, whose motivation was primarily to win, Reeves was motivated to just make money. While perhaps not as pure as Brown's, however, Reeves' rationale still helped shove the nation forward in race relations.

On the local level, in Cleveland, there were devils in the details. "When Paul signed us [Motley and Willis]," Motley remembered in 1995, "there were a few [Browns] who weren't too happy. Paul addressed that at the first meeting. He said, 'If you can't get along with your team-mates, you won't be here.' He didn't have to spell it out, everyone knew what he meant."[42] Jim Brown later recalled that, during his time in Cleveland, Paul Brown did not speak openly about race or integration, but instead put the team first, and integrated as necessary. The best players played. Period.[43] Finally, Brown had explained that he expected some criticism for breaking the informal, but rigid, race barrier, and that in especially racist hotbeds like Florida, "I know that I will not have my boys subjected to any form of embarrassment and will be assured of this before making any plans."[44]

"Once we began practice," Motley remembered in 1995, "the matter was settled. The other players saw that Bill and I could help the team, so they shut their mouths. As time passed, we got to be real close. The guys would stand up for us if they saw [opponents] pulling anything dicey."[45] Hall of Fame receiver Dante Lavelli believed that race was not terribly important in the locker room or on the field. Several the Browns' players, including the head coach, had competed with or against Black players in either high school or college, and many were sons of men who worked alongside Black men in the steel mills and factories.[46]

There were 60,135 in the seats at Cleveland Stadium for the opener against Miami. It was the first time more than 60,000 had paid their way in to watch a regularly-scheduled, non-exhibition pro football game.[47] The Browns outgained the hapless Seahawks 314 yards to 22, and outscored them 44–0. "Miami had nothing except nice white uniforms and these were only white until the Browns had rolled them in the dirt in the early minutes of the game."[48] Motley caught a 35-yard pass from Otto Graham to set up the Brown's first field goal, and "blossomed out as an offensive fullback threat last night. Hitherto he has been considered mainly a defensive power."[49] Graham, receiver Mac Speedie, and kicker Lou Groza, all future household names in both Cleveland and at the Hall of Fame in Canton, played key roles in the win. In fact, the single slight blemish on the entire evening came at halftime, when league founder Arch Ward delivered a few remarks to the crowd of that inaugural game and referred to the Browns as the Cleveland Rams.[50] The next day, the papers jibed Ward a bit about his gaffe, but that was all that was written concerning the error. The rest of the evening, at least in Cleveland, had been almost perfect.

The following week, in Chicago against Elroy "Crazy Legs" Hirsch and the Rockets, the Browns again dominated. In front of a reported 51,962 fans at Soldier Field, over 6,000 more than had ever paid to see a pro football game in the city's history, "Canton's Motley Stars as Browns Rip Rockets."[51] Motley, as a rookie, had only started on defense, and not at fullback, in the opener against Miami, although he took his share of reps in the offensive backfield. The regular starter, Gene Fekete, had injured a knee in the previous game, so Motley was given the start in game two on both offense and defense. "The big Canton Negro [again with the unnecessary identifier] carried the ball 12 times for a total gain of 128 yards and was by far the outstanding man on the field."[52] Embedded within that yardage total was a 20-yard touchdown run for the first score of the game.

The *Pittsburgh Courier* shared a few more details on Motley's afternoon. "Motley's brilliance became evident to the fans late in the first quarter when he broke through the center on the 49 yard line and ran 25 yards before being brought down by ... Hirsch. He then advanced to the 12 yard marker after receiving a screen pass from Otto Graham. The Browns were halted for two downs, then Motley got going again on a quick opening play through center [author's note: this was the "Trap" play for which Motley would become the perfect running back; more on the trap play in the next chapter] after which he whirled by Hirsch and went over the goal line standing up."[53] "He was equally effective on defense," continued the *Courier*, "and backed up the line during several crucial moments."[54]

In short, by the end of his second professional game, Marion Motley proved to be a football player like none that had ever before taken the field. He ran from scrimmage, he caught passes and ran, and from anywhere and everywhere he scored. He also played linebacker like his life depended on it. The following week, on a sweltering 87-degree afternoon in Buffalo, New York, Motley continued to awe. Of note, while the crowd was just over 30,000, it was still the largest gate in Buffalo's football history. That made three consecutive weeks of record-breaking attendance to watch the Browns play, and a sizable chunk of that was provided by the legion of non–White fans that Motley and Willis drew.

Motley caught a 33-yard pass from Graham for the second touchdown of the afternoon and helped the Browns to 28–0 shutout of the Bisons. Motley again started at linebacker and paced the Cleveland defense in the win. For the afternoon against the New York Yankees on September 29, Motley led a punishing 151-yard Cleveland rushing attack to a 24–7 win at home.

The October 6 game against the Brooklyn Dodgers, began under sunny skies in Cleveland, and soon turned into another Browns romp. More than 43,000 streamed into Municipal Stadium. The parking lot next to the stadium was jammed, in large part due to the regional fandom generated by the organization. Professional football games of that era were somewhat akin to college contests, with a marching band on the field before kickoff, and a bevy of high-kicking majorettes, along with a halftime marching concert. On this day there was also a "recreation" of *Casey at the Bat*, featuring a small man with an inordinately oversized bat mimicking the unlucky baseball player. The mayor of Cleveland and other notables were part of the festivities as well.

It was a microcosm of Cleveland's entire season. Not only was it coached by a Canton high school and Ohio State legend in Paul Brown, but it also showcased a brilliantly executed offense with Graham throwing to Dante Lavelli and Mac Speedie, and a rushing attack that featured Edgar Jones and the incomparable Motley. Black or White, it seemed, did not matter to the Cleveland fans nearly as much as the team's 4–0 record. The Browns wore their white jerseys and helmets, with orange and brown stripes on the arms, and kicked off to the Dodgers. After Brooklyn turned the ball over to the hosts, on Cleveland's first possession, Groza kicked a 15-yard field goal to make it 3–0. The uprights and goal posts were stationed on the goal line at the front of the end zone, unlike the more modern positioning in the back of the zone, and there was no netting behind the posts. Groza's kick was good, and the ball flew well up into the stands at the end of the field.

On the next Cleveland possession, Motley took a pitch to the left side and rambled 20 yards before being forced out of bounds. Soon thereafter, Don Greenwood scored the first of his two touchdowns on the day to make the score 12–0 after one quarter. Motley broke into the

Dodgers' secondary on two more trap plays in the first half, each net-ting 20-plus yards, and the Browns led 19–0 at the half. In the second half, again on Cleveland's first possession, Motley might have scored on a trap but for slipping and falling in the infield dirt of the stadium. Mot-ley had several more long runs that afternoon, but his real contribution to the passing game was keeping the Brooklyn pass rush far from quar-terback Graham. The existing videos of the game show Motley effort-lessly protect the pocket and keep Graham upright. Cleveland won the game 26–7.

After a 7–0 win in the rematch with the Yankees in New York, the Browns greeted the Los Angeles Dons under uncharacteristically sunny skies at Municipal Stadium. In front of yet another record-setting crowd, Cleveland triumphed 31–14. According to the *Pittsburgh Cou-rier*, Cleveland won easily, "with Motley, sensational sepia fullback, scoring two touchdowns."[55] The back's performance was even better than the reporter described. That day, October 21, Motley scored on runs of 48 and 68 yards, and logged 143 rushing yards on just eight car-ries, an average yards per carry of just under 18.

The following week, against the San Francisco 49ers, Cleveland's winning streak fell, 34–20. Motley was quiet on offense, with Don Greenwood taking the ball near the goal line. On defense, despite a fumble recovery by Motley, Frankie Albert's three touchdown passes were too much for the Browns. In the rematch against the L.A. Dons out in California a week later, the home team stunned Cleveland 17–16. "Big Marion Motley, Brown's stellar fullback, turned in a tremendous defen-sive game, making 60 percent or more of his team's tackles. He was slightly injured and had to leave the game just before the winning field goal was scored. He received an ovation from the fans."[56] A slight injury kept him off the field for the final plays of the fourth quarter, though, including kicker Joe Aguirre's game winning field goal with less than 20 seconds to play.

On the larger front, in the real world, the Browns made a decision that would impact part of their remaining schedule. When they were slated to play Miami in the penultimate game of the regular season, the reality of segregation again intruded. Per a Florida statute "prohibiting Negroes to perform with or against white teams," Motley and Bill Wil-lis were ruled out for the December trip down south.[57] "When I signed the boys last summer," Paul Brown told the press, "I made an agree-ment with the league that I wouldn't use them in Florida. I wouldn't do anything that might embarrass the boys."[58] According to the reporters, "Negroes are not permitted to enter the stadium, even as spectators."[59] The executive offices of the Seahawks were clear that they intended to support Florida law, especially since it might give the hapless Miami team any sort of competitive advantage.

Florida was segregated, severely so even for 1946 America. In 1962, 16 years after the incident with Motley, Willis and the Browns, Bill Bruton told *Sport Magazine* writer Bill Furlong that (as of that writing) most baseball clubs had restrictions on Black players even driving their personal cars as of the late 1950s.[60] "Negro players travelling from one city to another [in Florida] in chartered buses with the ball club," he continued, "could not enter a restaurant and eat with the team." "We'd have to eat in the kitchen ... [and if that didn't work at a hotel] we'd have to find a Negro cabdriver who can take us to a Negro restaurant."[61] Desegregation was hard, often life-threatening work, especially for the principal de-segregators. Woody Strode, UCLA star who was one of the first two Black players in the NFL, was later quoted as saying, "If I have to integrate heaven, I don't want to go."[62]

In Motley's case, with the Florida issue decided, the Browns remained in California following the loss to the Dons, and then headed up the coast to take on the 49ers at Kezar Stadium the following week. Film of this game is still available on the Internet, and one particular play demonstrates Motley's toughness and his desire to score. "Motley got his helmet ripped right off his head and still managed to gain 40 more yards ... [he also notched] a 63-yard run to set up a Browns touchdown."[63] Cleveland avenged their earlier loss to San Francisco, 14–7, and resumed sole proprietorship of first place in their division.

Motley did not play the following week, a 51–14 home win against the Chicago Rockets, as he was not healthy enough after pulling a thigh muscle in San Francisco.[64] The Browns then romped through their final three games, beating Buffalo 42–17 and hapless Miami 34–0 (making their two-game score against the Seahawks 78–0) and demolishing Brooklyn in the regular season finale, 66–14.

In mid–December, the United Press named the first All-America Football Conference team. Along with Otto Graham and Mac Speedie, Marion Motley was named first-team fullback. Cleveland also placed four on the second team: Lou Groza, Ed Ulinski, Mike Scarry, and Dante Lavelli. The 1947 *Pro Football Illustrated* named Motley first-team fullback on the all-AAFC offense and first team linebacker on defense. Not

IT'S A TOUCHDOWN!

Although there are many thrills in the game, always the biggest is when the ball is conveyed into the end zone

Hoofing around end, Marion Motley, Cleveland's all-league back, crosses the goal line up-right in a game with the Brooklyn Dodgers at Ebbets Field, Dec. 8, by eluding Art Vantone.

Marion Motley scoring in a late-season game against Brooklyn in 1946 (*Pro Football Illustrated*, 1947).

only did Motley play both sides of the ball, but he also was the league's best at both of his positions as well.

Motley's star continued upward in the AAFC Championship game against the New York Yankees. Both teams featured elite quarterbacks, receivers, and rushers, as well as stifling defenses. It was a chilly December 23 in Cleveland, two days before Christmas, the stadium blanketed in snow, the field a frozen mix of dirt, dead grass, and, in the end zones, snow. Flakes fell throughout the afternoon, and the weather doubtlessly affected the paid attendance, reported at a paltry 40,469.

CLEVELAND BROWNS—1947 ALL-AMERICA CONFERENCE CHAMPIONS: Back row, left to right—Ernie Blandin, Bill Willis, Lou Groza, Spiro Dellerba, Tony Adamle, Tom Colella, Lin Houston. Third row—Blanton Collier, backfield coach; Mel Maceau, Horace Gillom, Chet Adams, Lou Rymkus, Frank Gatski, Marion Motley, Alex Kapter, Bob Cowan, Morrie Kono, assistant trainer; Second row—Wally Bock, trainer; Paul Brown, head coach; Ray Piskor, Leonard Simonetti, Weldon Humble, Marshall Shurnas, Jim Dewar, John Yonaker, Mac Speedie, George Young, Dante Lavelli, Bill Lund, Mike Scarry, Dick Gallagher, end coach; Bill Edwards, tackle coach. Front row—Fritz Heisler, guard coach; Ray Terrell, Louis Mayne, Bill Boedeker, Ed Ulinski, Cliff Lewis, Lou Saban, Otto Graham, Ermal Allen, Edgar Jones, Bob Gaudio, Don Greenwood, John Brickels, backfield coach.

The 1947 Cleveland Browns, from the 1948 edition of *Pro Football Illustrated*, the largest, most popular pre-season journal for professional football in the 1940s. It ceased publication after the 1952 edition.

On both sidelines the coaches pulled their long, wool coats closer in futility against the Lake Erie breeze, and the players kept moving just to keep their feet from losing sensation. Tackling, contact of any kind, was going to hurt, and everyone dressed for the game knew it.

Given the weather conditions, coach Paul Brown's game plan called for Graham to avoid the longer downfield throws, instead relying on quick tosses into the flat or to specific spots on the field no more than about ten yards downfield.[65] The Browns made up the difference by turning to their rushing game. That afternoon, Motley led the Browns with 98 rushing yards on 13 carries, including a single 50-yard gain, and scored the first of Cleveland's two touchdowns, early in the second quarter. That two-yard blast, behind Lou Rymkus, had been set up three plays earlier on a Motley run from the 13-yard line.

Even though the home team outgained the visiting Yankees 315–146 yards on the day, and Motley shone on defense from his linebacker spot, the Browns needed to come from behind in the fourth quarter to secure the game. The drive was saved on a rare, 20-yard pass from Graham to Edgar Jones, who somehow managed to hold on to the icy ball as it nearly fell short of the mark. A perfect throw to Dante Lavelli, who had gotten behind his defender, turned into the final touchdown of the game. As the clock ran out, the head official handed the ball to defensive leader Lou Saban and the game was over. The net result was a 14–9 win, and the inaugural AAFC championship, for the Cleveland Browns.

It had been, in retrospect, as close to an ideal inaugural season as owner McBride, and certainly coach Brown, could have dreamed. On the year, as a 26-year-old rookie, Marion Motley ran for 601 yards on 73 carries (an 8.2 average), caught ten passes for 188 yards, scored six touchdowns, returned three kickoffs for 53 yards, and also played defense in all 13 games (including one interception). He was all–AAFC in every poll, and had announced himself to the entire football nation with enthusiasm, energy, and authority. His season totals, in terms of numbers of yards gained or tackles made or points scored, pale in contrast to the marks of modern players, but there can be no doubt that Marion Motley was an absolute superstar, a football immortal at the beginning of his professional career.

Paul Zimmerman captured the conundrum of evaluating Motley when he wrote about the 238-pound back:

> There's a statistical table at the end of this chapter [in his book on professional football], detailing the numbers that made up Motley's professional career, but it's a kind of meaningless way of evaluating this remarkable player. It would be like trying to describe a waterfall in terms of gallons per second, or a sunset in terms of light units. Never has there been a set of statistics to measure the force and intensity of a man's hitting power, or his effectiveness as a pass blocker, unless you use a seismograph.[66]

A purer statement of the impact of Marion Motley on the football field has yet to be written.

⧫ 5 ⧫

The First Repeat Champions
(1947)

Motley, like many of Cleveland's players, again spent the offseason working for Arthur McBride's taxi company. McBride was not simply the owner of the Browns, but he was also the owner of most of the Yellow Cabs in the state of Ohio. "I was just a field checker," Motley said about his job. "I would just check the cabs in the area. If we needed a cab in a certain area, like a fair, I would dispatch them to that particular area."[1] He spent almost all of his off-seasons working for McBride, as he still had Eula and three growing boys to support. They had rented a home at 1205 Gonder Avenue SE in Canton, and while the football income—about $4,500 per year—was terrific in contrast to that of many of his high school peers, growing families can always use more.

Many sports reporters, broadcast and print, have used the phrase "taxi squad" since the 1950s when referring to spare players within a particular team's organization. Teams generally keep a small cadre of such players under contract, allowing them to practice and participate but not actively on the roster, as insurance for sudden injury. If a regular on a team, perhaps a linebacker, is hurt too near to gametime to find a replacement in the open market, the team can tap the practice squad and immediately activate the substitute play without having to go through the vetting and negotiation necessary with a free agent.

Arthur McBride's ownership of both the Browns and his taxi company gave him a unique opportunity. He and Paul Brown selected and signed several potential replacement players for those positions in which potential for injury was higher than average, and at which a late-hour replacement would inhibit the team's efficiency in the upcoming game. McBride could put those relief players to work as taxi drivers to keep them salaried and available. The players could train with the regulars, but not count against the league's roster limits. The rest of professional football later adopted the concept, but McBride is the father of the modern "taxi squad."[2]

Motley continued to play a great deal of basketball in the offseason as well. Since before high school, and throughout college, Motley had been an outstanding basketball player, perhaps not on the level of Otto Graham but still talented enough to play at the major college level, and he had continued playing after his return to Ohio. Teamed with Horace Gillom, and a couple of McKinley alumni, Eddie Coleman and Jim Inman, the Canton United Musics played offseason exhibitions against teams throughout the area. Against such teams as the Tas Tees, who rostered major league baseball players Paul O'Dea, Joe Krakul and John Hitke, Motley used the game as a fun way to sustain both his conditioning and his competitive edge.[3] The football players were not fixated on filling specific roles, so they worked as interchangeable parts on a variety of basketball teams. From the Cleveland Browns to the Fifas and several others, the athletes just wanted to play, to have fun, to enjoy the mere act of competing.

In February, Motley was out driving the new car he had bought after the Browns' championship a few weeks earlier. His car "rammed into the rear of a car operated by Arthur E. Ritzman ... three miles south of Akron on route 8."[4] Motley was arrested on a charge of reckless driving. He scraped his nose and knee in the collision, while the other driver claimed back injury. Interestingly, another report noted, "Motley was quoted by highway patrolmen as saying he fell asleep at the wheel."[5]

At first blush, Motley appeared to be not just a poor driver, but an unsafe one, a hazard to fellow motorists. First had been the collision in California in 1940, when a Berkeley man had died and Motley had faced both jail time and a large fine for his recklessness. Now he was confronted by this most recent incident, a rear-end crash entirely his fault. It was the report that he fell asleep behind the wheel that is interesting. According to Motley's granddaughter, Bianca Motley Bloom, it wasn't until much later in life that the man was clinically diagnosed with narcolepsy, what used to be referred to as "sleeping sickness."[6] According to medical professionals, narcolepsy is a chronic problem, "characterized by overwhelming daytime drowsiness and sudden attacks of sleep. People with narcolepsy often find it difficult to stay awake for long periods of time, regardless of the circumstances."[7] There is no small irony in the fact that this enormous, athletically gifted human being was vulnerable to something as simple, yet incurable, as a sporadic attack of sleep. This would not be the last time Motley's narcolepsy interfered with his life.

Paul Brown, in his autobiography, wrote that Motley had problems staying awake in the countless team meetings and game preparation sessions he held throughout the season. "Once," Brown wrote, "he fell asleep driving, ran into another car, and bashed his nose. 'I don't care about your nose, but I do care about those legs, so you stay awake.' Sometimes he dozed off during our meetings, but I usually kept a wet towel nearby, and when I saw him beginning to snooze, I'd throw it at him and he'd bolt upright. The other players always laughed and razzed him, and he took it without offense."[8]

Fortunately for Motley, he was able to resolve the accident, did not sustain any long-term physical problems, and continued preparing for football. The AAFC was also preparing for season number two over the winter of 1946–1947, but that simple process generated controversy throughout the growing professional football world.

The older, more established National Football League had, in the 27 years since its founding in Ralph Hay's Hupmobile dealership in 1920, established a schedule, along with a geographic distribution of teams, that was slowly enabling the sport to take hold in the minds, and wallets, of fans across the country. The NFL had endured a generation of franchise instability and shifting fan bases, but as the Great Depression ebbed, the league found a solid footing from which it could climb. The appearance of the AAFC, especially the financial success of Del Webb's New York Yankees and Artie McBride's Browns, and the threat of a return to instability, was a sort of figurative chum in the water for reporters always hunting for story angles.

Competition among leagues was fodder for columnists and reporters alike. F.T. Kable, the publisher of the annual *Pro Football Illustrated*, wrote in his introductory editorial to the 1947 pre-season annual edition that the friction between the NFL and the AAFC could not be ignored. "In the current squabble between the NFL and the AAFC, thousands upon thousands of fans can't understand why the NFL didn't and still doesn't welcome the AAFC."[9] The tension between the national desire for even more geographically distributed football and the senior circuit's protectionism was palpable. "A monopoly so painstakingly built and so valuable as the NFL happens but once in a lifetime."[10]

The end of the essay set the scene for the following three seasons:

5. *The First Repeat Champions (1947)*

"if the AAFC carries on and makes preparation for 1948, which it is sure to do, it should convince the NFL that it has a permanent neighbor that bears cultivating."[11] Those words would prove prophetic when the leagues did merge in 1950, but in 1947 they were still obscured by the much more practical obligation of every team, every coach, and every player to deliver the best version of football possible and to do so every time a game kicked off. Paul Brown, and his Cleveland Browns, were ready to do their part. They were an undeniably talented team, and every success on their part detracted just a bit from the NFL's ethos of unquestioned superiority.

Robert Peterson, the sports chronicler who was largely responsible for an explosion in interest in baseball's Negro Leagues, and Black baseball in general, later turned his historian's gaze to the early days of professional football. His book, *Pigskin: The Early Years of Pro Football*, is one of the most concise narratives written about those earlier, pre-television years, including some consideration of the Cleveland Browns and their upstart AAFC. It is interesting to consider these early stars and their development. None had the public adulation or awareness of the elite college players of the 21st century. Instead, many were—literally—battle hardened, having faced death in Europe or Asia or at sea, and brought an edge to football and pain and suffering that few today could understand. For every Pat Tillman that has been honored of late, perhaps even immortalized in the Hall of Fame, many of the post–World War II players had endured four years of the horrors of war. The modern aphorisms like "football is like going to war" or "going into battle together" come off as woeful overstatements when considering the players of the late 1940s.

Even the AAFC's new commissioner, retired Navy admiral Jonas Ingram, embodied the martial connection between warfare and football, a linkage even more celebrated in the post-conflict euphoria following World War II. Ingram had played two years on the Naval Academy football team and after his post-graduation midshipman cruise, spent several years on various ships in the fleet. On April 22, 1914, during the battle of Vera Cruz, Mexico, he distinguished himself to the degree that he was awarded the highest military decoration in the nation, the Congressional Medal of Honor, for his heroism. He returned to the academy as the head football coach in 1915 and 1916. Ingram spent the next 25 years rising through the commissioned ranks, and in February 1942 he was promoted to vice admiral (three stars) and given command of the U.S. Fourth Fleet. In November 1944, after successfully prosecuting Nazi submarines and shipping in the southern Atlantic Ocean, Ingram was promoted to full admiral and named commander of the entire United States Atlantic Fleet. He retired in 1947, and took the reins of the AAFC, bringing along Navy buddy (and eventual successor) Oliver O. Kessing as his assistant. Kessing, himself, was a retired rear admiral, and when he took the job of AAFC commissioner in 1949, it marked the only military leadership succession in the history of the game. In 1947, though, Ingram's arrival not only gave the upstart league a patina of legitimacy, but it also brought a strong, combat-proven leader to the head of a group of largely self-interested team owners.

Cleveland's 1947 roster included a collection of names that are enshrined in the Hall of Fame in Canton. Lou Groza had played football at Ohio State, but his time in school was interrupted by a stint in the army. He survived the invasion of Okinawa, and after he was discharged in 1946, he returned to school, and then to Paul Brown's training camp. "Now I had never played college football except for three freshman games," he said. "I showed up at training camp and I said to myself, 'oh boy, what did I get myself into?'"[12] By the time Groza retired, he was the NFL career leader in points, field goals made, and extra points made, and he was the last of the original Browns to pack it in.

Star receiver Dante Lavelli had fought at the Battle of the Bulge, a sergeant in the Army's 28th Infantry Division. This was no casual combat—if there is such a thing—experience. The 28th ID had endured months of fighting across Europe leading up to the famous battle. Spread along a 20-mile stretch of the Our River in Belgium, the 28th took the full, withering assault from Field Marshall von Rundstedt's forces, at one time reportedly fighting elements of nine different German divisions simultaneously. It is still widely regarded as one of the finest stands in the annals of American military history. "I was shot in the foot," Lavelli told Peterson, "but I had my boots on and it wasn't too serious."[13] It was a typical dismissal from a veteran who had seen so much worse that August. Another Buckeye alum, Lavelli had a brush with professional baseball, but was ultimately told by Paul Brown to choose one sport or the other while in college (in Brown's case, that meant football). Lavelli did, and ended up with a bust in Canton.

One of Lavelli's receiving counterparts, Mac Speedie, grew up in Utah, and had been a scholastic track star as well football player. After the 1952 season, and a dispute with Paul Brown, he moved north to

Canada, and played for the Saskatchewan Roughriders and the British Columbia Lions of the Western Interprovincial Football Union for three years. In 1960 he went to work for former Browns teammate Lou Rymkus on the staff of the Houston Oilers in the upstart American Football League, and after that spent the rest of his professional life as a scout for the Denver Broncos. In 2021, he too was inducted into the Pro Football Hall of Fame.

Lindell "Lin" Houston had started as an old Motley nemesis during the former's time at Massillon High, and Lou Rymkus proved to be one of the best pass blocking linemen in all of football. Oddly, Rymkus' playing weight was about 231 pounds. Bill Willis played at a maximum weight 225 or so, and Houston starred at guard at 213 pounds. Motley, by contrast, was 225 on his lightest days, and bulked up to almost 240 by the time he retired.

In 1947 the Browns added a third Black player to their roster, Horace Gillom. Like Bill Veeck's baseball Indians, and their eager acceptance of Larry Doby and Satchel Paige, both contributors to the Tribe's 1948 World Series winners, Paul Brown defied the segregationists as he filled his roster with the best available players. Horace Gillom was just that. The AP article on January 3, 1947, began, "The football player tagged by Coach Paul E. Brown as 'the greatest athlete I ever coached' today became a member of the Cleveland Browns."[14] The original idea that coach Aiken had devised was that, since Motley still had eligibility due to the war, he could return and play in 1946. Paul Brown reached out to Aiken and told him he was going to sign Motley, but he was sending Massillon alum Gillom to Nevada in Motley's place.

At Nevada, Gillom had been a force from the outset. He, also, had come to the school after serving with the Army at the Battle of the Bulge, and had been awarded three bronze stars for valor.[15] He had backbone, and he was a gifted athlete. His "sensational punting, pass receiving and blocking drew rave notices from west coast writers and coaches. He dropped from school last month and returned to Massillon, where he has a wife and child."[16] Gillom had, in 1946, been named to several all-West Coast teams by local media and was endorsed as an All-American by writers in San Francisco. It's not clear whether stripping the University of Nevada of Motley, then Gillom after the 1946 season, by Brown actually led to Jim Aiken leaving the university, but in 1947 Aiken did just that, and took the head job at Oregon.

Writer Larry Smith enthused that, in Gillom, Brown landed yet another of the "best prospects ever to hit the professional ranks."[17] As a receiver, he would have been a predecessor of the modern array of athletically dazzling pass catchers. "Like Dante Lavelli and Mac Speedie, the Browns' pass-receiving aces of 1946, Gillom catches a pass with his hands only ... his specialty is snagging them with one hand, like an outfielder gathering in a long fly ball." Brown specifically observed, "Horace has a suction pump on the end of his arms [Brown referred to his long arms and unusually large hands] and he just sucks the ball in."[18]

While he was a fine receiving complement to established stars Mac Speedie and Dante Lavelli, Gillom made his lasting mark on football as an elite punter. More than 30 years later, a month before Miami's appearance in the Super Bowl (against AAFC alums the San Francisco 49ers) in 1985, when Dolphin's coach Don Shula was asked if he had ever seen a punter with a leg as powerful as three-time Pro Bowler and two-time All-Pro Reggie Roby's, writer Leo Suarez caught the coach's immediate bemused response:

> "Horace Gillom."
> "Horace who?" [The writer asked.]
> "You mean you haven't heard of Horace Gillom?" Shula snickered. "How long have you been a sportswriter?" The coach turned to several other writers standing nearby. "You've heard of Horace Gillom, haven't you?"[19]

They had not. But, as of 2021, Gillom still holds the Browns' franchise record for longest punt (80 yards, against the New York Giants in 1954), and is second—trailing only Don Cockroft—in team career punting yards (Gillom logged 21,206 over his tenure, impressive since throughout that time the regular season was only 12 games long, not the 14- and 16-game slates teams played afterward). Finally, his 1952 season average of 45.7 yards per punt, this time in the NFL and not the AAFC, is still the fifth best such season in the annals of the Browns, and his five top seasons are among the 25 best years ever by Cleveland punters. Running back Sherman Howard later described the punter's impact. "Gillom had such a powerful leg and kicked the ball so far; before that time, punters used to line up 10, 12, yards behind center.... He started the 15-yard drop. And with Horace, he would kick it so high that by the time the guys got down, the ball was coming down, so most guys had to fair catch."[20]

Not merely a third Black face in the team picture, the addition of

5. The First Repeat Champions (1947)

Gillom to the Browns, given his superb performance, made any internal team or player considerations about racial inferiority moot. Motley, Willis, and now Gillom were all front-line contributors to the Cleveland Browns, the 1946 defending AAFC Champion Cleveland Browns, and anyone having a problem with that was free to discuss it, preferably in a back alley, with the entire team roster.

The race issue was, at least publicly, resolved in the Browns' locker room, due in equal parts to the irreplaceable contributions of Motley, Willis, and Gillom, and to the direct, unflinching direction of Paul Brown. He had, he claimed, decided to sign Motley and Willis even before Branch Rickey inked Jackie Robinson, but he was not deaf to the likely reaction of at least some of the rest of the league. Motley later said:

> Paul warned Willis and me. He said, "Now you know that you're going to be in many scrapes. People are going to be calling you names. They're going to be nasty. But you're going to stick it out." It was rough, all right. If Willis and I had been anywhere near being hotheads, it would have been another ten years till black men got accepted in pro ball. We'd have set 'em back ten years. I still got many a cleat mark on the backs of my hands from when I would be getting up from a play and a guy would just walk over and step on my hand. I couldn't do anything about it. I'd want to kill those guys, but Paul had warned us. The referees would stand right there and see those men stepping on us, and they would turn their backs. The guy that finally broke it up was a referee out of Buffalo—one of the older referees [Tommy Hughitt].... When he caught a guy stepping on us, he wouldn't tell him nothing. He'd just pick up the ball and start walking off fifteen yards. They'd ask him why, and then he'd say, "For stepping on that man." The other referees saw what this ref was doing, and they looked around and saw that we were bringing in the crowds as well as the white guys, so they started to protect us.
>
> The opposing players called us nigger and all kind of names like that. This went on for about two or three years, until they found out that Willis and I were ballplayers. Then they stopped. The found out that while they were calling us names, I was running by 'em and Willis was knocking the [bleep] out of them. So they stopped calling us names and started trying to catch up with us.[21]

Motley continued: "We had a close-knit ball club, and I think this was why we won. Many times, the guys wanted to fight for Willis and me. They'd want to take care of the guy who was playing us dirty. But I'd say, 'What the hell, just let him go, because I'm going to run over him anyway.'"[22]

That tightly linked team started the 1947 campaign with a

preseason game against the Baltimore Colts in front of 35,106 in Akron.[23] The 28–0 victory, as with almost all preseason games, was most notable in that the Browns suffered no significant injuries. The regular season began in earnest on September 6, as the Browns smote the Buffalo Bills 30–14 in Cleveland. Motley's biggest offensive contribution came on a three-yard touchdown dash in the first quarter, making the score 13–0. His most notable defensive contribution came when he intercepted George Ratterman and returned the pick 48 yards for a touchdown that opened the gap to 20–0.

The following week, in front of a paltry crowd of 18,876 in Brooklyn, Motley ran for 111 yards on but five carries, a 22.2 yard-per-carry average. Embedded in those numbers were two touchdowns, a 13-yarder for the first score of the night, and a 51-yard run at the start of the second half, making the score 26–7. The final tally, 55–7, turned out to provide Cleveland's largest margin of victory for the whole season.

Motley played sparingly in the third game of the year, not due to injury but owing to the quick 21–0 first quarter lead that Cleveland took over Baltimore. He scored a one-yard touchdown later in the first quarter but was soon sent to the sidelines for the rest of the half. Horace Gillom smashed his record-setting 80-yard punt that afternoon, and his punting average on the day was 55.7 yards. It would have been higher, but he shanked a kick for only 34 yards late in the game. Paul Brown let Motley start the second half, but a "77-yard run by Motley was called back in the third period when he stepped out of bounds after reaching his own 44."[24] Motley continued to excel on defense over the next two weeks, victories over the Chicago Rockets and the New York Yankees.

In a crucial matchup on October 12, in Cleveland, Motley was the only effective cog in the Browns' scoring machine. Despite 253 yards of passing by Otto Graham, four turnovers led to a tough 13–10 loss to the Los Angeles Dons. Mac Speedie caught eight balls for 110 yards, but Motley produced the single Cleveland touchdown with a 14-yard run in the first quarter. The Dons' kicker, Ben Agajanian, produced seven points with his foot, and an L.A. fumble recovery on Cleveland's 28-yard line gave the Dons their only touchdown on the day. The result left Cleveland with a 5–1 record on the year, and comfortable control of their season and playoff destiny.

The Browns escaped a trap game against winless Chicago with 166 receiving yards, including a 49-yard touchdown catch by Mac Speedie and a 22-yard touchdown run by Motley. After extending their

ABOVE: Marion Motley, all-league back of the Cleveland Browns, gets off to a 35 yd. touchdown run. In chase is Glenn Dobbs (65) of the L.A. Dons.

Marion Motley, sans helmet, scoring against the Los Angeles Dons in 1947 (*Pro Football Illustrated*, 1948).

lead over the Rockets to 24–7 early in the fourth quarter, the Browns needed every point to escape a furious rally by the visitors, finally getting a 31–28 win. Otto Graham and Mac Speedie starred the next week, against the 49ers, with the former completing 19 of 24 passes for 268 yards, and the latter snaring 11 of those passes for 141 yards, including a 42-yard touchdown catch. The Browns' defense showed up again, and they escaped San Francisco with a 14–7 win.

To the casual observer, it appeared that Paul Brown had forgotten about his fullback. Motley was still dominating on defense in his familiar role as outside linebacker. Most teams did not even bother running in his direction, and that level of defensive influence seemingly made his offensive output almost incidental. Otto Graham threw for another three touchdowns in a 28–7 win over Buffalo, a 72-yard touchdown toss to Dante Lavelli in a squeaker over Brooklyn, and three more scores to Lavelli in a division-clinching rematch 34–17 victory over San Francisco.

On November 23, in front of more than 70,000 fans that had jammed into Yankee Stadium (at the time the largest crowd ever to see a professional football game in New York), Cleveland ran into a figurative buzz saw. Orban "Spec" Sanders channeled his best Marion Motley, and rushed for the first three touchdowns of the game, one on the heels of a critical Motley fumble deep inside New York's territory. The Yankees were already up 21–0 when their sole Black player, stellar rookie running back Buddy Young, added yet another touchdown to make Cleveland's deficit 28 points. A late touchdown pass from Graham to Bill Boedeker made it 28–7 at the half, and the reporters were already scribbling their post-game stories.

"Before the bewildered and disorganized Browns could regain their championship form, the New Yorkers had pushed four touchdowns across," wrote one.[25] Of course, as so often happens in sport, that sentence served to set up an abrupt reversal of fortunes after the break. "The smiling and confident Yanks opened the second half as if they were going to duplicate their superiority of the first two periods. But the Browns."[26]

"But the Browns..." was a perfect segue to an entirely different football game over the last two quarters. Cleveland's first offensive play, from their one-yard line after they had stopped the opening Yankee drive just three feet from yet another touchdown, was a 40-yard Graham bomb to Mac Speedie. The receiver galloped down to the New York 17-yard line, and then Motley caught a screen pass and rambled into the end zone to make the score 28–13. He followed that up with a ten-yard touchdown run before the end of the third quarter, cutting the deficit to seven. In the final frame, Jim Dewar raced five yards for a final, game-tying score. The final, 28–28, was even closer than the tied score suggests, in that a final Yankee drive stalled on the Cleveland 38-yard line. New York "took their time untangling themselves as time ran out, although coach Ray Flaherty had [his kicker] hurrying in from the sideline."[27] The Yankees had a time-out remaining but only got around to calling it as the clock ticked to zero. The tie was a lucky result for the Browns, and it reminded the entire team about the gossamer-thin margin between defeat and victory every week.

The game, although a tie, was significant enough to earn a chapter in Johnny Unitas' 1968 book *Playing Pro Football to Win*. Along with co-author Harold Rosenthal, they viewed the contest as one of the more spectacular non-victories in pro football history. The chapter, titled "When 28–0 Wasn't Enough to Beat the Browns," begins with Unitas reflecting on the game in the 1940s. "I'm told," Unitas wrote, "pro football after World War II was a really sock-'em game. The players weren't as big as they are today ... but they were just as tough in the '40s, maybe tougher. Most had come out of an experience known as World War II. A bloodied nose or a shot in the solar plexus didn't hold too much terror."[28] He closed his game summary: "Quite a man, Mr. Brown. No wonder the 1947 Yankees couldn't beat him, even with a 28–0 lead."[29] The very fact that the game was so interesting as to be reconsidered 20 years later, over a number of compelling NFL games, is testament enough to the significance of the players, the teams, and the AAFC to the future spread of professional football.

Four days later, on November 27, Motley scored the first Cleveland touchdown in a 27–17 win over Los Angeles. That victory avenged the sole Browns loss on the year, and they entered the season finale with a 11–1–1 record. In Baltimore, in front of 20,574 fans, the Cleveland Browns ran up 559 yards of offense, 334 of those on the ground, and put an exclamation point on their season by beating the Colts 42–0. After the Brooklyn score back in September, it was the second-widest margin of victory the team enjoyed all year.

After the game, the matchup between defending champion Cleveland and the dangerous New York Yankees moved to center stage among the press and the fans. The second AAFC championship game matched the two best teams in the league, and despite the atrocious pre-game weather forecast of a cloudy, 40-degree mid–December afternoon, every reserved seat in Yankee Stadium sold out. A few hours before kickoff, at 11 a.m., New York opened auxiliary bleacher seats and standing room only spots to accommodate the excessive demand.

The Akron paper described the playing conditions as "an ice-encrusted gridiron and in the face of constantly freezing weather."[30] The Yankees were a formidable host, featuring a roster that had won 11

games over the season, and were probably better than their NFL counterparts, the Giants. Only one team had bettered the New York squad
in points allowed and scored, though, the Cleveland Browns. The two
teams had met five times over the two-year history of the AAFC, with
Cleveland winning four of the contests while salvaging the lone draw a
few weeks earlier.

Cleveland Municipal Stadium

Opened in mid–1932, debuting with a heavyweight boxing match
featuring Max Schmelling, and then a July 31 Sunday baseball game
between the Philadelphia Athletics and the hometown Indians, the stadium not only served as the locus for Cleveland's major league sports
until Art Modell ferreted the Browns away in 1995, but it also became
a punch line for any number of low-rent comedians looking for easy
laughs in the 1970s. One of the classics—Question: "What do a Billy
Graham Crusade and a Cleveland Browns game have in common?"
Answer: "80,000 fans leaving the Stadium muttering 'Jesus Christ.'"[31]
The "Mistake by the Lake" was, in its time, however, one of the grand-
est multi-sport facilities in the nation, and hosted not just the last Indians World Series champions (1948), but also the AAFC and the NFL for
five decades.

The stadium was an engineering marvel. Built in just over a year, it
nicely filled an area of landfill that extended into Lake Erie. It cost just
over $3 million to build, and it could accommodate more than 80,000
ticket-buying zealots if needed. Technically, it opened for football use
on September 10, 1937, hosting the Cleveland Rams and the Detroit
Lions. The home team lost 28–0. With the arena filled to one-quarter
capacity, the Rams returned to the smaller League Park until they left
for Los Angeles after the 1945 season.

The location next to Lake Erie often became problematic in late
autumn and winter. Cold air from Canada would blow across the lake,
and as it hit the warmer lake waters and the air above, it did not take
much to turn that into devastating lake-effect snow, sometimes falling
at two to three inches per hour.[32] The winds alone could wreak havoc for
a football team, especially one so reliant on the passing game. The stadium was oriented for baseball, so that what was home plate in the summer faced east (to keep sunshine from the west from impairing batters

in late afternoon games). That forced the field to orient predominantly east to west. All the breezes and gusts from the north, from Canada, then, became crosswinds for passes and kicks. For players like Otto Graham and Lou Groza, it is impossible to estimate the cumulative effect of the stadium on their career statistics.

In September 1970 the stadium hosted Keith Jackson, Howard Cosell and Don Meredith for the very first Monday Night Football game. Blanton Collier's Browns beat Joe Namath and the New York Jets, 31–21, in front of 85,703 in the seats. Twenty-five years later, Art Modell packed up the team and relocated to Baltimore. The NFL assured Cleveland that it would have a new team within four years, but when the new Cleveland Browns kicked off in 1999, they did so in a brand-new facility, one located right next to the popular Rock and Roll Hall of Fame. Municipal Stadium, demolished in 1996–1997, was consigned to memory.

During its active service, the stadium was home to five professional football championship teams, a World Series winner, several movies, the Rolling Stones, and several high-profile college games. Today, though, it exists as a residuum of wet rubble, turned in to several artificial reefs along the Lake Erie waterfront.

Back at the Game

Broadcasting immortals Mel Allen and Russ Hodges (the lead radio voices of baseball's Yankees and Giants, respectively) shared play-by-play duties on both television and radio. This was still a decade before the infamous 1958 Colts–Giants game that cemented the relationship between professional football and the nation of watching fans, but it was—as were so many features of the AAFC's brief tenure—a harbinger of the future. Del Webb, owner of the Yankees, had personally ensured that two of the top sports broadcasters in the business were charged with calling this game, of putting pro football's best foot forward on the big stage.

The pregame festivities included on-field performances by the Marine Corps band from Quantico, as well as the Baldwin High School band. The field was a slippery floor, snow-free but damp and frozen, and sharp cuts by the players were almost impossible. Although just under 62,000 ticket holders actually passed through turnstiles, providing a gate for less than $210,000, but that group included local luminaries like Cleveland mayor Burke.

The opening kickoff went to the Yankees, but they failed to earn a first down. Motley set the tone for his day when he blew through the line and made the first tackle of the game on the Yankee runner for a short loss of yardage. Once Cleveland took over, they sent Motley and the football up the middle on the notorious Cleveland trap play. After Graham failed to complete his third-down pass, the Browns kicked the ball back to the Yankees. On their next possession, though, Graham lateraled to Motley from the Cleveland 36, and the big back took off on a 51-yard ramble across the—literally—frozen tundra. He moved to the sidelines to evade the Yankee defenders, but defensive back Harmon Rowe caught his leg and Motley stumbled out of bounds. After a few plays, Graham scored on a one-yard sneak.

In a key series before the break, Motley was playing linebacker deep near the Cleveland end zone. On the first Yankee snap, he laterally pursued the New York runner and forced the latter to move so far to the right that on his upfield cut, again on the slippery, frozen turf, he lost his footing and Tony Adamle was able to bring him down with no gain. The defense held, repelling an otherwise near-certain touchdown, and forced New York to kick. The second quarter Yankee field goal made the halftime score 7–3. A third quarter touchdown by Edgar Jones then provided the final tally. On the ice rink that was Yankee stadium, Cleveland won 14–3 and captured their second AAFC crown.

Motley's defense that afternoon was brilliant, perhaps abetted by playing conditions that made scoring even more difficult than usual, and it would have demanded post-game attention had not his offensive contribution been so spectacular. During one particular play, a Yankee counter, Motley sprinted from his outside position toward the middle of the field. As the play direction reversed, he pivoted and followed the ball carrier, eventually making the tackle himself after only a very short New York gain.[33]

On offense, for the day, he ran for 109 yards on 13 carries (8.3 yard average). In the crowd that blustery afternoon was football writer Paul Zimmerman, later better known as "Dr. Z" to *Sports Illustrated* readers in the '60s, '70s, and '80s. He wrote about the afternoon:

> I watched the Yanks play the Browns for the AAFC championship. I sat in the upper deck, in the end zone above home plate, and my binoculars

caught Motley coming right at me, 51 yards on a direct handoff over the middle, with the Yanks' Harmon Rowe riding his back and slugging him in the face for the last 20 yards.

After the game a photographer asked Motley to smile.

"I can't," he said. "My teeth were knocked out."[34]

It isn't clear that this interaction occurred on the 51-yard run, on a play in the third quarter when he had four Yankees piled on him while still running, or that the tale is anything more than an apocryphal anecdote, but Zimmerman continued to tell the story for years. At the end of the day, and this was indisputable, the Cleveland Browns had again been the better team, and despite not scoring, Marion Motley was the star of the game.[35] Per one local account:

But after all the backs have been slapped and all the songs of praise have been sung, the Clevelander who must be singled out for the greatest praise is broad-beamed, bull-necked Marion Motley. The giant Cleveland Negro [there's that qualifying adjective again] fullback carried the Browns to victory. It was Motley who carried 13 times for 109 yards of the Browns' 172 net yards by rushing. It was Motley who broke loose in the first period for a gallop from his own 36-yard line to the Yankees 13 and who definitely set up the Browns first big touchdown. It was the unstoppable Motley, more often than not, carrying three, four or five Yankees on his rugged back, who set the stage for the Browns' other touchdown in the third quarter.[36]

The game was an exclamation point on a terrific sophomore season for Motley. He was not just regarded as one of the AAFC's best linebackers, but he also finished the season with 889 rushing yards (third in the conference in both total rushing yards and in yards per game), along with nine total offensive touchdowns to go with his one defensive score. He returned 13 kicks for more than 300 yards. On other leader boards for 1947, Motley was fourth in rushing attempts, rushing touchdowns, yards per rushing attempt, and touchdowns. He finished sixth in points scored, seventh in yards from scrimmage, and his 48-yard interception return was the third longest all year. He was named first-team all-AAFC by the conference, the AP, and UPI, and second team by the parochial *New York Daily News*. It was the championship, though, that made his year a success in his own mind. Paul Brown wrote in his autobiography, in describing Marion Motley's biggest contributions, that "no one ever cared more about his team and whether it won or lost, rather than how many yards he gained or where he was asked to run."[37]

Marion Motley and Bill Willis endured pain, to be sure, as much about their race as their rookie status. Just about every time Motley hit the ground, someone stepped on his hand. When he ran, he was assaulted well beyond the norms of football, occasionally by members of his own team. He was held. He had phantom penalties called on him for obscure offenses imagined only in the mind of some of the White officials. Yet, eventually, his superiority on the field, and his value to his team, caused a behavioral change. Now, after an opponent stepped on him, or flung an epithet his way, there were White teammates ready to fight with him. It proved to be a seminal season in the history of professional football.

Year later, the *Pittsburgh Courier* synopsized Motley's early contributions beyond the field: "The image of a new world, the expanding, post-war U.S. world for Negroes, had taken shape. The great, two-platoon Browns, with Otto Graham in the T-slot, out-drew every pro eleven in the nation, week after week."[38]

It was also a tumultuous time in race relations. Washington, Strode, Willis and Motley had just finished their second seasons as Black men in pro football. Jackie Robinson, Larry Doby, Hank Thompson, Willard Brown and Don Bankhead had each spent part or all of 1947 playing major league baseball (with Robinson pacing a world champion, and Doby set to join that small club the next season). Post-war America, writ large, was coming to grips with the idea that racial segregation was not only illogical, but also immoral. The nation was undergoing a sort of sociological tectonic shift, demonstrably paced by professional athletes starring in formerly White leagues and in formerly race-exclusive games.

Marion and Eula, though, while playing their small but critical role in the national change, remained focused on what mattered most to them. They retreated to their Canton home, their three boys, and for Marion another winter of playing basketball and working for Arthur McBride's cab company. Life was good, but there was little reason to anticipate that 1948 would end up being the best year of Marion Motley's football life.

6

The First Perfect Season
(1948)

On January 1, 1948, the *Akron Beacon Journal* posted a brief advertisement that the "Browns' new promotional movie [was] scheduled for next week in Chicago.... Early theme will feature the family life of the Browns' players. Shown and explained by slow motion and voice will also be the trap play made famous by Marion Motley."[1] Motley was a multi-faceted, lethal weapon in Paul Brown's arsenal, but despite the hype, many of his greatest contributions to Cleveland's successes came without the football. The offensive production could be neatly captured in recognizable statistics. His defensive presence could not. Motley had been the AAFC's premier left linebacker during the 1946 and 1947 seasons, and his ability to move with the football was a matter of statistical record. Still, albeit to a lesser degree, his defensive contributions could be counted as well. But it was his blocking, that final tool in his bag, that made Motley perhaps the finest fullback, if not the finest all-around player, in the history of professional football.

A brief exploration of each of Motley's contribution "skill baskets," movement with the ball, blocking, and defense, may be useful in understanding his aggregate football value. In this chapter, it makes sense to start with his play with the football. Throughout the stories written about Motley as ball carrier, both during his playing days and after, there are three basic plays in which he was featured, and it would be conservative to guess that the three made up more than 90 percent of the schemes in which he was used.

A brief description of each is useful in understanding just how effective Motley's power was as a counterpoint to Otto Graham's passing. The first play, the one most often associated with Motley and the Browns, is the trap. In his obituary in the *New York Times*, the story included the phrase "peerless runner on the Browns' famed trap play."[2] Motley's biography on the Pro Football Hall of Fame website states that "with his powerful running on Cleveland's famed trap and draw series, made the Browns' ground game go."[3]

The trap play is so dubbed not because of the runner's role, but because of the movement of one of the offensive linemen. According to football player and analyst Sam DeLuca, along with many others, the play frees the runner up the middle, on either side of the center, because of a block, a trap block. "A defensive lineman is trapped when blocked by a player approaching from the side, provided that the person blocking him is not the player on either side of the offensive lineman is directly opposite."[4] Now, this is football, but that very precise description almost sounds legalistic in verbosity.

In a simpler form, it means that the guard or tackle on the side opposite of the intended direction of the run, such as a left tackle or left guard if the play is supposed to run to the right of the center, pulls out of his position, explodes immediately behind the center, and puts his shoulder directly into the defensive rusher. The block was originally referred to as a mousetrap, with the trapping guard making contact as low as possible. In the times predating Motley, some coaches even considered the block "inherently tricky" and thus unsportsmanlike, and as such, they argued, it should have been outlawed.[5]

An example of how a trap play progresses: On a run to the right, the center would push forward or even a partial step left to block a defender, and the opposing defensive tackle would try to shoot into that gap—between center and right guard—to penetrate the backfield and cause a loss on the play. In the trap, in this example, the left guard would drop his right foot back, pivot to the right, and effectively blindside the supposedly free rushing, but isolated, defensive tackle. A perfect blindside block, in the vernacular, is close to ear-holing the defender, getting such an unexpected shoulder block on the rusher that he ends up on his back with the play going past him.

When properly executed, the interior defender is not just taken out of the play by the trap block, but that very action opens the space, the hole, that the defender vacated. The rusher then has a gap into which he can carry the ball in free space. For a mere mortal running back, and if the defense isn't expecting it, the play design can gain at least two or three yards, and perhaps more. For Motley, who was both bigger than the linemen and faster than the defensive backs, even a small hole in the line was a potential 20-yard gain every time the Browns ran the play. Complicating the defensive problem even further was the fact that Otto Graham could also run if the defense took away the opening, and he was so agile that even if the play fell apart, it still might turn out to be a downfield pass to Speedie or Lavelli or a screen dump to running back Colella.

There was almost no advantage for a defense in stacking an extra person on the line to stop the Cleveland run, because of the concomitant sacrifice of coverage of the receivers, or in dropping an extra linebacker into coverage and allowing Motley to plow through the line. Once into the defensive secondary, the smaller, speedier defenders then had the additional, health challenging problems associated with tackling Motley. In one particular case, in 1948, that exact scenario played out in semi-tragic form. Paul Zimmerman, writing about one of his interviews with Motley, remembered a conversation with the aging star. Zimmerman began: "I was in the Stadium the day you knocked Tom Casey out of football. Casey was a gutty little defensive back, the only man I ever saw stop Motley head-on when Marion had a full head of steam." The blow sent Casey to the hospital with a concussion, and he never played again. "Good old Tom," Motley said, smiling. "He's Doctor Casey now. I see him once in a while, and he says, 'You S.O.B, you ended my career.' And I tell him, 'I couldn't help it if you got in front of me.'"[6]

In his book on the T formation, Otto Graham wrote about another somewhat amusing example of the trap play gone bad.

> One time we called a trap play against a defensive five-man line and I was to hand the ball off to Motley. After we had lined up, the other team shifted to a six-man line and Marion didn't notice it at the moment. Of course, that changed the hole as far as the offense was concerned. Marion came barreling through where he would have against a five-man line and there I stood with the ball, right in the line of his progress. He hit me like a ton of bricks and propelled me on through the endzone for a touchdown. Unfortunately Marion was called in motion which prevented us from taking six points.[7]

The Motley legend grew throughout his football career. Unlike mythology, unlike players and feats whose magnitude grows over time like fishermen's tales, the stories about Motley were often rooted in either pain, scars, or both. Charlie Powell, a 6'3" multi-sport star who later played minor league baseball and boxed professionally against Cassius Clay (Muhammad Ali) and Floyd Patterson (albeit losing both), described an encounter with Motley in his book about his 1952 rookie season as a San Francisco 49er:

> Another guy who could hit was Marion Motley. We went to Cleveland for an exhibition game my rookie year and they gave Motley the ball on a draw play, and when he came through the hole he sounded like a rhinoceros. I said, "Oh, shit," because if he got going for even two steps, you knew he was going to be a handful to tackle. But I hit him low, got him down, made sure I still had all my teeth, and got up feeling pretty good. People ask me, and I tell everybody: There has NEVER been anybody who came through the line like Marion Motley. I'm telling you, that's exactly what he sounded like, a rhinoceros.[8]

Powell's description of the draw, and its potential consequences, is apt. "The draw play, in contrast to the trap, is a running play designed to look like a ... pass."[9] The quarterback drops back from the line with the football as if to pass, and as the defensive linemen charge across to rush the passer, the quarterback simply hands the ball to the blocking running back, who then takes off forward through the area vacated by the defenders. With wider line splits than in the 19th-century version of the T formation, defenders had more room to rush, but committing to a particular hole in the line again opened a different gap somewhere else.

Cleveland's draw play came about, if the memories of the participants are to be believed, by accident. In a 1946 game, coach Paul Brown remembered, "Otto [Graham] got such a hard pass rush that he handed the ball to Motley in desperation. The defense had overrun Motley in their desire to get the quarterback and Marion swept right through them for a big gain. We looked at the play again and decided it couldn't help but work. In a short time, it became Marion's most dangerous weapon."[10] "Marion's tremendous running ability," Brown later wrote in his autobiography, "made our trap and draw plays so effective. When he ran off-tackle, players seemed to fly off him in all directions. He possessed tremendous speed for a big man, and he could run away from linebackers and defensive backs when he got into the open—if he didn't trample them first."[11]

In later years, writers delighted in recounting anecdotal conversations with some of Motley's opponents. In one 1955 off-season coaches meeting in Pittsburgh, the story came up about the time Motley, close to 260 pounds (for storytelling purposes ... much like that fisherman's yarn about the size of "the one that got away"), rushed down the field for a touchdown. Otto Schnellbacher, who was 80 pounds lighter, tried only to grab him from the side. "Why didn't you tackle Motley from the front?" a coach asked him. The player replied: "There's nothing in my contract about committing suicide."[12]

Last, but not least, was the screen pass from Graham to Motley. A deception, as with much of Paul Brown's playbook, makes a properly executed screen looks like a slow-developing long pass, but one in which the defenders on (what will be) the screen side have a clear lane to chase the quarterback before he throws. As they close in on what appears to be an easy sack for a loss, the quarterback tosses the ball over the pass rush to a back or receiver in the open space called the "flat," who should then have a wide-open field through which to romp unimpeded.

"The secret to running the screen well," DeLuca wrote, "is to have a bunch of hams on the team … the defensive linemen must believe that the play is a pass and that they are legitimately beating the offensive lineman to the passer."[13] On most designed passes, Brown normally kept Motley in the backfield as a blocker for any rusher leaking through the line. His presence would actually help sell the pass play. His elite speed, though, made him virtually unstoppable once he got the football.

Paul Brown and the team officially convened the 1948 preseason camp at Bowling Green on August 4 with the first scrimmage of the summer. The reporters saw the "usual amount of ragged play and missed assignments" but enthused about new running back Dub Jones from Brooklyn.[14] The had also brought in Ollie Cline as a backup fullback for Motley, as well as Tony Adamle to shoulder more of the linebacking responsibilities and to give Motley a few more breathers during games. With the offensive nucleus still healthy, and the return of Bill Willis, Lou Groza, and Lou Rymkus, prospects for the season were bright.

With the draw, the trap, and the screen in the toolbox for Motley, and Graham having a pair of targets like Lavelli and Speedie to snag his lethally accurate passes, the Browns began the 1948 season with a pre-season win over Buffalo in Akron, but followed that with a rare loss to Baltimore in Toledo. The 13,433 that watched the 21–17 Browns defeat were united for the rest of the season; they saw the only loss Cleveland would suffer in 1948.

The Browns made a few adjustments for the new season, includ-ing making star kicker Lou Groza a functioning tackle.[15] The team lost the incumbent, Ernie Blandin, to the Colts, and Coach Brown decided to fill from within, rather than try to find the right body type and atti-tude that late in the preparation phase. They also decided to give punter

Horace Gillom a shot at offensive right end (a receiver, in modern parlance). Dante Lavelli suffered a broken leg, and the pure athleticism of
Gillom was simply too tantalizing to resist.[16]

With Lavelli out, Motley coddling a strained back, and Graham
nursing a sprained wrist on his throwing arm, the Browns took the field
on Friday night, September 4, against the Los Angeles Dons in front
of 60,193 in Cleveland. The Browns won 19–14 (although it was 19–7
until the final moments), but Paul Brown's first post-game comment was
an understatement. "It was a long evening."[17] In reality, the game was
Cleveland's from the outset. The Browns took the kickoff and Motley
made the first two first downs, on a nine-yard catch and then a run, and
while he did not score that evening, he was a persistent presence that
kept the Dons' defense honest.

The following week, in Buffalo, Cleveland won 42–13 and one headline the next day read: "Brownies Hoist Warning After Blasting Buffalo."[18] With the opening game rust knocked away, Cleveland unloaded
the whole arsenal on their hosts. Graham tossed two touchdowns,

**Happy Browns players following the 1948 triumph over the Buffalo Bills.
From left: Edgar Jones, Lou Saban (front), Otto Graham and Motley. Motley's uniform number changed from 76 to 36 after the AAFC and the NFL
merged (*Cleveland Press Collection*, Michael Schwartz Library at Cleveland State University).**

6. *The First Perfect Season (1948)*

Motley ran 18 yards for another, and running backs Tom Colella and Dean Sensanbraugher each plowed into the end zone as well. It was, the papers reported, "a 'no-contest' affair after the first half, if ever."

Six days later, in Chicago, the Browns topped the Rockets 28–7. A week after that the teams conducted a rematch in Cleveland, this time the Browns winning 21–10. Successive wins over Baltimore, Brooklyn and Buffalo set up a rematch of the 1947 championship game in New York. This time, however, there was no drama, as Cleveland moved to an 8–0 record with a 35–7 shellacking of the Yankees in their home stadium. Some of northeastern Ohio's collective sporting attention may have been diverted elsewhere as well. It was not only that Cleveland's Browns were making a mockery of the AAFC with their unexcelled dominance of every team they played, but on October 11, the Indians won their fourth and final game of the World Series, beating the Boston Braves in six games. It was difficult for many fans to pick a favorite sport, with both organizations performing so well, but the city on Lake Erie dominated the sports pages across the region.

Owner Bill Veeck's 1948 Indians club was special in a variety of ways. It was the first American League and World Series champion in Cleveland since 1920. The starting center- and right-fielder was a Black man, Larry Doby, the first in the American League. Notably, Jackie Robinson's Dodgers had won it all in 1947, and now Larry Doby's Indians captured the crown in 1948.

Of note, 41-year-old (or, perhaps, 48-year-old … part of the mystique is that there is no universal agreement on precisely when he was born) Satchel Paige, one of the greatest pitchers in baseball history, but whose feats had been confined to the Negro Leagues and barnstorming exhibitions, finally got a chance to pitch in the established World Series. Paige tossed two-thirds of an inning with no decision but in so doing became the first Black pitcher in Series history. Cleveland teams, owners, and fans displayed a sincere, ongoing affection for success, and did not allow the race and ethnicity of players get in the way of championship celebrations.

Paul Brown had demonstrated a clear demand for competitive success, even if it meant breaking unwritten rules or so-called gentlemen's agreements about Caucasian purity in football. Indians owner Bill Veeck had a similar perspective. In the early 1940s, before he bought the Tribe, Veeck had purportedly conceived a plan to buy the moribund Philadelphia Phillies and fill the lineup with Negro League stars. In private, he effused about the possibilities of absolutely dominating not only the National League but the entire sport as well with a team of Josh Gibson, Pat Patterson, Jimmie Crutchfield, Satchel Paige and the like. Veeck was squashed by the collective weight of the other owners and the commissioner at the time, but in 1947, ten weeks after Jackie Robinson started at first base for the Brooklyn Dodgers, Veeck had Larry Doby on the field in a Cleveland uniform. Veeck hired Paige for the final weeks of the season, as well. An outstanding team was improved, not an easy feat, and they easily won the second World Series in franchise history.

The city of Cleveland's collective appreciation for excellence, for outstanding players who not only looked like Graham or Speedie or Rymkus or Groza, but also like Motley, Willis, and Gillom, continued to pay dividends on the gridiron. After beating Baltimore 28–7, the undefeated Browns were once again officially installed as favorites to win the AAFC title. At that point they had gone 18 straight games without a loss, and had lost but one of their last 30 contests. There has been a degree of tacit agreement among historians that the overall talent level in the AAFC was below that in the National Football League. Whether or not the assertion is fair or accurate is a discussion for a different venue. There is an argument to be made, however, that the Cleveland Browns of that era were every bit as good, perhaps even better, than the best teams in the NFL. If nothing else, the Browns were inarguably the dominant team throughout the four-year history of the junior circuit.

By the time the San Francisco 49ers came to Cleveland for a mid–November game, the press had labeled the afternoon as a "Game of the Century." The gate was advertised at 82,769 in Municipal Stadium, the total yet another single-game pro football attendance record. Unlike some similarly advertised games, this time the fans actually got their money's worth. Cleveland was 9–0 on the year, but San Francisco, having started the season on August 29, was 10–0. It shaped up be a titanic battle of the two best teams in the AAFC.

As happens all too often, though, the game that was predicted quickly deviated from the game that was played. This one started with San Francisco's Forrest Hall fumbling on the opening play. Within a minute after kickoff, Cleveland held a 7–0 lead. The "luckless lads from the City by the Golden Gate," as the San Francisco opined in the game recap, played well enough, but a few key breaks let Cleveland walk off with a 14–7 win.[19] Motley did not score, but contributed to the 179 Cleveland rushing yards, his blocking keeping Otto Graham upright in the pass pocket to complete critical passes to both Bob Cowan and a young Ara Parseghian on the winning drive.

The following Sunday, at Yankee Stadium, Motley scored two touchdowns and paced a 34–21 Cleveland win. That decision gave the Browns an 11–0 record, and control of their playoff destiny. Paul Brown allowed the players to keep the tone of the locker room light, not allowing his team to worry about the long season, but rather continue to concentrate on the next opponent. He wrote of that year, "Marion came in for his share of good-natured ribbing, too. We defeated Los Angeles handily in a game in 1948, but Marion atypically lost three fumbles in the first half. After the game, the players took some tape, made a handle from it, then stuck it on the ball and handed it to Marion. It was so unusual for him to fumble the players felt it might be their only chance ever to kid him about it."[20]

On the Sunday after Thanksgiving, November 28, the Browns made the trip to San Francisco for a rematch with the 49ers. The 'Niners needed to win the game to remain in the hunt for a slot in the AAFC championship game, while the Browns knew that they merely needed to beat Brooklyn the following week to clinch their own berth in the finale. Perhaps on their minds, as well, was the fact that they had not lost a game, and that only San Francisco and Brooklyn stood between them and a perfect year.

Kezar Stadium was filled to capacity, with a crowd advertised at over 61,000 (the final tally was recorded as 59,785) in the stands on a sun-soaked Bay Area afternoon. Cleveland kicked off to Forrest Hall, the same Forrest Hall that had fumbled to open the game in Ohio, and as he ran down the sideline, a Cleveland defender nearly decapitated him. Hall held on to the ball, though, and San Francisco set up in much better shape than in the earlier contest.

In yet another example of history repeating itself, quarterback Frankie Albert handed off to Jim Cason on the first play from scrimmage, and he lost the handle as well. Tony Adamle recovered the ball, and Otto Graham tossed a 41-yard touchdown pass to Dante Lavelli on the very next play. After another San Francisco fumble, a Groza field goal gave Cleveland a 10–0 lead after the first quarter. Joe Perry and Alyn Beals both ran for touchdowns in the second, though, and San Francisco led 14–10 at halftime.

Cleveland failed to convert a fourth down on their first possession of the second half. Motley was stuffed twice at the line, and Paul

Brown's daring call to try and pick up a first down came up short. On the next play, from Cleveland's 29, Albert hit Beals for another touchdown, and extended the 49ers' lead to 21–10. Then, as if on cue, the Browns took over. On San Francisco's next possession, they tried to convert on fourth down as well. Motley was in at linebacker, and clogged the middle as Frankie Albert's jump pass missed his mark. Graham wasted no time, connecting with Edgar Jones for a first down on the San Francisco 48. Jones ran for four yards, Collins picked up three, and Jones reversed for a first down on the 40. San Francisco was flagged for pass interference on the next play, and two plays later Motley caught a flare and ran six yards for a touchdown.

By the end of the third quarter, Cleveland led 31–21, and after weathering a short Albert to Perry touchdown connection, the final gun gave the Browns their 12th win of the year. With a spot in the championship game secured, the final regular season tilt against the Brooklyn Dodgers was almost anti-climactic. The score was 31–21, but all three Brooklyn touchdowns came after they trailed 31–0. The Cleveland Browns had finished the regular season without a loss or tie and looked ahead to the game against Buffalo as the final piece of a perfect campaign.

Two days before the championship, the Associated Press named their All-Pro football team. The AP list was selective—both the AAFC and NFL players were considered—and Cleveland's successes help the team land three players on the list. Mac Speedie, Otto Graham, and Marion Motley were all first-team selections, with Bill Willis and Lou Rymkus garnering second-team recognition. The text of the story underscored both the ongoing feud between the two leagues while also acknowledging the extraordinary ability and achievement of each player chosen. "The fact that ... the Browns ... placed three men on the [first] team does not necessarily mean that these elevens completely dominated the play in their respective circuits," the writer stipulated, "however, it does show that these players were highly regarded."[21]

A day earlier, the United Press International (UPI) had released its All-America Conference all-star squad, and Graham, Speedie, Motley, Rymkus, Willis and center Lou Saban all made the first team. The writeup on Motley was notable not for the statistical summary of his brilliant season, but because of what was omitted from the text: "The 238 pound Motley is the man who does the running for Cleveland when Graham is not passing. Together they form an unbeatable combination.

The league's best rusher with 964 yards and a 6.14 average per play this season, this former Nevada university star is especially great bursting into the clear on a trap play."[22]

Throughout Opotowsky's paragraph Motley's race was neither exposed nor discussed. The writer's word choices and diction were completely accurate, yet at no point did he feel compelled to somehow qualify, and thus diminish, Motley with unnecessary, amplifying and irrelevant description. While likely not noted by the reading audience, this story was refreshing in that it compared the best players in the league, White and Black, without discriminating by race.

Back on the field on Sunday, December 19, Motley and the Browns put an exclamation point on their unprecedented perfect season. Lake Erie seemed to try her best to make the day miserable. Snow had fallen all morning in the lead-up to kickoff in Cleveland, and not only were the sidelines coated in white, but so were the endzones. The thermometer topped out at 33F, and 22,981 braved the arctic conditions to watch the season's denouement.

By halftime, despite Motley running with some degree of abandon, Cleveland led by only two touchdowns. In the third quarter, one series after an Edgar Jones score from the nine, Graham handed off to Motley on a straightforward "fullback blast" from the Buffalo 29-yard line. Motley was virtually untouched as he glided into the endzone to make the score 28–0.

Buffalo picked up their lone touchdown on the next possession, but Cleveland turned Motley loose in the fourth quarter. On an off-tackle run over the right side, he plowed 31 yards for another touchdown, and on the succeeding drive he scored on a five-yard lateral to the left. Cleveland won 49–7, and as lopsided as the final score appears, had the clock not run out Cleveland would have continued to rack up the points. It was a drubbing in every sense of the word, and an apt end to the perfect 14–0–0 season. They were, again, the first professional team to "play an undefeated season without defeat and ever to win three titles in a row since Green Bay did it in the National Circuit from 1929 to 1931."[23]

Most contemporary football fans know that the 1972 Miami Dolphins went 17–0–0 and were the first—and still only—NFL team to run the table throughout the regular season (14–0), then win all of their playoff games (against Cleveland and the Pittsburgh Steelers, respectively) before defeating Washington 14–7 in the Super Bowl. That

17–0–0 mark remains the finest complete season in football history, as Mercury Morris has repeated any, and every, time he had the opportunity. Morris' bluster notwithstanding, the achievement is unparalleled. The only other time a team has enjoyed a year without a loss, and ended with a championship, was in 1948 by the Cleveland Browns.

Yet another intriguing little side note to the stories of the '48 Browns and the '72 Dolphins came in the person of Don Shula. Shula also grew up in northeastern Ohio, in the town of Painesville in Lake County. He played football at tiny John Carroll University, just outside of Cleveland, and ran for 125 yards in their 1950 upset of Syracuse University. He was drafted in the ninth round of the 1951 NFL draft by the Cleveland Browns, and along with fellow John Carrol alum Carl Taseff were the only rookies to make the team after training camp. In his year and a half with the Browns he made a notable defensive impact with four interceptions in 23 games. He played for Paul Brown, and alongside Motley and Graham and Willis and Speedie and Lavelli, many of the stars of the 1948 team, and the sum of those experiences likely shaped his future coaching philosophy, the one he displayed as head coach of the 1972 Miami Dolphins.

In 1948, though, appearing in the papers the day after Cleveland trounced Buffalo, the AP published a story with a headline that was more portent of the future than news of the day: "Pro Grid Peace Near? Rival Loops to Meet to Discuss Problems."[24] Three Browns on the AP All-Pro team, along with the renown attached not only to Motley and Graham but also to Lavelli, Speedie, Groza, Gillom, Rymkus, and the rest of the Cleveland juggernaut, continued to show the nation and the press that the AAFC was not just an aggregation of rough-necked, talent-less buffoons, unable to stay out of their own way, a group of gifted athletes. And, best of all, they were athletes that drew a paying crowd. This reality prompted NFL commissioner Bert Bell to convene a meeting of NFL and AAFC leadership in Philadelphia to begin to talk more seriously about what a unified pro game could offer.[25]

The story went on to note that Bell's attitude toward the AAFC, in general, had been dismissive from the outset, much akin to that of his predecessor, but the attendance marks in Cleveland and San Francisco were spectacular. There was, it seemed, money to be made in merging the leagues. Bell was clearly not driving that action, but the AAFC's success had created a "football cold war that has skyrocketed player salaries and other expenses and driven several franchises in both leagues into the red."[26] There has been one constant throughout the long history of professional football, and that is that money always wins. Race? Black players? Black star players? Sure. Radio and Television coverage? Why not? But losing money? That was never an acceptable outcome, regardless of how much crow the Commissioner might have to consume. That story line would play out in 1949, and lead to the mega organization that is the NFL today.

Marion Motley had enjoyed what proved to be the finest professional season of his football life in 1948. It was not simply that the team romped to an undefeated 14–0 record, and a third AAFC title, but Motley led the league with 964 rushing yards, logged another 192 yards receiving (14.8 yards per reception), and returned 14 kickoffs for 337 yards. For those 1156 yards from scrimmage, every time he touched the ball, Motley's average gain was 6.3 yards. *The Sporting News* named him to their 1st Team All-NFL/AAFC team, and the AAFC dubbed him 1st Team All-Conference as well. It was, by any standard, by every standard, a career year.

⑾ 7 ⑾

The Last Days
of the AAFC (1949)

Along with their three boys, Marion and Eula had settled into residences in both Cleveland and in Canton and were enjoying a few conventional off-seasons. Athletes in all sports of that era worked at off-season jobs like the McBride cab empire, but in Motley's case, to supplement his income, he worked for a beer distributor as well. With increased fame came better off-season opportunities, both more interesting and more lucrative, and Motley was all too happy to exploit his football notoriety if he could convert it into financial security. Those who remembered him after his death would routinely comment on Motley's maturity and absence of ego throughout his life. If a job as routine as working for a beer distributor brought in some additional cash for the Motley clan, then the All-AAFC running back was ready to distribute some beer.

Continuing to draw on his pre-professional athletic experience, Motley never really let himself get too far out of playing shape, either, sustaining his conditioning over the winter by playing basketball with his teammates in the evenings. The 1948–49 offseason marked his third with the Brown's semi-pro team, playing alongside Mac Speedie, Horace Gillom, Dante Lavelli, Lou Groza, and Otto Graham on the Cleveland squad.[1] Graham had played basketball at Northwestern, and Motley at Nevada, so both often starred in these games due to their fusion of size, strength, speed, and agility. On the football field Motley was the epitome of a physical player, and on the basketball court he was every bit as unstoppable. The Browns hoopsters played all comers in Ohio, West Virginia, and Pennsylvania, and sold out almost every game.[2] Not only did all of those hyper-competitive, elite athletes get the chance to keep their collective edge during the winter, but their celebrity drew quite a few to the games. That most of all those admission dollars from the spectators went to charity only ennobled the games, and those more intimate connections with fans served to improve the aggregate community perception of the team.

In January 1949, Motley was invited to, and attended, an honorary affair at *Sport Magazine*'s headquarters. It was the first (of what would become an annual event) awards dinner at the Hotel Astor in New York City.[3] The magazine had also invited fellow Cleveland stars Bill Veeck (Indians owner) and Lou Boudreau, and Cleveland native Harrison Dillard, the 1948 Olympic champion in the 100-yard dash. The last local luminary to attend was University of Kentucky basketballer Alex Groza (brother of Browns kicker Lou Groza).[4] Later that year, 1949, Alex Groza would be chosen in the first round of the NBA draft, and he would average more than 23 points per game as a rookie. It would later come out, though, that Groza and two of his Kentucky teammates were engaged with gamblers in point shaving in college, the largest such scandal in University of Kentucky history. Due to the mere implication of association with gamblers, the NBA banned all three for life in 1951. But in 1949, Alex Groza was still one of the bright stars in Cleveland's athletic galaxy.

In an awkward news story the day following the dinner, after Motley failed to return home on schedule, Eula called the Cleveland police and filed a missing person's report. Later that day, he told reporters in Ohio that he definitely was still in New York, and not "missing. I'm leaving tonight. I'll be in Cleveland tomorrow. I don't know anything about being missing. It all sounds phony to me. I just stayed over."[5] He told one reporter from the United Press that "he had remained in New York to appear on Jackie Robinson's radio show."[6] It was interesting, though, that Motley only learned of his status, that of a missing person, after being contacted by the local press. He promised reporters that he was going to "telephone his wife immediately to straighten things out."[7]

Motley and Eula had been married for seven years at that point. He was 29 years old, she 32, and they were in the midst of parenting three boys. The marriage, though, would last just 16 more years, and that January there may already have been more than the mere concern for the player's health that compelled Eula to call the police. Motley could have been tracked down at his hotel, or by the team, but instead she engaged the police in a search for one of the most famous (and, physically, the largest, most recognizable) Black athletes in America. Throughout his married life there were whispers of infidelity; whether this was such an occasion will likely never be known, but it was a private matter that created a new public distraction once it crept into the sports pages.

Motley returned home without incident, resumed his basketball work, and nursed the various dings he'd suffered over three years of pummeling by frustrated AAFC tacklers while skidding around on frozen ground in Cleveland and New York. He left Eula and the boys and reported to camp in Bowling Green on schedule, and began getting ready for his fourth season as a pro. As training camp wrapped up, Motley's role on the team morphed a bit. Paul Brown told him that he would see reduced linebacking opportunities due to some nagging, but minor, knee problems that were re-aggravated in pre-season scrimmaging.[8] Even so, Motley remained the finest blocking fullback in the league, and could rip off a long run if the opportunity arose.[9]

As well, the AAFC's operating stability had become a much more public issue. In January, the Brooklyn Dodgers and the New York Yankees amalgamated, with Dan Topping (of the Yankees) as president and Branch Rickey (Dodgers) the board chair. Two days later, conference commissioner Jonas Ingram resigned and tossed the reins to the deputy commissioner. Notably, and probably reflecting the increased financial pressure on some of the owners, team rosters were pared from 35 players to 32. Three fewer contracts may not have amounted to much of a savings, but it was better than nothing for some of the struggling ownership groups. The Browns, the Dons, and the 49ers were solvent, but in places like Chicago, where the Rockets had to compete with the NFL's Bears, finances were precarious. On February 1, a small consortium bought the Chicago Rockets, renaming them the Hornets, and at the same time absorbed much of the old Brooklyn Dodger player pool.

Within the ongoing maelstrom that would be the AAFC's final season, there was still some outstanding football left in the collective tank. After defeating the new Chicago Hornets in their first preseason game, Cleveland welcomed rival San Francisco to Cleveland in mid–August but managed only a 21–21 tie. In general, preseason games scores are the least relevant part of the entire training phase, as coaching staffs need to evaluate players, create a roster for the year, and—mostly—keep the main players healthy. Motley, Lou Groza, and guard Bob Gaudio were all banged up in this game, and missed the final tune up, known regionally in northeast Ohio as the Rubber Bowl, against the Yankees on August 26.[10] Injuries to Motley and Groza, key cogs in the Browns' machine, were the greater concerns.

Groza was held out of the exhibition finale, Motley played sparingly, but Cleveland still won 28–21. Motley was invisible for the regular season opener in Buffalo on September 5, and the Bills tied the Browns 28 apiece.[11] It was the first time Cleveland had failed to not only win, but dominate, their season opener. The following week, in Cleveland, Motley was held out for the entire game as the Browns romped over the Colts, 21–0. After two more wins over New York and Baltimore, Marion Motley arrived for the 1949 season.

Paul Brown had eased Motley back into the practice regimen, and by the time Cleveland kicked off against the Los Angeles Dons, he was ready to go. "Warning to all clubs in the All-America Football Conference: Marion Motley is back in form."[12] So opened the game summary the next afternoon. It continued: "Mashin' Marion was the big gun in the attack as he rammed his way to two of the Brownies' six touchdowns and accounted for 139 of the 242 yards they gained on the ground."[13]

Motley's touchdowns came in the second and third quarters. The early one came on a two-yard blast and he "scored standing up." The second was a 33-yard gallop in the third quarter, when "he ran straight through the middle of the line on the trap play and there wasn't a man within five yards of him at any time."[14] It was a glorious and triumphant return to the center stage for Motley, and Cleveland appeared to be primed for the following week's matchup in San Francisco.

The hype then fizzled. For the first time in nearly two years, the Cleveland Browns lost a regular season football game, this time in front of 59,770 49er fans in Kezar Stadium. Unlike their two 1948 meetings, there was no catastrophic San Francisco fumble in the early part of the game, no easy touchdowns for Graham and Motley. Johnny Strzykalski scored twice, and Joe Perry once, before the end of the first quarter. Down 21–0, the Browns fought well, keeping the margin at a touchdown until Frankie Albert hit Nick Susoeff to make the score 35–21 at the end of three quarters. On the day, Albert tossed five touchdown passes, breaking the AAFC single game record.

Despite a 12-yard Motley touchdown run early in the fourth quarter, making the score 42–28, San Francisco clamped down on all phases of Cleveland's offense. Additional scores by Joe Perry and Eddie Carr were more in the category of insult to injury than of game-changing feats, and San Francisco enjoyed what was arguably their finest hour during the entire AAFC tenure.

Thirty years later, the monthly *Football Digest* ran an account of the game as recalled by Frankie Albert. "The Game I'll Never Forget" was a frequent feature in the magazine, and the fact that this was Albert's most prominent memory said as much about Cleveland's reputation among the rest of the league as it did about the 49ers. "I would have to admit," Albert told writer Dave Payne three decades after the fact, "the Brownies had a bit more talent than us—not much—but enough to get the best of us seven of the nine times we played in the AAFC. Heck, the Browns probably had the best team in football during those years ... one of the most satisfying games of my career came midway through the 1949 season when Cleveland came to San Francisco."[15]

He continued: "As for Motley, he was a bruiser. Graham would get a team thinking so much of his passing that he would suddenly give the ball to 240-pound Motley up the middle. Sports writers in those days described him as a runaway beer truck. He ran kind of straight up, but he still punished you. You had to hit him low to bring him down.... We were probably as ready for Cleveland as we had ever been when they came into Kezar that October day in '49. And I admit, everything went our way. I completed 16 of 24 passes for 242 yards and five touchdowns."[16]

At this point, given the attention that his formidable running ability attracted week in and week out, it is worth a quick examination of Motley's third superpower. His ball handling and defensive skills were unquestionable. As a runner of his time, there had never been anyone in his class in the history of the game, and with the exception of Jim Brown, Barry Sanders and maybe a few others, perhaps none since. As a defender, he had been one of the best linebackers in football, an all–AAFC selection and one of Paul Brown's favorites, and would have continued to play at the position throughout his career if his running had not been so critical to the Cleveland offense scheme. Still, it was the least glamorous, the most underappreciated skill of the three, blocking, that has truly differentiated him from every other great running back in the game. Even to this day, those who saw Motley play almost universally agree that his blocking aptitude and ability were the reasons that Graham stayed upright, and that the Cleveland receivers often had decent passes to catch.

Blanton Collier was often effusive in remembering Motley and talking about his skills. "He had no equal as a blocker; yes, he could do it all."[17] In the packet of material generated by the Pro Football Hall of Fame supporting Motley's induction, more attention lingered on his blocking skill. "What helped make Graham so expert a passer was the protection he received as a result of the ferocious blocking of his chief bodyguard, Motley. No static blocker: Motley, however. He also served as the perfect foil for Graham. Whenever enemy defenders became too impetuous, they would get chopped down on trap plays while the huge Motley would rumble through the suddenly opened holes."[18]

In a very real sense, Motley's love of, and ability in, lead blocking for halfbacks and pass blocking for Graham helped create the opportunities he exploited as a runner. He gave himself freely to the blocking duels. "Marion Motley never thought about Marion Motley," recalled teammate Tony Adamle, "only the team."[19] Motley may not have thought about Motley, but defenders certainly did. "It was said, Otto Graham was the key to Cleveland's greatness. If that was true, then Motley was the key case. If a pass rusher penetrated the front line, he would find an overpowering brick wall named Motley between himself and Graham ... this not only relieved the pressure from other linemen, but it also let Graham, the key, work at maximum capacity."[20]

Motley was a large man for the time and got bigger as he aged, and he used his heft to protect his teammates. "I was the biggest man on the team at 232 [pounds, in 1948]," said Motley. "When I first started, [I played] at 228 to 230." When he no longer started at linebacker as well, he climbed to 232 pounds, and ultimately reached 245 by the time he retired. It was not until 1949 that any other player on the team exceeded 250 pounds.[21]

When it came to discussing his mental approach to football, Motley would often tell interviewers, "I just enjoyed playing the whole game. Blocking was no effort to me. It just came to me. A part of the game. It wasn't a task."[22] In the late 1980s, he talked about the art, science, and attitude of blocking with Stuart Leuthner:

> A lot of [today's players] want to know what I think about football today, and I don't think there's a real way to compare the game today with the one we played. Our hands had to be on our chest, and if they moved from there, you got called for holding and it was fifteen yards. Another thing, blocking is atrocious today. I don't care how strong these kids are, that doesn't make any difference. You can't just take your hands and push the other guy around and expect to get him out of there. That's the reason you see so

many field goals kicked today. They get down near that goal line and want to push and don't go anyplace. Down there we used to eat dirt. You'd root your way in, down on your knees, and use your shoulders and hit that guy.[23]

Those words convey a tinge of a get-off-my-lawn, grumpy-old-player ethos, but the proof is on the remaining game films and in the collective, recorded memories of those he blocked, and those he protected. Paul Brown, in his autobiography, shared his true feelings about Motley's skill.

Marion became our greatest fullback ever because not only was he a great runner, but also no one ever blocked better—and no one ever cared more about his team and whether it won or lost, rather than how many yards he gained or where he was asked to run. No one reached our passers when he was blocking, and we often let him take on a defensive end man-for-man because he was big enough to handle anyone. After he hit a guy a couple of times, that player began looking for Marion before he went after our passer.[24]

Motley's blocking was palpable, corroborative evidence of one of his core attributes, his innate and sincere humility. He simply did not need all the attention on the field, did not crave the spotlight. Football is a team game, and Motley was always more concerned with the final score than his individual statistics. In later life he never entered a room or started a conversation by announcing "who" he was or "what" he'd accomplished in football, even though his enshrinement in Canton drew the interest of almost everyone he encountered. But his humility, echoed in the words of Tony Adamle, Paul Brown, and so many more, was his shield and his motivation, and his keel. It kept him upright throughout his life both in and after his playing days. Protecting his teammates, doing everything within his span of control to help his team win, that was the elemental greatness that propelled Motley. It is not uncommon to find teams with a terrific blocking fullback, but never does that player show the burst, the speed, the instincts, and the ability with the football in the open field, that Motley displayed. There have been fullbacks who could run the ball very effectively, as well, but none were capable of punishing leaking pass rushers the way Motley did.

The sole significant, published repudiation of the notion that Motley was a superior blocker comes from established football historians Kenneth Crippen and Mat Reaser. In their book *The All-American Football Conference*, they agree with the wider summary of Motley as runner and receiver. The deviation arises in their judgment that he struggled in pass protection. "Only about a third of the time was he able to hold his ground. The rest of the time, the defender either pushed him back or easily slid off him."[25] They are equally dismissive of Motley's run blocking, stating that if Motley was not meeting a defender head on, he "would either not block anyone or he made a weak block."[26]

Crippen and Reaser cite extensive film study as the foundational reference for their judgments, but game film of the day was nothing like it is in the 21st century. It is often grainy and episodic, and the camera frequently follows the movement of the football instead of maintaining an 11-on-11 perspective. Both writers have long experience and demonstrated expertise in studying and writing about earlier football, but their judgments may be fairly questioned in view of the decades of consistent consensus among coaches like Paul Brown and Blanton Collier, quarterbacks like Otto Graham, opponents from just about every team the Browns played, and reporters who covered Motley from high school in the mid–1930s through his final game in 1955. Almost universally, the in-the-moment conclusion was that Motley was a devastating blocker, and that the careers of Brown, Graham, and his teammates were all demonstrably improved by Motley's ability to block. This discussion is moot today, as Motley has been a Hall of Famer for more than 50 years, but it is interesting to note that his name can still induce quasi-controversy more than two decades after his death.

While Motley was well aware of his value to the team, that knowledge apparently did not stoke his ego, nor did he allow it to set himself above anyone. Throughout his career, and his life, he was a quiet, almost humble man when it came to evaluating his athletic skill. When it came to comparing salaries from his time with those of the more recent game, Motley was a bit less sanguine later in life. "I don't have any feeling of resentment toward the players who are making big money. The thing that upsets me is the fella who gets $100,000 before he comes to camp. My bonus was $400. That was what I got, and I didn't get it until I got to camp. My salary the first year was $5,000."[27] The most he ever earned in a single season was $12,000.

Returning to the 1949 season, and the aftermath of the blowout loss to San Francisco, the Browns took out their frustration on the Los Angeles Dons by inflicting a 61–15 whipping on the southern Californians. One significant note in this game came in the form of an otherwise insignificant fourth-quarter touchdown by one George Taliaferro.

Taliaferro had been an offensive star at Indiana University. That fact, in and of itself, is not particularly compelling. A three-time All-American, he led the Hoosiers in rushing, passing, and punting in various seasons, and in 1945 had led the entire Big 10 in rushing for the year. George Taliaferro was also a Black man, and that made his story not only fascinating but socially relevant. Taliaferro's football ability opened a door, in 1949, when he became the first Black player ever drafted into the NFL. The Chicago Bears took him in the 13th round that year, but he was also offered a contract by the AAFC's L.A. Dons. Taliaferro opted for California, and by the end of that rookie year logged nearly 500 yards rushing, 790 yards passing, 982 yards punting, and 366 return yards. Motley, Willis, Washington, and Strode had broken the race barrier back in 1946, and now Taliaferro—and so many that followed—benefited by inclusion in the player draft. To be sure, Taliaferro would not have been drafted at all were he not a tremendous football player, but the opportunity existed largely because of the path cleared by those first four.

Cleveland welcomed the San Francisco 49ers to Ohio for a rematch on October 30, and managed a 30–28 win to even their season series. Motley ran for two more touchdowns the following week in a 35–2 win over Chicago and added another two weeks later in a 31–0 shutout of the Yankees. Cleveland beat Buffalo in the division round of the AAFC playoffs, earning a slot in the 1949 AAFC championship game against Frankie Albert, Joe Penny, and the rest of those pesky 49ers.

While the action on the field continued according to schedule, the foundations of the AAFC, in truth those of professional football writ large, were shifting. On December 10, Herb Altschull of the Associated Press broke the news that the AAFC was merging into the NFL. "Thus ended," he continued, "one of the most costly wars in the history of athletics. Losses to club owners soared to upwards of $2,000,000 in the protracted battle."[28] The league press conference was evidently called abruptly, with little warning to the press and even less to the general public. Bert Bell would retain his role as commissioner of the expanded entity, initially designated as the National-American Football League, or NAF, and three AAFC organizations were integrated into the new structure. Cleveland and San Francisco were the two obvious choices for assimilation, given their talent levels and the broad ticket-buying fan support. After a good deal of back and forth haranguing, and copious appeasement to Washington owner George Preston Marshall, the Baltimore Colts became the third.

7. The Last Days of the AAFC (1949)

Of interest, much of the public credit for brokering what many had considered an un-makeable deal was accorded to the owner of the New York baseball Giants, Horace Stoneham. His stake came from his ownership of New York's Polo Grounds. Two NFL teams played there in 1949, and both lost "a considerable amount of money."[29] Commissioner Bert Bell and AAFC representative J. Arthur Friedland "told newsmen that Stoneham started the merger by summoning [both] to New York last Friday." The men worked through the weekend and produced the merger within 72 hours.

The Sporting News story on the merger noted that the agreement came in the nick of time. "Interest in college football had taken a remarkable jump while the pros had suffered. It is doubtful if any of the AAC clubs will show a profit while many could not have survived another year."[30] During the press conference, Bell explained the speed of the proceedings. "We do things in a hurry when we do them." A reporter added, "Especially when there's a lot of money involved." Bell laughed, and added, "You're darned right."[31]

The merger announcement may have drained a bit of enthusiasm for the upcoming Cleveland–San Francisco championship game. Due to that, and the prosect of miserable, frigid weather that included the chance of snow, fewer than 30,000 tickets were sold. At least one visiting reporter dreaded the upcoming afternoon beside Lake Erie. "Fully equipped with tennis shoes, hand warmers, cotton gloves, long underwear and a sideline kerosene heater," the 49ers readied for the game. "The gear," the story continued, "usually worn by ice fishermen, home gardeners, and down easterners" was needed "when the weatherman predicted cloudy and colder with snow probable."[32]

On the Cleveland side, receiver Ara Parseghian was the only player not listed at full strength, which meant that Paul Brown was confident in Motley's health for the game. On a snowy day, with an icy field, better to not have to rely on Graham's arm and his receivers' skill in the challenging conditions.

The game, in front of 22,500 hardy football fans, went largely as the oddsmakers had predicted. The betting line gave Cleveland a seven and a half point edge at kickoff, and the Browns did their part when they scored in the first quarter as Edgar Jones barreled into the endzone from the two-yard line. Motley uncorked the play of the game in the third, a 68-yard touchdown run off a trap that made the score 14–0. Graham threw for only 128 yards on the day, but rushed for 62, most coming off seven quarterback sneaks. The teams traded touchdowns in the final frame, and when game ended, the Cleveland Browns had captured their fourth consecutive AAFC championship, 21–7. San Francisco head coach Buck Shaw offered the most succinct summary of the game, the year, and the conference. "Aw, hell! What's the use of analyzing?" he asked. "We just weren't good enough. You can't afford to make any mistakes against them. They're a great team."[33]

Hal Lebovitz, a Cleveland sports scribe talented enough to be inducted into the National Baseball Hall of Fame's writer's wing, covered the game's aftermath. He opened with "At exactly 4:16 p.m., Sunday, December 11, a gun sounded at Municipal Stadium to mark the end of a glorious era of football for Cleveland—and perhaps the start of a new one."[34] Paul Brown shook hands with his "lifetime champs" of the AAFC, and the fans interrupted their exit in the muck and the mire to laud the players with a long, loud stream of applause. "Appropriately," Lebovitz wrote, "the ground crew chose this instant to lower the flag and the band played taps. It seemed to signify the final moment of the All-America Conference."[35]

The following week, on December 17, Motley and his Cleveland teammates took on an AAFC all-star amalgamation at Rice University in Texas, in what organizer Glenn McCarthy named the "Shamrock Bowl." McCarthy, a wealthy oilman in Houston, had hoped to earn an AAFC franchise for his home city, but the merger with the NFL had killed that aspiration. Nevertheless, McCarthy pressed on with the game, and despite the rain that afternoon almost 12,000 fans watched a game that Hall of Fame quarterback Y.A. Tittle later called "one of the great memories of my life. We were treated like movie stars."[36]

The location of the game provided yet another jab at professional football's racial integration scheme. It took a relaxation of local laws, not the informally binding Jim Crow policies but actual, written law, to allow the Black players like Motley, Gillom, Joe Perry, and New York's Buddy Young to play. Motley and Willis did not experience the same star treatment as Tittle, either, instead staying in a private residence in a part of town predominantly occupied by non–White minorities.

On the morning of the game, Motley and Willis took a taxi to Rice's stadium, but when they tried to enter, the guard told them that players were not allowed through that gate. This despite the fact that the entire Browns team had used it the day before at practice. "It was pouring rain," Motley told Ray Didinger, "and we were getting soaked. We told the guy we used that gate all week. He said, 'Damn it, don't you listen? No players come through here.'" When the team bus arrived a few moments later, the Browns walked through the gate, and Brown asked Motley and Willis why they weren't already inside. "I told Paul, 'That little so-and-so wouldn't let us in.' Paul was furious. He went and got the man who was sponsoring the game, told him the story. He fired the guard on the spot. I told [McCarthy], 'The reason you're playing this game is you want to bring pro football to Texas. If you do, you're gonna have black players. You'd better change your ways down here, or else there's going to be hell to pay."[37]

Even after the four were permitted to take the field, Black fans were still barred from the stadium. In short, one of the more integrated teams and leagues were playing for pay in Houston, but the local minority families and fans were denied admission. Y.A. Tittle recalled that organizer "Glenn McCarthy really took a fascination with Buddy Young. I remember him just pulling money out of his pocket and giving Buddy $2,000 or $3,000."[38] The Browns lost to the All-Stars, 12–7, and Motley's season came to an end.

The end of the season, and of the AAFC, offered an opportunity for reflection. On balance, the 1949 season signaled that Marion Motley might, after all, be mortal. After the various dings and a few minor injuries, he started just ten games and rushed for only 570 yards on 113 carries, his lowest seasonal total as a professional. He did lead the entire AAFC in touchdowns, with eight, and his rushing yardage was still good for third in the circuit behind Joe Perry and Buffalo's Chet Mutryn. Notably, though, he also finished in the top 20 in the conference in pass receptions and eighth in kickoff returns. His 48 points tied him for fourth in scoring, and he was again selected to the All-Conference list, but for the first time was named to the second team, not the first. At the age of 29, it appeared that Marion Motley was beginning to fray a bit at the edges.

While Motley was not one to share much of his inner pain, words from his successor, Jim Brown, very well describe what it felt like to play fullback in Cleveland. Brown's career started two years after Motley played his final down, but the essential elements of Brown's description, as the fullback in Paul Brown's offense and playing in a northern city by Lake Erie, were still quite apt. After every tackle, he shared, "I'd get up slowly, deliberately ... there were times I had no choice, had to get up slowly." In an age when a forearm shot to a runner's head, or a

helmet-to-helmet collision, the sort that would be illegal in the contemporary game, he was in pain. Often, he wrote, "my arm was bent as
God had not intended or the nail on my big toe had been bloodied and
knocked right off ... almost everything hurt." As expected, and difficult
to understand unless experienced, it was the—literally—frozen ground
at Municipal Stadium that often inflicted the greatest damage. "Sometimes what hurt the most was the ground. When the field was frozen,
you banged it with a frozen elbow, it would hurt right to your teeth."[39]

Brown's description is relevant not only because he and Motley
played the same position, but also because they did so in the same arenas and in similar weather conditions. Brown had a single face bar on
a slightly improved helmet, one that may have protected his teeth and
jaw a bit, and he did not get the brunt of the first Black star abuse from
opponents that Motley did, but his description of the violence and pain
inherent to playing football in the 1950s remains illuminating. Working for Paul Brown under the conditions that Jim Brown describes, with
the collisions, the weather, the pressures, and the still-extant racism
that pervaded much of society and the fans that attended games, Motley
could be forgiven for aging.

With the demise of the All-America Football Conference, and
the looming introduction to the National Football League, the entire
Browns team was embarking on an uncertain path. Edgar Jones, the
best halfback on the team during their AAFC years, retired due to lingering shoulder issues. Defender Lou Saban retired to get into coaching, a decision that ultimately led to head jobs in both the AFL (Boston
Patriots and Buffalo Bills, 1960–1965, including AFL championships
in 1964 and 1965) and the NFL (Denver Broncos and the Buffalo Bills,
again). Offensive line stalwart Bob Gaudio called it a career as well.

Just 26 years old, Ara Parseghian left football due to a late-season
hip injury. Parseghian made out well after his playing days ended. The
following year he took an assistant coaching job at his alma mater,
Miami University in southwest Ohio, and moved into the head coaching office the next year. After seven years leading Northwestern's football program, he accepted perhaps the most prestigious job in college
football, the head coach at the University of Notre Dame. At the time
Parseghian took the reins, the Irish had not had a winning season in the
preceding five. Two years after, starting in 1966, he led the university to
a national championship. He added another in 1973 before moving to
the broadcast booth for good.

7. The Last Days of the AAFC (1949)

Summarizing the league's denouement, the single, final word on Cleveland and the Browns' four-year era in the AAFC is dominance. Their overall record, including their four championships, was an almost unbelievable 47 wins, four losses, and three ties. According to the Pro Football Hall of Fame's Cleveland Browns website, "The teams of the AAFC basically were of comparable quality to those of the NFL but, in the first 10 years of post–World War II pro football, the Cleveland Browns proved to be the best in either league."[40] They had desegregated the AAFC without undue fanfare or attention seeking, and afforded genuine dignity to Motley, Bill Willis and Horace Gillom, accepting the athletes as team members, not merely Black team members. Their excellence had lured fans to the stadium, and brought money to owner Mickey McBride, and in conjunction with the San Francisco 49ers they had created a genuine rivalry that they could take with them to the NFL in 1950. In 2020, *Sports Illustrated* ran a story naming the members of the all-time Cleveland Browns team.[41] On that list were, naturally, Jim Brown and Marion Motley at running back, but also on the squad were the original luminaries Otto Graham, Dante Lavelli, Bill Willis, and Lou Groza. The AAFC iteration of the Cleveland Browns was the greatest grouping in the history of the organization. They were dominant.

ᛁᛚ 8 ᛁᛚ

New League, Same Outcome

Joining the NFL (1950)

As 1950 dawned on the professional football world, both the game's landscape and its future path were obscured in shadow and fog. Sports like baseball and boxing and horse racing, games competing for the aggregate fan dollars and time, were solid in the minds of the ticket-buying, newspaper-reading pubic. The new pro football federation, however, still had not found its footing. That external angst and turmoil had no effect, though, on the Motleys and their off-season lives. Marion and Eula even spent the time and money to drive to Paterson, New Jersey, to spend New Year's Eve with Cleveland Indian star Larry Doby and his wife.[1] The two stars had met in Cleveland, and since their respective seasons barely overlapped, they had found that they enjoyed the time spent in each other's company. It was a small club, the one populated exclusively by Black athletes (in a largely segregated world) whose membership criteria seemed to include a large and potentially intimidating physical presence, professional athletic stardom, and at least one championship in their sport. Doby, Motley, Gillom, and Willis were the only four such men in the Cleveland area that met all of those standards, and it was a natural that they and their families were friendly among themselves.

Back in Cleveland, columnist Joe Cooterton asked Motley's opinion of the upcoming season. "We're hoping to turn out another winner," he answered. "The Browns should do well in the new league and the competition should be tougher ... the new league should draw well and I believe our attendance will be much better, especially playing against the Chicago Bears and Philly Eagles." Motley laughed as he added, "I'll be ready."[2]

126

8. New League, Same Outcome

Later in the month, the fullback once again laced up the basketball shoes for his off-season conditioning. After four years of winter basketball, the team sponsored by the Cleveland Browns had grown to 16 players, nearly half the football roster, and actually assigned line coach "Weeb" Ewbank as head coach.[3] Motley, even though he was now weighing in upwards of 232 pounds, still loved basketball and running the floor, and even as he approached the old age of 30, played quite well. In late February, Motley and Otto Graham were picked to join a group of NFL players forming an exhibition team to take on the Harlem Globetrotters at the Cincinnati Gardens.[4]

The Cincinnati Gardens, in its day, was no tiny, underfunded arena. It had opened just a year earlier, and with 11,000 seats, at the time it was the seventh-largest indoor arena in the United States. Between 1957 and 1972, it would be home to the NBA's Cincinnati Royals, a team that featured the immortal Oscar Robertson, and hosted the league's All-Star game in 1966. The opportunity to play against the Harlem Globetrotters, especially in such a professional forum, was an honor for Motley, and a testament to his basketball ability and athletic reputation.

Still, in the real world, and especially in the 1940s and '50s, there are few results more consistent and predictable than those of Globetrotter basketball games. This night was no different, as the Marques Haynes– and Goose Tatum–led Trotters won their 119th game of their preceding 120 (the sole loss was to George Mikan and the professional Minneapolis Lakers, a team amid a two-year professional basketball championship streak, a week earlier). The Globetrotters' Clarence Wilson hit five consecutive shots from beyond 25 feet, and the footballers trailed 35–15 at the half. The second half was largely a replay of the first, and the Globetrotters won 60–33.[5] The score would have been much worse had Chicago Hornets rookie defensive end George Benigni, who had also been drafted by the NBA's Philadelphia 76ers out of Georgetown University, not scored 13 by himself. Motley and Graham were both held scoreless, but they returned to the Browns' basketball season with chests puffed and heads held high.

Thus, in a real sense, Marion Motley experienced one of the more fascinating athletic careers ever lived. It was not just that he was an elite, all-time football player, one who excelled on offense, defense, and special teams in high school, college, and in the professional ranks, but he'd also had the chance to compete with and against some of the finest Negro teams and sportsmen of the 20th century. He'd pitched with the Kansas City Monarchs in college, and now taken the court against the greatest barnstorming basketball team in the annals of the game, all while continuing to trample the opposition in college and professional football. Motley, even as he passed his 30th year, had established himself as one of the greatest athletes to ever play sports.

Such achievement provided little consolation once training camp began. The aggregation of aches and pains, the nagging, chronic discomforts that make even simple chores, such as merely getting out of bed in the morning, far more challenging than they are for the most of us. Compounding those maladies was the daily reality of those violent collisions with some of the most talented tacklers in football history. If that was the price of playing another year, though, Motley was eager to pay.

The Browns embraced their admission to the new league in their traditional fashion, by winning. Their first three exhibitions were all victories. They beat Green Bay 38–7 in Toledo, knocked off their familiar AAFC rival Baltimore Colts 34–7 in Cincinnati, and topped Detroit 35–14 in Akron. Their pre–Labor Day weekend tune up against the mighty Chicago Bears took place in Cleveland and generated the expected level of press interest beforehand.

"It took four years to arrange it, but the Cleveland Browns finally get the chance they have been waiting for tonight—a chance to knock off one of their proud but dangerous National League rivals, the Chicago Bears."[6] So began the game day hype in regional newspapers. Yes, in one sense it was just another preseason opportunity to evaluate the respective rosters and finalize player decisions. In another, though, it was George Halas on one sideline and Paul Brown on the other, each ready to "pull no punches in their efforts to prove the other team inferior."[7] The final score would not matter, but the unfettered, testosterone-fueled competitive juices of everyone on the field, from aging coaches on down, was going to foster an in-season level of violent intensity.

The game did not disappoint; 51,076 watched in Municipal Stadium—a crowd that, a decade earlier, would have been almost record setting for a championship game—and were treated to a legitimate, grudge match football game. "Last night's game was the first major test for the Browns, new to the National League. The Bears, five times champions of the circuit since 1933, have symbolized National League power for the last 30 years."[8] The United Press story continued, terming the game an aerial battle between Graham and Johnny Lujack.

Lujack threw the first touchdown pass of the game, to Jim Keane, a short drive that started after Motley lost a fumble in Cleveland territory. Graham retaliated with a score of his own, but Chicago re-took the lead on a field goal by a young kicker named George Blanda. A Graham-to-Dub Jones touchdown and a Groza field goal restored Cleveland's advantage. Cleveland took a 27–10 lead in the fourth and needed the points to weather two Lujack touchdown tosses to Ken Kavanaugh, scores that made the final total 27–23 in favor of the Browns. Despite the fumble, Motley was still Cleveland's best running option, gaining 52 yards on only seven carries.

A few days later, in their final pre-season game in Buffalo, Motley had yet another excellent game, scoring a touchdown on a 13-yard screen pass before giving way in the second half, as the Browns beat the Steelers 31–21 to close out a perfect 5–0 exhibition campaign. The most important game, though, in terms of overall team confidence, had been the win over the Bears. Pundits and prognosticators across the country were in near-universal agreement that, while the Browns certainly had some talented players and an excellent coach, their domination of the AAFC over the preceding four years was as much a function of the absence of any credible competition as it was Cleveland's competence. "Just wait," they seemed to say, "and see how you do when you're facing the big boys, actual NFL teams, week-in and week-out ... then we'll see just how glittery your record looks." To Motley and his teammates, the opinions of a collection of sportswriters were just opinions, and not very informed ones at that.

"Everybody get out of my way! I'm coming through," shouted Marion Motley at his teammates one August afternoon at the Browns' Bowling Green training camp. Paul Brown answered with "If they don't get out of your way, Marion, run over them."[9] Philadelphia writer Mort Berry, embedded with the Browns for the three weeks leading up to the game, in recapping Motley's 1950 pre-season noted that "it was against the [Detroit] Lions that Motley had one of his better days. He left cleat marks on their backs and chests as he gained 139 yards on 14 explosions through the line. The biggest single gain was a 41-yard touchdown run." The words were part of an article intended to hype interest in the season-opening game between the defending NFL champion Philadelphia Eagles and the four-time AAFC champion Browns.

For an introduction to a new league, Cleveland's opening game was not going to be an easy greeting. NFL Commissioner Bell had been on the record, before Horace Stoneham's deal-making blitz, as minimizing the skill and ability of the entire AAFC. If the Browns were the acknowledged champions of the old conference, then in Bell's view it was time to administer a reality check to the Clevelanders, and who better to do that than the current kings of the NFL. This game was scheduled by design, Bell's vision being a clear demonstration of NFL superiority, a reminder to any doubting writers or fans that even the best of the deceased league were no real match for the best in the senior circuit. At least, that was the plan.

"My theory," Motley told Berry, "is that if I run over them the first time, they'll be kind of cautious about grabbing me after that."[10] The writers were not shy in appreciating Motley's pass blocking, either. Berry wrote, "Two-hundred and thirty pound defensive ends, coming in at full speed with the intent of bowling over the stationary Motley ... simply bounce off the iron-hard blocker." Motley explained that he tried "to make a study of blocking the different types of ends. That helps me to be able to run into people."[11]

For their part, the Eagles were a great team. "Bucko" Kilroy and Hall of Famer Steve Van Buren, both later named to the All-Decade team (1940s) by the NFL, spearheaded a Philadelphia rushing attack that had led the team to consecutive NFL titles in 1948 and 1948, and any defense that featured Chuck Bednarik was a challenge of the highest order. They were coached by future Hall of Famer Alfred Earle "Greasy" Neale, and he was convinced that his team would dominate the upstarts from Ohio.

Neale's athletic career was compelling in its diversity. A multi-sport star, he had been a starting outfielder for baseball's Cincinnati Reds between 1916 and 1924, including a world championship with the 1919 Reds. That title, of course, is one of the most notorious in sports history, as the opponent was the Chicago White Sox, a team that lives on in popular memory as the Black Sox. The knot of allegations of fixed games and curious play will never be completely untied, but Neale hit .357 in that series, including a double, a triple and four runs driven in. He did his part in legitimizing Cincinnati's pennant, regardless of Chicago's level of effort. By the time Neale left the diamond for good, after an eight-year major league career, he had finished in the top ten in National League base stealing four times and had notched 50 career triples.[12] While he was playing baseball, though, or, more accurately, when the season ended, he played professional football with the Canton

Bulldogs, Dayton Triangles, and Massillon Tigers before the founding of the NFL, and in 1941 returned to the professional game as head coach of the Eagles. By 1969, he was a member of both the college and professional football Halls of Fame.

Neale did not suffer from a lack of confidence. "We'll beat the Cleveland Browns Saturday night," Neale told the writers, "if our team plays the game it is capable of. We'll win if our boys carry out their assignments, if we block like we should."[13] Neale sincerely believed his team the better of the two. His coaching counterpart, Paul Brown, was a bit more circumspect. "We never said we could beat the Eagles. We never even claimed we could beat a low ranking NFL team. All we asked for was the chance. We've got it."[14]

Saturday evening, September 17, in Philadelphia, the 1950 NFL season kicked off in front of 71,237 fans. The die appeared cast when the Eagles broke the scoring seal with a 15-yard, first-quarter field goal, good for a 3–0 lead. The home team would not score again until the fourth quarter. The AAFC champs did not merely defeat their NFL counterparts, they destroyed them. Motley carried the ball 11 times for 48 yards and caught a pair of passes for 26 more. Otto Graham also completed 21 passes for 346 yards, including three touchdown tosses, and the Browns almost coasted to the 35–10 victory.

Motley, though, also contributed on defense. One of the two major rule changes that had been approved prior to the season was making permanent the free substitution rule. Before, coaches were limited in their ability to shuttle players on and off the field, a forcing factor for the two-way players up until 1949, so moving key defenders around as the tactical situation dictated was impossible. In 1950, the unified NFL removed those restrictions, and in key goal-line situations, must-stop scenarios, Brown was able to insert Motley on defense as a stopper. On one late-game Philadelphia possession in this contest, Motley went in at linebacker and made either solo or assisted tackles on four consecutive plays to keep the Eagles out of the end zone.

Both sides showed immense degrees of class afterward. Neale did not make any excuses, even though he was missing Van Buren, and Brown left it at "We're happy. We're not going to gloat when we win a ball game."[15] After the build-up and anticipation surround the clash of football titans, the final score represented a bit of an anticlimax. Yet, simultaneously, the result quietly but unmistakably informed the football world that the Cleveland Browns were as good as their reputation.

In later years, Motley considered that game one of the top three of his career, "the ones I always tell people about." He told Stuart Leuthner:

> Greasy Neale was telling everybody, "The high school kids are coming to play the pros." You know what I think gave us the incentive to go out there and play the game we did? A Philadelphia *Enquirer* sportswriter came up to camp to live with us the three weeks we were in camp, and he was going to write a story about it. He used to get the paper sent up from Philadelphia every day, and he'd cut out the sports column. Pretty soon the board was full of those articles, all of this shit about how they were going to do this and that to us.
>
> When we walked out on the field that evening, we wanted to beat them because we wanted that guy to have to eat his words. We kicked off to the Eagles and held them, and then they kicked to us. A little back we had, "Dopey" Phelps, went all the way in for a touchdown but they got Lenny Ford for holding. The Eagles kicked to us again and Phelps took it to the thirty-five. From then on, the Eagles couldn't do a thing.[16]

The following week, Motley ran for 19 yards on three carries, but did catch a 22-yard screen pass in a 31–0 shutout of the familiar Baltimore Colts. At 2–0, the Browns looked to have measured the NFL just as they had the All-America Conference. The next week, against the New York Giants, Cleveland suffered a dose of reality, a reminder not to take winning for granted.

The *Cleveland Plain Dealer* announced the bad news: "Before 37,647 of Cleveland's faithful and 40,000 vacant seats—seats that might have been filled had the fans known in advance what was about to happen—the Browns were dropped from the unbeaten, invincible class yesterday and failed to score a point for the first time in 62 games."[17] From the outset, the game looked like it was going to be all offense for 60 minutes. The Giants scored after a 52-yard drive on their first possession of the game, grinding out the rushing yards and not relying on quarterback Charlie Conerly.

Motley led the ground attack with 53 yards on 17 carries, but New York kept him in the middle of the field and held his longest single run to nine yards. He even fumbled a handoff from Graham in the first half, killing what was Cleveland's best scoring opportunity of the day. The key to New York's win, though, was taking away Graham's passing game. On the afternoon, the Browns' quarterback was 12–30 in passing, for only 127 yards. Under the modern passer efficiency rating system, in which the maximum possible score is 158.3 and a Pro Bowler's average game score is around 75, Graham managed a 13.5. The Giants intercepted him three times, largely due to the defensive scheme change they made to rush the ends instead of dropping them into pass coverage, an early iteration of the blitz. Graham and his receivers weren't ready for the tactic, and it showed. None of that is to imply that Graham was less than stellar overall. In 1954, he would become one of the first quarterbacks ever to post a perfect 158.3, that time against the Cardinals. But against the Giants, on that Sunday, Graham endured a bad day at the office.

Now humbled, the Browns roared back the following week in Pittsburgh, beating the Steelers 30–17, and then topping the Chicago Cardinals 34–24 in Cleveland. Motley's two-yard, fourth-quarter touchdown provided the final cushion and margin of victory against their close geographical rival.

The 4–1 Browns travelled to New York for their rematch with the Giants the next weekend. In their AAFC days, the Browns had never been swept by another team in any season, so there was a sense of eager anticipation in the locker room prior to kickoff. The Browns managed to score 13 in the game, a vast improvement over the earlier shutout, but they gave up 17, and took their second loss of the season, both to the Giants. New York had not run the same defense against Graham that they had a few weeks before, and the otherwise unflappable Graham had another three-interception game, and netted a 36.1 passer rating. Motley was little help, again held to only 21 yards rushing (and eight receiving) and did not score.

Motley had struggled in both games against the Giants, and he may have begun to hear—or imagine—whispers about both the team and his skills. He needed a chance to set the public record straight. Football, like most sports, captures our collective attention and passion in part because it does occasionally offer opportunities for redemption. One of those occurred on Sunday, October 29, 1950.

The thermometer in northeast Ohio peaked near 75F that afternoon, with a few clouds. Overall, it was a comfortable day for mid-autumn and a great day for football. This was a home date for the Cleveland Browns, and they took the field in Cleveland, with its white lines chalked neatly over infield dirt so recently used by the baseball Indians, in front of 40,713 partisans. Most were seeking a win in the very first game with their new, geographic rivals, the Pittsburgh Steelers, but also wanted a modicum of relief and assurance after their team's 17–13 loss to Steve Owen and the New York Giants a week earlier. In that defeat, Cleveland had only gained 82 rushing yards, on 32 plays, and the entire offense provided one touchdown. It was a lackluster showing at best and seemed to confirm some the suspicions of the New York press.

Jim Schlemmer wrote, "Last Monday ... there was a lot of talk that the Browns were 'over the hill.... There was much talk, too ... that the Browns possessed no ground attack and consequently were impotent now that Otto Graham had been disarmed.'" Former New York Yankee coach Red Stader, an alum from the AAFC, went so far as to say that "now that Motley has been stopped from going up the middle, the Browns are powerless."[18]

Given that the Browns' quarterback, Graham, completed just five of nine passes, for only 157 yards, that afternoon, the naysayers should have been proved right. The team had fallen into third place in their division, trailing the Giants and the Eagles, and doubters were seemingly everywhere. By the time of the kickoff on this pre–Halloween gameday, the Browns had posted a respectable, even surprising, 4–2 record, but it was predictable, the media decided. The AAFC team was good, but not better than the NFL's best. In fact, this Browns team's winning window was probably just about ready to close, as their stars had begun to fray at the edges. Approximately one football minute after kickoff, a huge chunk of the over the hill narrative collapsed.

Cleveland received the ball and returned it all the way back to the Steelers' 32-yard line. After a tipped Graham pass, off play-action, that fell incomplete, and then a halfback dive, Motley went to work.[19] The *Akron Beacon Journal* reported: "He went for 12 yards on each of the first two times he carried the ball. He took a pitchout from Graham for 50 yards to the Steelers' 2-yard line where he was ruled to have stepped out.... He exploded on a trap play to go 69 yards for another touchdown and he went 20 yards on still another trap through the line, as he gave the lie to Strader and all of the 'over the hill' crowd."[20] "Motley was chased by [defensive back Bob] Gage, but the speedy Pittsburgh halfback conceded when Marion was still 25 yards away from a touchdown."[21]

That afternoon, Motley also caught a 33-yard screen pass that he ran in for a touchdown, a feat all the more remarkable in that a Steeler defender knocked Motley's helmet off about five yards into the run after the catch, yet the unprotected big man still survived two attempted tackles before finally rumbling into the end zone. The play came about as an act of desperation. Graham dropped back to pass, found "himself surrounded by Steelers" and weakly tossed to Motley in the left flat. From there, without any lead blocking and working independently behind enemy lines, Motley showed that the rumors of his demise were a tad premature.

Most significantly, perhaps immortally, that afternoon, Motley rushed for 188 yards on only 11 touches for an average of 17.1 yards per carry. It was, and still is, one of the most efficient single-game rushing performances in the history of professional football. That single game mark for anyone rushing for more than 150 yards has only been excelled once in the annals of the NFL, in 2002, when a young Michael Vick ran for 173 yards on only ten carries.

With the win, Cleveland moved back into second place in their conference, and with a rematch against the first-place Eagles remaining, the team was once again in control of its playoff destiny. They eked out a tough 10–7 win over the Cardinals at Comiskey Park in Chicago in early November. The win put the Browns back into first place, and they cemented their grip on the spot a week later when they beat San Francisco 34–14 in Cleveland.

Perhaps it was familiarity with San Francisco, or possibly the Steeler game simply reinvigorated the team's commitment to the running game. Regardless of cause, Motley ran for another 114 yards (21 carries) and a touchdown against the 49ers, and then 178 (on 27 attempts) against the Washington Redskins (now the Washington Football Team). The Eagles came to Cleveland on the first weekend in December, and had clearly taken a page from the Giants' defensive playbook as they held the Browns' fullback to a mere 16 yards, 11 of those on a single carry. Cleveland did not attempt a single pass that day, but still managed a 13–7 victory and season sweep of the defending NFL champs.

Motley: "We beat them throwing the ball in that first game, and Greasy Neale started saying that we weren't nothing but a basketball team. The next time we played them, we never put the ball in the air and beat them again. We ran that ball right down their throats. That's the kind of guy Paul Brown was, stubborn, especially if he got something on his mind. We were on the side lines screaming, 'Throw the ball, throw the ball,' but he wouldn't let Otto throw it one time."[22]

The last weekend of the regular season saw the Browns paste Washington 45–21. Motley carried the ball four times, but still gained 48 yards. But Graham returned to form with three touchdown passes, including one to Lou Groza, and when the game ended, Cleveland finished its first NFL tour with a 10–2 record. For a team many expected to fail under the brightest of spotlights, the team had done just the oppo-site. The lone blot on Cleveland's season, the Giants, also at 10–2, were coming to Cleveland for a playoff game the next week, a game that rep-resented another of those chances for gridiron redemption. The choices were win or start the off-season. It was, truly, as simple as that.

As the Browns had learned through harsh experience over the pre-ceding four seasons, December weather in the city by Lake Erie could be uncomfortable at best. Nightmarish was the norm, and the December 17 conditions lived down to expectations. The field in Municipal Sta-dium was frozen, and the icy wind off the lake gusted to more than 25 miles per hour. As such, the aerial games were largely grounded, and the contest was decided by straight-up, man-versus-man blocking, tackling, and running. The two teams had already demonstrated that they were well matched, even though New York held a 2–0 advantage on the year, and this game was no different.

Motley ran but seven times, gaining 12 yards in the process, and the entire team racked up only 153 on the day. Graham was held to 43 yards passing as well, but the weather and the defense, and Lou Gro-za's toe, combined to grant Cleveland an 8–3 win and a shot at the NFL championship.

The AAFC's Los Angeles Dons, as part of the merger with the NFL, had sent many of their best players to the L.A. Rams, and together the new group had played brilliantly throughout the 1950 season. They and the Chicago Bears, like the Browns and the Giants, had finished the year with identical 10–2 records, and after a coin toss the two were sched-uled to play their sudden-death game in Los Angeles. Much like the frigid winds and icy field had possibly given the Browns an edge against New York, the Rams and Bears kicked off in 90-degree heat and bright sun, conditions foreign to the Chicagoans. The Rams' two losses, again paralleling the Browns' losses to the Giants, had both come at the hands of the Bears, but the third time proved a charm for the Rams and they won 24–14.

The Rams presented a new challenge to Paul Brown. Their offense, to that time, was considered the most effective in the NFL's three-decade history, and featured a veritable murderers' row of Bob Waterfield, Norm Van Brocklin, Tom Fears, Elroy "Crazy Legs" Hirsch, and former Heisman Trophy winner Glenn Davis. The game was set up in the press as a football version of the unstoppable force versus the immovable object, in this case the unstoppable offense versus the immovable defense. Regardless of where the game was to be played, it would match two of the greatest units in the game. Unfortunately for the Californians the 1949 NFL title game had been played in the Western Division champion's stadium, Los Angeles, so the 1950 version was played in Cleveland.

On Christmas Eve, 1950, the Rams took the opening kickoff and returned it to their 18-yard line. On the next play, the first from scrimmage, Bob Waterfield found speedy Glenn Davis cutting across the middle of the field, toward the left sideline, and connected on an 82-yard touchdown pass to put L.A. ahead 7–0. Later, Graham responded with a 27-yard touchdown pass of his own, to Dub Jones, to even the score, but the Rams went ahead again, 14–7, just before the end of the first quarter. Motley netted only nine yards of rushing for the game, as every time he carried the ball there were at least three Rams in on the tackle. Los Angeles' coach Joe Stydahar, later inducted into both the college and professional football halls of fame, understood that the crummy weather favored the ground game, but he was not going to allow the Browns' greatest rushing weapon to beat them.[23]

Regardless of how defenses stacked up against him, Motley was always ready to block, and Graham was never touched by the Rams' pass rushers on the fullback's side. In an episode of the television series *The Way It Was*, this one remembering the 1950 NFL championship game and hosted by Curt Gowdy, featured a panel that included Graham, Lavelli, Groza, Waterfield, Hirsch and Davis, along with announcer Bob Neal. Twenty-four years after the game, Graham was still making a point of praising Motley's blocking for giving him the space to find his receivers, and to take off running when the defense allowed.

Graham took advantage of that extra time and finished the game with 22 completions in 33 attempts, 298 yards passing, and four touchdown tosses. He also used the Rams' zealous commitment to containing Motley to his own advantage, rushing 12 times for 99 yards out of the quarterback slot, including a critical sprint in the final two minutes of the game. Dub Jones, Dante Lavelli and Rex Bumgardner all found the end zone, and despite a costly Motley fumble in the third quarter, one that soon turned into a Rams touchdown, Lou Groza kicked the deciding field goal with fewer than 30 seconds remaining in the game. He was outwardly calm, but back in the locker room afterward, he pulled off his kicking shoe and kissed it.

The crowd held their collective breath on L.A.'s final play as Van

Brocklin launched a 55-yard Hail Mary heave, but Warren Lahr ended the game with his second interception of the day, this one carried into the end zone, and then out of the end zone by the players' combined momentum to clinch the victory. There was a moment of panic on Cleveland's sideline as they waited for the officials to rule on the play. Had they ruled that Lahr's catch caused a formal change of possession, and then Davis moved him out of the end zone, the play could have been ruled a safety. In the ages before replay, though, and given the home crowd, the weather, and the fact that the original call was an interception, the officials did not reverse the decision.

Cleveland thus won the notional turnover battle, 6–3, and claimed their first NFL championship with the 30–28 win. "Storybook Finish Provided by Groza" screamed the headline on Christmas day.[24] The Browns had endured a season of disrespect by much of the league, and this win legitimatized not only their first year in the NFL, but their reputation earned over the last four years. AAFC or not, the Browns were the best team in football.

Along with the 1947 game against the Yankees, when Cleveland rallied back to close out a 28–28 tie, and the first game of 1950 against the Eagles, Motley called this first NFL championship one of the three great highlights of his career:

> Late in the game we got the ball on an interception, and Groza kicked a field goal with twenty-eight seconds left in the game. I was somewhat of a goat in that game because I fumbled, and they scored. The ground was frozen, and we came out in our cleats and Los Angeles was wearing gym shoes. We finally had to go to the gym shoes, but before we did, I was running up the sidelines with the ball. When I went to stop my feet skidded, and when I tried to catch my balance, they knocked the ball out of my hands.... We fought back and stayed in the game and won it on Groza's kick.[25]

That was a typical Motley assessment. Even on the biggest stage in his profession, and despite making a critical error that could have cost the Browns the game and the season, it was the team-first nature of the comeback, and ultimate victory, that made this game one of his great memories. As teammates listened, the Brown's captain repeated an oft-shared meme when he told a reporter, "Marion Motley never thought about Marion Motley—only the team."[26]

The gate that afternoon totaled 29,751, but those tough enough to endure the windy, 29-degree weather, and the omnipresent clouds, had been treated to a championship game for the ages. After the gun, some of those fanatical souls rushed the field and tore down the goal posts in the end zone where Lahr had performed his miracle, and there were rumors that some even set a celebratory fire in the center field stands. The Browns split a winner's pot of $41,186.98 ($1,113.16 per player), and the Rams $27,457.98 ($686.42 per player). While the money was welcomed, this was about legacy. It was their fifth title in five years, and this time they left no doubt about the identity of the best team in football. That laurel rested in Cleveland.

Nineteen fifty, clearly, was an epic rookie (NFL) season for the Cleveland franchise. Motley led the team, and the league, with 810 rushing yards, and yards per carry (5.8), while also catching passes for another 151. Back on defense for the year in the new league, not for the whole game but as a situational substitute, he also recovered three fumbles in the regular season and one more in the playoffs. For his efforts, he was named 1st Team All-Pro by the Associated Press, the UPI, and the *New York Daily News,* and selected for the Pro Bowl for the first and only time of his career.

As for Marion Motley, he had proven himself the best fullback, the best blocker, and one of the stellar defenders and special teams players in all of football. That 1950 season, defeating the rest of the league and enjoying victory in a championship game still considered one of the greatest games in NFL history, was another pinnacle in his professional life. As 1951, and the following seasons, would show, though, he was quite mortal. The backside of his career was already looming on the horizon.

9

Decline and Fall
of a Legend (1951–1955)

On January 14, 1951, the NFL played the first-ever Pro Bowl, an all-star game between the American and National conferences, the respective teams led by conference champion coaches Paul Brown and Joe Stydahar. There had been all-star games earlier in the league's history, beginning in 1939 at a baseball park, Wrigley Field, in Los Angeles. That first game matched the 1938 champion New York Giants against the best of the rest, and while the nature of football of that era skewed toward running, Washington's Sammy Baugh and New York's Ed Danowski both threw touchdown passes as part of the day's airshow. Interestingly, the Rams' coach, and National Conference coach in the 1950 game, Joe Stydahar, had also played tackle and kicked for the All Stars in the 1939 version.

The NFL All-Star game, as it was called, was again played in 1940 (in Los Angeles), and the 1941 and 1942 iterations in Philadelphia, but the concept was cancelled after that due to wartime travel limits. In re-establishing a new version of the contest, the 1950 game was deviating from the old template of champions-versus-stars by making the game all about the individual players. Renamed the Pro Bowl, the game was sponsored by the Los Angeles Publishers Association, and for 20 years, until 1971, it would be held in Los Angeles.

Both the Browns and the Rams had constructed their respective offensive schemes around the T formation, and both 1950 squads featured starters who were well versed in the approach. Cleveland's Graham and L.A.'s Waterfield and Van Brocklin made the team, along with fullbacks Tony Adamle, Marion Motley, and Dick Hoerner as the underappreciated cogs that allowed the quarterbacks exploit the formation's full potential. This familiarity flattened the learning curve in the brief game preparation interval, and made a close, competitive and enter- taining show almost inevitable. On game day, though, it was Otto Gra- ham who claimed top billing in the American conference's come from behind 28–27 win in the L.A. Coliseum.

Since the defense on both sides showed up ready to hit, neither team gained more than 24 rushing yards. Graham and Bob Waterfield did not miss a beat in the air attack, executing their familiar offenses to a T. With the American conference down 27–14 in the second half, Gra- ham passed, ran and sneaked his way to two unanswered touchdowns, and earned MVP honors in the game. Still, Motley played, and blocked well for his quarterback. It was the only Pro Bowl in which he would play, and it was a win for his team, for his coach, and quarterback.

Sometime in February, Marion and Eula escaped tragedy when their car was hit—this time not Motley's fault—by a truck from Meeks Motor Freight Company of Louisville, Kentucky. Motley sued for $50,000 and claimed that his football career "has been affected seri- ously by injuries." Eula sued for a separate $50,000 in damages, claim- ing that her injuries led, in part, to her developing tuberculosis. She was later compelled to enter a sanitarium as a reaction to her tuberculosis symptoms following the collision. The other two passengers in Motley's car, Edward and Ollie Mae Coleman of Canton, sued for an additional $75,000 for their injuries.[1]

During the abbreviated offseason, after recovering from their inju- ries as much as possible, Marion and Eula also prepared to invest in their future by buying a bar, bowling, and restaurant facility in the Kinsman neighborhood in east Cleveland.

The business foray would not succeed. In a 1968 piece on Motley, Tom Melody wrote that "his investment in a Cleveland tavern brought him nothing but debts." "Marion was too good natured; he let too many of his friends work there," a close associate confided.[2] The bar failed after a few years, but it was a testament to Motley's realization that fame is fleeting. Better to take a shot while he was still a relevant and pub- lic personality than to wait until after his playing days ended. As events soon proved, that sentiment bordered on prescient. Motley's days of football stardom were ending. Motley said years later,

> You know, during half of my eight years with the Browns—in fact, the whole four years I played with them in the National Football League—I had bad trouble with my knees. Geez did I have trouble with them. And the way Paul handled the situation, he really shortened my career. In 1951 we were

in training camp, getting ready to play the College All-Stars, and Paul was giving us fundamental drills in blocking and tackling. In one of those drills a player's knee hit my knee, and as soon as he hit me, well, I was hurt. By the time practice was over, my knee was like a balloon. The trainer told Paul to give me a couple of days off, but Paul said, "No. No, he can come out and run a little bit. If he can't run, he can hop around." So that's what I did. I ran on one leg. The ground at that particular time was like cement, and running on that one good leg, I wound up with both knees full of water.[3]

Motley explained the accident in a bit more detail: "It was a real fluke accident. We were practicing a reverse body block, where you step in and put your knee between the guy's legs and then let your leg whip. Tony Adamle and I were working together, and his knee hit my knee, that was the beginning of my problems."[4]

The scenario degraded from there for Motley.

Our team doctor was on vacation, so they sent me to see a doctor in Cleveland who's [now] one of the top surgeons in the country. A Dr. Lambright. He took two pans of water off my knees and then called the training camp and told our trainer I shouldn't run for three or four days. So I went back to camp thinking I'm going to get a rest, but after I'd stayed off the field for one day, Paul Brown told me, "You get your suit on and be out here." I put on my equipment and stood around for a while, and then Paul said, "All right, Motley, get in here. I want you to run some." I tried to, but my knees locked up on me and swelled up big as a balloon. I had to have water taken off again. I went to Chicago and played in the All Star game, and after the game I couldn't walk out of Soldier's Field. I had to lean against a wall while they brought my car to me. I couldn't move. I always had knee trouble after that, and football became a job.[5]

While the incident might make Paul Brown appear callous, even unfeeling, the perspective he displayed sprang from the same single-minded drive to win that propelled Cleveland's integration in 1946. Brown had a job, to win the next game. His assets were his players. Everything else was distraction. Salaries, racial quotas and unwritten rules, the press, each were generally ignored in the build-up to the next kickoff. In Motley's case, it is quite likely that Brown saw the fullback as an aging weapon. A powerful weapon, to be sure, but one that was closer to exhausting his playing value than he was to revealing his potential. After age 30, even in today's modern game with exponentially better medical technology, running backs are unreliable from one season to the next. If Motley could at least block and play the occasional short-yardage defensive down, he was still useful to the team's greater

Motley sheds a would-be tackler in a 1951 game against the Chicago Bears (*Cleveland Press Collection*, Michael Schwartz Library at Cleveland State University).

The Chicago Bears tackle Motley in a 1951 game. Note the six Chicago players closing in on the Cleveland star. Solo, unassisted tackles of Motley, especially in the open field, were rare (*Cleveland Press Collection*, Michael Schwartz Library at Cleveland State University).

efforts. Better to wring every last ounce of football out of Motley, before he aged out of utility, than to let a bad knee sap his remaining value by wasting his few seasons remaining.

The season began well, with the Browns whipping the College All Stars 33–0, and the sole preseason smirch came in a 21–20 loss to the Lions in Detroit. In their first regular season game, though, the defending NFL champions lost to old rival San Francisco 24–10 to start the season with an 0–1 record. With Motley's knee issues, Brown gave Harry Jagade and Emerson Cole opportunities to compete for the starting fullback job.

While the collective memory of that early season has faded with time, it appears that Motley's professional career had reached a crossroads, at least in Paul Brown's eyes. "Big Marion Motley's future as a Cleveland Brown was hanging in the balance," reported the *Akron Beacon Journal* a week before the game against the 49ers. After a poor showing throughout the preseason, Brown mulled cutting the star from the roster. "It's a tough decision to make. Motley has had eight weeks to get into shape," mused the coach, "but he hasn't come around. We certainly need whatever help he can give us, but he will have to do much better" than he had done in the final preseason tune-up against the Rams.[6] Brown later added, "If he can't cut it in these two games [San Francisco and Los Angeles, in California, over consecutive weeks], we'll have to drop him. We can't let sentiment enter into it."[7]

The mood was not quite grim after the opening loss in San Francisco, but the locker room atmosphere was far from relaxed. Not only did the team fail, but Motley carried the ball just twice for 12 yards, and caught a single pass on the afternoon. The following week in Los Angeles, against the Rams, though, Motley allowed a glimpse of his inner, though aging, warrior, and racked up 106 yards on 13 rushes, including a long run of 19 yards. Cleveland won the championship rematch 38–23, and proceeded to run off ten more wins to finish the regular season with an 11–1 record. That was enough to earn the Browns a slot in the NFL championship game, again against the L.A. Rams, although this time the game would take place in California.

After Cleveland's five consecutive titles, including their win over L.A. in the 1950 championship game, it was understandable that the Browns were a favorite among the gambling crowd. Since the Rams had already lost to Cleveland, earlier in the year, and posted a pedestrian 8–4 record on the season to reach the final, Cleveland's path to #6 appeared open and flat. Of course, this was professional football, where nothing is guaranteed.

The *Plain Dealer* captured the result, and the general feeling, that evening:

LOS ANGELES, Dec. 23—However fantastic it may seem, Cleveland tonight is without a pro football championship for the first time in seven years. The city's six-year reign in professional football, started by Bob Waterfield and the old Rams back in 1945 and prolonged by the Browns through five glamorous seasons, ended today as Waterfield and the new Rams squeezed through to a 24–17 victory before 59,475 in the Coliseum.[8]

While not the all-time classic that was the 1950 championship, the 1951 iteration was still exciting, and not decided until late in the fourth quarter. The DuMont Network had paid $75,000 for the television broadcast rights to the game, so the 1951 NFL championship became the first coast-to-coast televised championship in professional football history, and the broadcasters got their money's worth. There was no assurance that, 70 years later, the NFL championship would become the biggest television in not only sports, but in American broadcasting, and that the DuMont instincts would prove startingly prescient over time.

In this game, though, and after a scoreless first quarter, Dick Hoerner put L.A. up 7–0 with a blast over the goal line in the second period. Cleveland pulled ahead on a 52-yard Groza field goal and a 17-yard Graham-to-Dub Jones touchdown pass. In the third, one of the figurative heirs to Motley's position, Dan "Deacon" Towler, rushed for a touchdown of his own to put the Rams back in front. Graham had fumbled in their own territory, and Andy Robustelli recovered and would have scored had Motley not hauled him in from behind and tackled him on the one-yard line. It still took Towler three attempts, but he pushed across the line on the last one.

Towler was a big, strong athletic player and a gifted runner, somewhat in the Motley mold, from Washington and Jefferson college in Pennsylvania, and his contributions all season were a big part of the reason that the Rams were in the final game. Towler was also Black. Had there been no Motley, no Willis, no Washington, and no Strode, gifted, Black football players like Towler might not have had their moment in the spotlight, their chance at football fame. Towler was unique in that he truly did not care about football nearly as much as he did about his faith in God, and he left football after a few years to serve as an ordained Methodist minister in California for the next 40 years. But in 1951, he was part of a Rams offense that has remained one of the greatest in football history.

Late in the third, with L.A. on Cleveland's one-yard line, Paul Brown put Motley in at linebacker. The Browns stopped a Hoerner charge, and then Motley led a penetrating rush and dropped Towler for one- and two-yard losses. After a penalty on Los Angeles, the quarter ended with the Rams backed up to the Cleveland 17-yard line.

Although the defense held on that occasion, the Rams outscored the Browns 10–7 in the final frame to recapture the title they'd last won in 1949. It was also, likely, a moment of small vindication for the non–AAFC team owners. "Their" boys had finally given Paul Brown and his upstarts their comeuppance, had shut down Motley, and had even exposed the football mortality of Otto Graham. Motley and his teammates made $1,483 each as their share of the pot, and even that was a bit of a victory in that it was the highest "loser's" pot ever.[9]

Despite the lingering knee problems, and now serving as backup fullback, Motley still managed to run for 273 yards on 61 carries and caught ten passes for 52 yards as well. Those marks were good enough for third place in the team rushing category, behind Dub Jones and Ken Carpenter, and sixth in receiving. He remained a devastating blocker, Otto Graham's bodyguard, as some referred to him, and found himself in kickoff returns and on defense when the situation dictated. It was no Pro Bowl year, but it was a very good season, nonetheless. The Browns did not win their sixth championship, but they came within a touchdown in the final game before yielding. It was, in short, the first indication that the great team, the great players, might have peaked. As an aside, Dan Towler did get the opportunity to play in the Pro Bowl, so well in fact that he was named Player of the Game. One of the Motley early successors, his heir apparent, had not simply arrived, but had underscored the sense of just how much talent had been squandered during the NFL's lost, segregated years.

Marion Motley's 1952 season was notable for several reasons. Most visible among those, he was forced to change jersey numbers, from 76 to 36. In the modern NFL, the league has a set of policy guidelines for jersey numbers. Receivers, for example, are generally in the 80s, while linemen are in the 60s and 70s, and running backs below 40. In the AAFC, quarterbacks were numbered in the 60s, fullbacks in the 70s, halfbacks in the 80s, and linemen in the 20s, 30s, and 40s. In 1952, given the reality of national television and the need to keep things simple for the casual viewers, the NFL "strongly" encouraged each team adopt the more standardized numbering scheme.[10] Thus, quarterback Otto Graham adopted number 14, Motley switched from 76 to 36, and Lou Groza took over 76 (as a tackle, and this jersey number was eventually retired by the Browns). There are a number of images of Motley in his Browns uniform, in museums and the internet. In those in which he's wearing 76, they are from pre–1952 games, and 36, the years 1952–1953.

Wearing the number 36 did not seem to be a problem for Motley, and his 1952 campaign frequently inspired comparison to those of his younger years. Although he was now 32 years old, he was now healthier, and not only regained his starting fullback job, but led the team in rushing with 444 yards (on 104 carries). He caught 13 passes for 213 yards— fifth on the squad—for a 16.4 average, and in his three regular-season kickoff returns netted 88 yards.

Though the team had managed a relatively poor 8–4 regular season record in 1952, poor in contrast to the glittery standard the franchise had established since it began play in 1946, they still found themselves hosting the championship game again, this time against Bobby Layne, Doak Walker and the Detroit Lions. The game, played on a frozen Cleveland field, was a tightly contested affair, the final score notwithstanding. Motley played well in all phases, despite the pre-game reporting that his performance had slipped.[11] He ran the ball six times but gained 74 yards, 42 of those on a single carry in the third quarter. "Big Marion Motley sparked this drive by carrying a pitchout 42 yards to the Lions' 5," wrote the papers.[12] He also caught three passes for another 21 and returned two kickoffs for 49 more. On the day, his 144 yards of production led the entire team, save Graham. But it was not enough, and Cleveland fell to Detroit, 17–7.

Over the winter, the NFL changed the respective conference names from American and National to Eastern and Western, and in June 1953, Browns founder Mickey McBride sold the team to Cleveland Indians executives David R. Jones and Ellis Ryan, along with a small group of subordinate investors. The new ownership interfered with Paul Brown's approach not one whit, and the 1953 season seemed to promise the team and the town the opportunity to regain some of the luster lost in two straight title game losses.

On a social front, the crack in football's segregated wall that had opened in 1946 with Motley, Willis, Washington, and Strode, was now—at least—an open window. The Pittsburgh Courier's Bill Nunn wrote a story that highlighted some of the 49 Black players seeking one of the 400 or so positions in the league. George Preston Marshall's Washington squad, as well as the Detroit Lions, were the exceptions in bringing in Black players, despite the relatively high population of Black families in both cities. Cleveland had ten non–White players in camp, Chicago eight, and every other team at least three.[13] It was progress. Glacial in pace, but it was progress, nonetheless. In October 1953, the Bears' Willie Thrower would, in fact, become the first Black NFL quarterback in the "modern" game.

On the field, Cleveland returned to their dominating form and posted and 11–1 mark in the regular season. Motley was now sharing fullback duties with "Chick" Jagade, the new team rushing leader, and he ran the ball just 32 times all year. Marion Motley failed to score a single touchdown in 1953, the first season of his career in which he failed to score.

The championship game, the Browns' annual rite of winter, was a rematch against the Buddy Parker's Lions in Detroit, but the home team won their second straight title with a 17–16 heartbreaker (for Cleveland) of a win. The day had been Cleveland's until the last two minutes, when Bobby Layne found an open Jim Doran, who had somehow gotten past 1950s hero Warren Lahr, on a 33-yard pass for Doran's only touchdown on the season. Motley was limited to special teams, and did not touch the ball on offense. He had, in the parlance of the print media, acquired football knees over the last few years, and was clearly did not invoke fear in opponents, at least as much as he had in his younger days.

Although an aging athlete, Motley and the Browns returned to the basketball court over the winter. With 6'8" Doug Atkins on the team, and the tandem of Motley and Gillom at forward, they once again sold out a number of smaller gyms and auditoriums on their good will "hoops" tour of the region.[14] On the family front, the Motleys had expanded their investment portfolio to include a small, four-unit apartment building in Cleveland. Evidently it was more of a fixer-upper opportunity than a gilded guarantee. In February, the Cleveland Sanitation Department sent the police to bring Motley before a judge regarding whether the building had been brought up to regulatory standards. The police statement noted that "the Cleveland Browns player had been ordered to 'clean it up, provide adequate garbage and rubbish cans and fix a faulty gas stove.'"[15] Almost everyone on record, those who actually knew Motley, would be loath to accuse him of being a slumlord, but he was an aggressive investor, even if he did enjoy a mixed bag in terms of results.

In March, Motley signed his ninth contract with the Browns.[16] He was one of five original Cleveland Browns, and the changes to the core roster of champions was obvious. Star runner Dub Jones retired to his lumber business in Louisiana, although he later returned for both the 1954 and 1955 campaigns. Fellow Stark County high school star and Browns teammate Lin Houston retired, as did longtime roommate Bill Willis, George Young, and defensive tackle Derrell Palmer. Groza, Graham, and Lavelli remained, along with center Frank Katski, from the original cadre, but beyond that Paul Brown found himself working with an entirely different cast of characters.[17]

The more significant departure, though, was the early retirement of Harry Jagade. The fullback who had displaced Motley as starter in 1951 and 1953, opted to move forward with his business career in Chicago.[18] The unexpected, and somewhat abrupt, move left Paul Brown scrambling. He had resigned Motley, but at 34 with a pair of gimpy knees, there was no assurance that the former All-Pro could even make it through training camp. As one writer noted, "Still on hand at fullback with the Browns in big Marion Motley, but he hasn't the intense speed he once boasted when he made the trap play a thing of beauty.... Motley may see some service at fullback, but the chances are he'll do most of his playing on defense."[19] Like Jones, Jagade later rescinded his retirement, but played the 1954 and 1955 seasons closer to home, for the Chicago Bears.

On August 7, in a full-contact intra-squad scrimmage, Motley's knee smashed into a defensive scrum, and he did not rise. Unable to play in the preseason games, he entered September on the sideline.[20] Paul Brown, ever the efficient manager, intimated to reporters that he was close to cutting Motley. The team had added Maurice Bassett in the backfield, and prepared Curley Morrison to fill the Motley/Jagade void at fullback.[21]

Given the slow pace of his rehabilitation and knowing that—sentiment be damned—Paul Brown would release him if the coach felt he was not among the best 33 players for the roster, Motley tackled the issue head on. On September 20, a week before the season opener at Green Bay, the *Akron Beacon Journal* reported that "Marion Motley, fullback for the Browns since the teams was formed in 1946, today announced his retirement from professional football."[22] "The old knees just won't take the gaff anymore," Motley told the writers. "The rest of me's young enough, but the knees feel like a hundred."[23]

Motley was left to join the throngs seeking entrance into the Browns' locker room, his former haven, on December 26, right after the Browns had pummeled the Lions, 56–10, and regained their place at the top of the football ziggurat. Instead of leaning on Motley, Brown had spread the ball to nine rushers and receivers, and Grahams' three touchdown tosses (and three rushing scores) put Cleveland back on top.

By this time, the retired Motley was, essentially, managing his tavern full-time, yet even that segment of his life was not immune to challenges. One evening in early December, one Samuel Williford was in the establishment, evidently playing a mechanical bowling game. For some reason, still unknown, Williford determined that the machine had not paid out the $1 he believed it owed him, and he challenged Motley to pay him his perceived winnings. Motley said no, and then asked Williford to leave. Williford left, but soon reentered and again demanded his spoils. Marion's sister Dorothy, who was working there at the time, called the police, and Williford waited outside. When the two officers arrived, Motley pointed out Williford and as they started to arrest Williford, he drew his revolver and shot officer Henry DeZort in the leg and arm and then turned to run away. The other officer, Sergeant William Kahoe, promptly drew his pistol, dropped to a knee, and shot the fleeing Williford in the head and back, killing him.[24] It was, undoubtedly, incidents like this that contributed to the tavern's demise soon after.

Even though he was off the football team, Motley still joined the basketball Browns in their now-annual winter tour.[25] His knees seemed to have responded well to the respite, and as it turned out, football was perhaps safer than managing a bar. "I still haven't made up my mind definitely on whether I'll make the attempt," Motley told writers. "I think that maybe I could help out the Browns as a linebacker." If he could carry through on that little medical miracle, it could help Paul Brown fill a gap on defense for the upcoming season. Throughout his all-star rushing career, he was still a go-to linebacker inside the five-yard line, in a goal line situation. Both players drafted as linebackers, Kurt Burris and Ken Locklear, opted to play in Canada, and Tony Adamle, who had come out of retirement at Brown's behest to play the role, had broken his leg and had decided to leave the game for good.[26]

The money would not hurt. His three sons with Eula were now

teenagers. Philip in particular was showing signs of genuine football aptitude, and Motley's outside endeavors were struggling. Not only was the tavern now under continuous financial pressure, but Motley's real estate holding were failing. In March, "in a 'get-tough' move against substandard tenements, the city [of Cleveland] law department ... filed warrants against 24 landlords. One of those accused was Marion Motley."[27] It was tough enough having a patron shot in your restaurant's parking lot, but that was only exacerbated by a press report calling the apartment building he owned a "tenement." Slum lord was not a moniker in keeping with either his football reputation, or with his actual character as a human being. The walls probably felt like they were closing in on both Marion and Eula.

Of course, those who truly knew Marion Motley also believed he had never intended to become a real estate predator. In one of many examples, in June 1954, Motley entered one of his favorite local clothing stores, and found the manager, and his friend, Charles Avner, "trying to stall a customer he thought was giving him a forged check." Avner was hoping for some sort of intervention, and Motley's arrival was just that. The newspapers noted that the "proprietor introduced his customer to Motley who engaged him in conversation while the proprietor could investigate the validity of the check." The police arrived, arrested the man, and Motley was again a hero.[28]

Motley's football legacy continued to build in 1954 despite the man never taking the field. Cookie Gilchrist is a name and associated reputation that has faded over the decades, now known mostly to football historians, and perhaps a few Buffalo residents. In the early 1960s, however, he ran the football with the same physical intimidation that Motley had displayed throughout his career. Gilchrist was an all-league player between 1962 and 1965, and was named the American Football League (AFL) MVP in 1962. He helped lead Buffalo to the AFL title in 1964, was part of the player's leadership cadre in the AFL All-Star game boycott of New Orleans in 1965, and in 2005 was selected to the All-Time AFL team.[29]

Gilchrist's story, though, began in 1954, when Paul Brown signed him directly out of Har-Brack High School in Pennsylvania. The signing was likely illegal, since Gilchrist had not yet graduated, and when Brown failed to commit a starting slot to his new running back, Gilchrist left the team and spent the next eight years in the Canadian Football League. In his autobiography, Gilchrist wrote warmly about his experience at the Browns' training camp, and especially with his first mentor, Marion Motley. "When I arrived in camp I was clearly there to be Marion's replacement, but, putting team first, he took me under his wing. Meeting Marion would be one of the few times in my life that I would be starstruck. He had been one of my football heroes, and I tried to emulate his playing style on the field and his professional demeanor off the field."[30]

Cookie Gilchrist became a tremendous football player, one raised in the informal Motley school of physical play. It was Motley, Gilchrist said, who drove the young back to become a better pass blocker, and the relationship lasted a lifetime. "After I retired," Gilchrist said, "Marion and I ran into each other on the banquet circuit, and I still felt like I was talking to my older brother."[31]

The next summer, after his year-long sabbatical, Marion Motley decided to come back to the game he loved. "Marion Motley, who holds most of the Cleveland Browns' ball-carrying records, is coming out of retirement as a backer for the defensive line."[32] Paul Brown looked at the opportunity as a low-risk investment for the team, and a win-win scenario should Motley succeed. "If he's still the linebacker he once was, Marion certainly would be a big help to us. He has maintained his weight and appears to be in good condition and he'll be given every chance to make it."[33] The mood brightened further once Motley got to camp. "Marion is in such good shape that we decided to use him at full-back, too," said Paul Brown in late July.[34]

All those good feelings evaporated once the preseason started. Motley took a few hits to his knees in training camp, and by mid–August some were speculating that his spot on the team was tenuous at best.[35] The Pittsburgh Steelers, the Browns' closest geographic rival, were in the market for Black players of their own, having seen the attendance boosts afforded teams by stars like Marion Motley and Dan Towler, and while they invited "nine negro candidates" to camp, were on the lookout for any name-brand players as well. Marion Motley filled that bill.

On September 7, the Browns traded Motley to the Steelers in exchange for fullback Ed Modzelewski. Paul Brown addressed the writers: "Marion is in good shape and I suppose that Pittsburgh wanted someone of his size. Apparently Modzelewski hasn't been impressive, but we want a look at him."[36] Years later, in his autobiography, Paul Brown tried to articulate his actual feelings at the time:

The toughest moment of that year was to have to let Motley go in a trade to Pittsburgh that brought Modzelewski to the Browns. Marion's injured knee had kept him from playing in 1954, and I had thought he would retire from football, but come training camp, there he was, wanting to play. I knew his days as a fullback were numbered, so we used him as a linebacker during our preseason games, but his legs still caused him problems. Since Marion needed an extra year's salary to help him bridge a new career, we traded him to the Steelers. I didn't handle the situation well, though, because I didn't have the courage to tell Marion firsthand that we had traded him, and before I could think of a better solution, he found out from another source, deeply hurting him.[37]

Motley was a bit less emotional in his memory. "During training camp in 1954, I was running downfield on a kick and felt something tear in my knee. I stayed out that year and knew Cleveland wouldn't want me back. They had all those young backs like Curley Morrison and Dub Jones and Chet 'the Jet' Hanulak, so they traded me to Pittsburgh in 1955. I hurt my knee again. Since I was thirty-five years old, I quit."[38]

Later, Motley added a few details about the way he learned of the trade. Brown wrote Motley a letter, rather than confront him face to face. "The way it was done," Motley remembered, "it left a bad taste in my mouth. Paul Brown was the greatest coach I ever saw and I liked him. He taught me a lot about life, but I felt he could have handled my trade to Pittsburgh a little different." Even in a darker memory, though, Motley could almost always find a silver lining. "I liked Pittsburgh. Mr. Rooney and I struck up a friendship that has lasted [until death]. He always [sent Motley] a box of cigars, and I never go to Pittsburgh that I don't call him."[39]

It was an interesting deal, one with finer details that will likely remain hidden forever. The Washington Redskins head coach, Joe Kuharich, was stunned at the trade. Steeler coach Walt Kiesling later told reporters that he had contacted every team in the league about Modzelewski's availability but had no takers. "When I read that he'd [Modzelewski] been traded to Cleveland, I couldn't believe it," said Kuharich later. "We wanted Modzelewski," said Washington owner George Preston Marshall. "The Steelers promised us that they'd talk to us before they did anything about him. But they traded him to Cleveland without even discussing him with us."[40]

With Pittsburgh, Motley tried to regain his position in the offensive backfield, getting several opportunities in the remaining preseason games. The exhibitions only exacerbated the pain in Motley's game knees, and along with coach Walt Kiesling's aggressive practice approach ("Man, that coach ... worked that team to the bone. They left all their football on the practice field"[41]) and he carried the ball twice in the regular season. The first time, against the Chicago Cardinals, netted an eight-yard gain and a glimpse of past greatness. The second, a no-gainer one week later against the L.A. Rams, on October 2, was his final carry in professional football.

By late October, the papers were reporting that Motley had lost his back-up linebacker slot to Vic Eaton. Unable to play most games due to the chronic effects of his injuries, the Steelers finally gave up on their experiment. "Marion Motley, one of the original Cleveland Browns, was a man without a team today following his release by the Pittsburgh Steelers.... He appeared briefly in five of the Steelers' six league games, mostly as a blocker on punts and field goal attempts."[42] There was a humorous aspect to the transaction, as well. Ed Modzelewski, the fullback for whom Motley had been traded, was thriving in Cleveland. When a Cleveland writer, Herman Goldstein, wrote: "Told that with Motley placed on waivers and finally released, the trade could be cancelled and he'd have to return to the Steelers, he [Modzelewski] scowled, 'I'll quit first.'"[43]

Cleveland enjoyed the productivity from Modzelewski, but at least one player missed Motley's presence. Otto Graham, in what would be his final season as a player, complained publicly about what he viewed as dirty play by various pass rushers. Dick "Night Train" Lane had his own thoughts. "I can understand Graham squawking because they've really been giving it to him this season. They've been storming through the Cleveland line and laying him flat. In other years they didn't do that because you just couldn't get to him." Again, these are the words of one of the best defensive players in football history, and one who had chased Graham since the Browns entered the NFL. "Fact of the matter is that Otto doesn't get the protection he once did. When he had Bill Willis and Marion Motley in front of him, knocking off would-be tacklers, it was just a breeze. All he had to do was take his time, find a receiver, and fire the ball. You couldn't get through those guys [the Cleveland pass protection] with a howitzer. Sometimes, if the other team sent five or six men after Graham, Lenny Ford would drop back to help Willis and Motley. They formed a stone wall for Otto ... that's enough beef to flatten a charging bull." He added, "Graham's just getting a taste of it for the first time. Motley and Willis aren't around to protect him and he misses them."[44]

9. Decline and Fall of a Legend (1951–1955)

Thus it ended. The spectacular playing career of Marion Motley was over with a few flicks of a pen. The Steelers finished with a 4–8 record, good for last place in the NFL Eastern division. The Cleveland Browns, sans Motley, managed to win the NFL title again in 1955. They beat the Rams, 38–14, and the game marked the tenth consecutive appearance in a league championship, the final game of each year, every year since the team had been born in 1946. Otto Graham retired after the game, winning his third NFL Most Valuable Player award and the Hickok Belt, a prize given to the best professional athlete in the United States, along the way.

Motley's quantifiable football contributions were stark. His Pro Football Hall of Fame file summarizes it thusly:

> Deadly pass blocker, peerless runner on Browns' famed trap play.... Also played linebacker early in career.... All-time AAFC rushing champ.... Top NFL rusher, 1950 ... All-AAFC three years, all-NFL in 1950...Lifetime rushing: 828 carries, 4720 yards ... 5.7-yard career average all-time record.... Caught 85 passes, scored 234 points in nine years.... Played in 1951 Pro Bowl.

That distillation is as laconic as it is complete, as the power of his achievement still emanates from every phrase. It was, arguably, the most remarkable career enjoyed by any football player, ever.

⫴ 10 ⫴

Life After Football
(1956–1998)

Life after football proved challenging to the former star. Too old and gimpy to play effectively, Motley sought to peddle his knowledge into a second life on the sideline. His former allies, like the head coach he had—in part—made famous, were not as helpful as they might have been.

> When I finished playing, I asked Paul [Brown] for a job coaching, but he said I didn't have enough experience. That's the kind of bullshit you got. For years after I quit, the Browns used my moves to teach my pass protection block, the trap, and the draw play. We basically had four plays that I did and that was all—an end run, a buck up the middle, a trap play, and a screen pass. I'd only carry the ball eight or nine times a game, and I always thought I could have carried it a lot more, but Paul Brown was the coach and he was also a winner. He didn't need any advice from me. I was the first back ever to run the draw play, and the Browns told me I didn't have enough experience to coach. Paul also made some statements which I will never reveal, but they left me with a bad taste in my mouth for a while. I was very bitter for many years, and then I thought to myself, "There's no use going around carrying a chip on your shoulder, Marion."[1]

This new version of life in retirement, an existence not executed within the seasonal rhythms of the sport or curated by coaches and the demands of conflict, was not very easy for Marion Motley. His Cleveland tavern had failed, he had not finished college, and his football celebrity had arrived in an earlier era, a time when football greatness did not necessarily confer a lifetime of fame, fortune, free drinks, guest spots on major sports networks, or book deals. His pedestal of prominence had been knocked over, felled by his failing knees and the inexorable drain of time, and now he was preparing to resume life in the real, non-football world as a 35-year-old Black man. That latter trait presented an additional challenge. In 1955, almost a decade before the Civil Rights Act was enacted, Jim Crow was not only alive and well, but thriving, throughout much of the country. To be a Black man in certain parts of the country and in certain social circumstances, was a challenge not easily described to those who did not walk in those figurative shoes. While well past the age of legitimized lynching, and almost nine decades after the eradication of slavery, much of the nation remained stove piped by race.

There are bookshelves filled with volumes of sociological and economic history centering on race in the United States in the 1950s, but it is in some of the specific examples of abuses that the worst-case behavior toward Black Americans evinced itself. At the time, the nation suffered from a severe case of the "presence of the past." Gone were the lynchings, the legal school segregation, the whole legally-justified doctrine of separate but equal, but remaining were the echoes of centuries of the established norms of social interaction. Some of those echoes were more tangible than others. It was never that all non–Black people were racist, but that those that did believe in the tenets of segregation were occasionally capable of terrifying behavior. One of those examples, in 1950, had played out in Martinsville, Virginia, a small town near the Virginia–North Carolina border. In a case that garnered national attention, and revulsion, the "Martinsville Seven" became one of the more notable examples of the worst outcomes inherent to racism.

In that case, seven Black men, six aged between 18–20 at the time of the incident, were convicted of raping a White woman in town two years earlier. After six hasty trials, every one before juries of all-White males, none deliberating more than two hours before reaching their respective, guilty verdict, the seven accused were sentenced to death. No White person had ever been sentenced to death after being convicted of rape, and despite the NAACP's appeal for a stay of execution, the final sentence was carried out on February 5, 1951. "Never before had a state executed so many men, nor had a lynching of that magnitude for men accused of rape ever been reported."[2] That the incident generated widespread outrage was a sign of progress, especially in contrast with the climate 30 years earlier, but it was just another example of the challenge of being a Black man in certain parts of the country.

This was a time that is difficult to imagine today, just a figurative moment just after the 1954 decision in *Brown vs. the Topeka Board of Education*, which set aside the guidance of the 1896 *Plessy vs. Ferguson* decision that had instantiated the notion of separate but equal. It was getting easier, and safer, to be Black in America in the mid–1950s, but the scales were still tipped against Marion Motley's prospects outside football. He did not even merit a pension from the NFL until 1988, when the league approved a monthly payout, specifically for pre–1959 players, of $60 per month for every month played. That would work out to about $6,480 per year for the Hall of Famer.[3] In the late 1950s, though, Motley needed to work. But job hunting was not easy, regardless of location. Throughout the Midwest, while not as stratified as the Deep South, there were still large swaths of exclusion. As former MLB star pitcher Jim "Mudcat" Grant wrote about his time with the 1955 Keokuk (Iowa) Kernels: "From the time the Keokuk team photographer said, 'You black boys do strange things to the lighting [for photographs],'[4] I was ready to explode." He later summarized his feelings, saying, "In Keokuk they didn't want you in some places if you were black."[5] It was not just in Iowa that those walls remained solid.

Thirty years earlier, the best Motley might have hoped for would have been to find work as a janitor or theater attendant or, perhaps, as a Red Cap on a railroad. In a relative sense, though it was fortunate that he was reentering the working world at the time he did. It was not, and never has been, a perfect world, but the opportunities for employment had expanded considerably in contrast to the time when Shakvol Motley had moved his family to Ohio to escape the fields. "When I left football," Motley later recalled, "I went to the post office for a couple of years, and then I sold whiskey and worked for a construction company as their safety director."

In 1958 he found himself coaching what he called a "sandlot" team, a squad of fewer than 20 players, incomplete uniforms and equipment, yet sharing Motley's unquenchable love of the game. Tom Fitzpatrick of the *Lima* (Ohio) *News* caught up with Motley for a quick story, Motley's remorse bubbled up to the surface. "As far as I can remember the toughest day of my life was when the doctors said I had to quit [football]. I'd had this bad knee for awhile but thought I could get by on it. Then one day I slipped in the mud.... I knew in my heart then that it was all over.... I sat waiting in the doctor's office, knowing what he was gonna say and yet hoping that he'd tell me I was gonna play again." That, Motley reiterated, was his toughest moment in sports.[6]

He worked as a parking lot attendant and then for the Stark County tax department initially, followed by a brief stint as a dump truck driver for an excavation firm, and then spent two years delivering packages with the post office. In 1960 he took the job with the James Barclay and Co. Distillery, and he stayed with them until 1966. It "wasn't too tough for me [to take the lower-skilled jobs] because I ... it was somewhat of a letdown, but it wasn't as tough as it seems because I had my home, I owned my home. Then I had another piece of property. Because I had lived this way before, I adjusted myself and went back. One of my philosophies was 'I'm not gonna lose what I have. I'm gonna keep this ... do whatever I have to do to keep it.' I'd work anywhere as long as I could make it. Takin' it in stride."

He had taken those jobs with the intention of improving his lot in life with each new opportunity. "After Barclay, I resigned out of the whiskey business, then I did some remodeling. Home remodeling. I stayed in that for a while and it didn't pay off."[7] He and Eula divorced in 1962, after the boys were out of the house, and he always needed money for the divorce settlement, for providing a residence for his ex-wife. The jobs provided a reasonable standard of living, especially since he already owned his home, but the idea of coaching or scouting football was never far from his mind.

The divorce between Eula and Marion was not an easy one. The two had separated in 1959, after she discovered Marion's secret. In her testimony to the divorce court, "Mrs. Motley said her husband told her he 'had another woman.' She said that he was a dictator-type of person." In all, she was awarded their home on Earle Avenue in Cleveland, and $217 per month until their youngest son graduated high school. After that, the monthly support dropped to $100 per month.[8]

As time passed, there were moments of frustration. In an interview on file at the Professional Football Hall of Fame in Canton, recorded in the late 1960s, he went on the public record. "Every other ball club gave all their players a break. But Cleveland, both Willis and I came out of this thing and we never got anything from Cleveland. I asked for either one, a scouting position or a coaching one. And [right after that] I was going around the country, matter of fact I went to New York for a program by *Sports Illustrated*, and they were askin' me 'Did they give you anything?' I said this is what happened: I ain't got anything from them."[9]

Referring to an exchange in 1963, Motley noted: "I asked Paul Brown for a scouting job. And I asked Modell [in 1963]. The thing that burns me is that I was talking with Modell one year ... this was a time when white scouts were having trouble getting into Negro schools, getting information, so I went and talked with Modell. I give 'em this idea.... I came to talk to you about scouting the Negro schools; information from them, and I think I'm well enough known that I could help you."[10]

Motley added more detail to his thoughts on the job situation, and about how it played out over the years.

> Dante Lavelli was scouting for the Browns at the time, so I said to Lavelli, "What the hell's happening? Nobody's calling me. If they don't call me soon and send me out to scout, I'm going to call the newspapers." I guess Lavelli told 'em right away, because that Friday they called me and told me they wanted me to go to Wilberforce [a small, historically black college in southwestern Ohio]. But Wilberforce had nothing. Neither of the teams in that game had anything.[11]
>
> The Browns just kept sending me there as appeasement, to keep me from saying anything. I made two or three trips that year, but all this was appeasement. One day I caught Modell at the practice field. Modell, I says, what about the scouting thing we talked about? He's kneeling on one knee, looking at practice. He doesn't even look around. He looks out on the field and tells me, "Well, Motley, you know what? The only thing you can help us with is signing the ballplayers." I says, is that what you think? He says yes, and I tell him well, I thank you, and with that I walk off the field.

When Art Modell and his staff hired Bill Nussbaumer as an assistant coach, the latter a former Detroit Lions player who had coached for eight years, without even interviewing Motley, the latter's pride would not accept the slight without speaking out.

In February 1965, Motley met with Bill Nunn, of the *Pittsburgh Courier*, about his prospects. Motley, with a bit of editorial help from Nunn, wrote an open letter describing his perception of his personal situation. Just as he had on the football field, Motley lowered his shoulder and plowed ahead. The letter was an explosive satchel of charges, and if Motley's intention was to hit a nerve in the Browns' ownership, it worked. While there is some validity to Cato the Elder's assertion that "it is hard to have lived with one generation and to be tried by another," Motley's words resonate throughout the national conscience even today. Excerpts from letter:

> About one year ago, I inquired at the Browns' offices about a coaching job or some sort of affiliation in any meaningful capacity.... I was ... turned down by the Cleveland Browns, namely by Paul Brown ... his only reply was... "Have you tried the Steel Mill?"[12]

160

Motley continued in that vein, noting that he had friends of both races who continued to ask him (Motley) why he was no longer affiliated with the Browns. He described a 1963 encounter with new owner Art Modell in which Motley asked if he could work scouting "Negro Schools," and help in signing their otherwise undiscovered athletes. Modell dismissed Motley, according to the letter, intimating that Motley was qualified for little more than coercing the players to sign after someone else, presumably better qualified, had scouted them and found them worthwhile as prospects. Motley closed with his observation that Modell doubted the ex-player even possessed the qualifications, experience, and general knowledge to truly know a football player.

Motley's later reflection on his letter was unrepentant.

> I blasted 'em. I wrote in a newsletter, a long [letter]. I had a colored writer send it out. After that, I'm watching practice one day and Modell came over and he saw me and he says, "Hey, I'd like to talk to you." So I say OK, we talked.
>
> He says, "You know, I think you did me an injustice." I said, "No, I don't think that I did. Because I asked you for a scouting job, I sat down and talked with you and you even ignored me when I went to talk with you on the football field and then came along and hire a guy who never gave Cleveland anything.... Now they put this guy [Nussbaumer] in as a coach."
>
> He [Modell] went on ranting and raving. He says, uh, "You know, I'm not prejudiced. 'Cause I always try to help Negroes." He says, "I give to all their community funds." He says, "I do all this stuff."
>
> I said, "Look, I don't know about that. What you give is out of your pocket. But what you give me? Nothing." He said, "I don't think you wrote that letter." I said, "So you calling me a dummy?" He said, "No, no, no.... I didn't call you that." I said, "Yeah, you just called me a dummy. This is what you've felt all the way along about my mind." I said, "You think that I was a dummy when I was just asking for a scouting job, that I couldn't do it. You told me the only thing you thought I can do was help you sign ballplayers. Otherwise, you were telling me I was a dummy, that I can't go write up a kid."
>
> Then, one word led to another and he got hot. Red in the face. And I stood there and laughed at him. Then I walked away. He's a bastard ... the guy is not right.[13]

The exchange with Modell was not a case that was unique to Motley. In Jim Brown's second book, *Out of Bounds*, he relates a conversation he had with the owner as well, this time about how roommate assignments were being handled on the road. As Brown wrote, "Art got mad at me. He said, 'Jim, I'm not prejudiced. I give more money to the

NAACP than you do!'"[14] While that fact was almost certainly true, it was also irrelevant to the players. Modell was not bigoted on the level of many prominent Americans. Alabama governor George Wallace had famously preached "segregation now, segregation tomorrow, segregation forever" in his 1963 inaugural address, and much of the cheering crowd agreed. But Modell, the team owner, was a victim of his own hubris.

The perception that guilt-relief could be monetized, could be purchased like a 16th-century indulgence from the Catholic church, that spending some amount, less than 100 percent, of a resource like the money that Modell possessed in excess, was the rhetorical giveaway about the team owner's conception of the issues Motley and Brown each addressed. To Modell, and this is not a judgment of his individual level of racial bias, it was evidently enough to spend money on worthy causes. That, to him, appears to be what he believed in doing to ease a social problem. He was blind, though, to the obvious manifestations of the problem within his sphere of control, on his team and among his players. Modell's perceptual blind spot, natural evidence of that hubris, was to the friction within the very corporation that he managed.

The 1960s were a time of change in larger public perceptions of Black athletes. This was the decade in which Muhammad Ali polarized a boxing audience by choosing prison over service in the war in Vietnam. Ali was a devout Muslim, and had registered as a conscientious objector when originally eligible for the military draft. When ordered to report for induction into the U.S. Army, he declined. While he was sentenced to five years in prison, he was able to avoid incarceration, but was still banned from boxing for three years. Dr. Harry Edwards, a Bay Area sociologist, has concluded that the world changed in the 1960. "In the 1950s, the model black athlete had been established around the attitudes toward Joe Lewis and Jesse Owens and even Jackie Robinson, where they go out on the field, go to the track, went to the ring, do their job and then go back to the Black community and don't say anything."[15] In Cleveland, this began to change with Jim Brown's public dispute with Modell and Motley's frustration at not being able to find a job in football.

In Motley's case, the Browns' collective unwillingness to give him a shot at coaching did not go unnoticed among Black football players around the country. Willie Davis, Green Bay Packers Hall of Fame defensive end who had starred for coach Vince Lombardi during their glory years, told *Black Sports Magazine* later that he took a path to business after he retired, rather than coach. "I started with Cleveland and something happened to Marion Motley that really put a fear in me.... Motley was near the end of his career and he supposedly went to Paul Brown and asked for him to help him get a job.... Brown, I was told at the time, recommended Motley try the steel mills."[16]

Motley's gifts as a running back, his ability to dominate the opposition so thoroughly, probably made his skills look intuitive rather than learned, instinctive, something that he couldn't explain to those less talented. While Motley was an imposing athlete, much of his success came because of diligent dedication to study and practice. Blocking was a skill he studied for years, and at which he was one of the finest practitioners, ever. In 1978, star Miami Dolphin fullback Larry Csonka shared that he had patterned himself after Motley. "Many people ask me what man I styled myself after as a runner. I styled myself after a style of running. I had the opportunity to see films of Motley running for the Browns when I lived in Stow. My father said, 'If you can run like Motley and run as hard, you will do well.' I tried to style my running after Motley."[17] With such a testimonial, it is difficult to believe that Motley would not have made an effective coach if he had been given the opportunity.

In 1966, Motley approached new Washington Redskins coach Otto Graham about a position on his staff, but aside from a few scouting opportunities, more appeasement, nothing came of the request. While he had successfully coached youth football since he retired from the NFL in 1955, he seemed to have little credibility among the professional coaching fraternity. In 1967, desperate to prove his capability, Motley agreed to coach the Cleveland Daredevils of the startup Women's Professional Football League.[18,19]

At this point, a brief examination of women's professional football is necessary, if for no other purpose than offer context for Motley's decision to accept a coaching job in the game. While there had been women's football games used as halftime entertainment at men's games as far back as the mid–1920s, there was no organizing construct in which to market the game to a ticket-buying public. That changed in 1965, when a Cleveland theatrical promotor, and the one of the sponsors of the Miss Cleveland pageant, named Syd Friedman created what historian Stuart Kantor later called, accurately, a two-team "gimmick" league for women and tackle football.[20] Originally envisioning "a Harlem Globetrotters–type team" to barnstorm against men's teams in other cities, the female players' collective passion, and ability, convinced him to focus on the gender-specific game and build credibility within.[21]

Motley shared the gist of his first conversation with Friedman with *Cleveland Plain Dealer* writer Hal Lebovitz. "I'm going to organize a professional football team. I want you to coach it," Friedman told Motley. "I'm interested," said Motley. "Keep talking." Then Friedman dropped the other shoe. "A girls' team," he said. Motley could only respond, "You're putting me on."[22,23]

Friedman continued his pitch: "This is going to be an all-girls team. They'll get paid for playing and you'll get paid for coaching. I want you to prepare them to play men's professional teams." Motley could only snort, "Now I know you're kidding." After a long conversation, Motley finally disabused Friedman of his original dream, and talked him into something more feasible, like women playing women.[24]

This was almost ten years before Billie Jean King won the televised spectacle the television networks called the "Battle of the Sexes" tennis match against Bobby Riggs, but Friedman still thought he could make a profit putting women on the field, facing off against each other. The first two women's teams, one in Akron and one in Cleveland, the latter named the Daredevils, played each other in four regional exhibitions in what was called the Women's Professional Football League, and cleared a path to expansion that would include teams in Pittsburgh, Toronto, and Detroit.

The women were not some frail, physically incapable athletes. Susan Riley, 305-pound dominated the offensive line, and Cleveland's Marcella Sanborn could throw a ball 35 yards on a line, and punt the ball over 40, and Motley came to respect his players. "The 300 pound girl is fast on her feet. The big trouble was getting her a pair of pants. I finally went to the Browns and asked them to let her use Chubby Grigg's old suit." When asked about the "weaker sex," he answered: "Weaker nothing. They play just like men. The other night I showed one of the girls how to block and then I had her demonstrate on me. I weigh 250. She weighs 185. I braced myself and, man, she bumped me so hard I got out of there. She is a cashier in a food market and nobody is going to sneak past her."[25]

The new head coach had to relearn some traditional, fraternal behaviors, like not casually slapping his players on their backsides after a good play, and he had to knock before entering the locker room. Still, Motley took a group of women who had, by definition, never played organized football before, and turned them into a functional team. "We use regular plays, some of the same ones we had when I was with the Browns. We even got my old draw play. The first time we tried it, the defensive tackle began to scream and holler. I asked her what was wrong. She said, 'That's not fair! You've got two girls blocking me.' I had a time convincing her it wasn't poor sportsmanship."[26]

The Daredevils tied Detroit, 6–6, in their first official game, and the idea grew from there.[27] The league garnered momentum over the following years, and after the aforementioned tennis spectacle, or the 1972 enactment of Title IX's provisions guaranteeing equal opportunities for women in intercollegiate sports, and earned enough recognition to entice the writers for the television show *Charlie's Angels* to write an entire episode that centered on the sport.[28] That was the sport in which Motley finally got his chance to build a team. Motley would stay with Cleveland, while Tex Mayhew headed up the Pittsburgh squad, and former New York Giants receiver Frank Liebel took over the Erie, Pennsylvania, team. Motley stayed with the team for just two seasons, but the league was still too young, too wobbly, to provide him with the credibility he sought as a reference for convincing an NFL team to take a chance on him as a coach.

The coda on the Women's Professional Football League was largely positive. One of the league's stars, running back Linda Jefferson, was named *Women's Sports* Athlete of the Year in 1975, and in 1976 the enterprise grew to 14 teams in cities ranging in size between Middletown, Ohio, to Los Angeles, California. By the mid–1980s, the National Women's Football League had weathered a spin-off attempt by one of the early owners, but neither survived until 1990. After an attempted reanimation in Europe, the women's game finally took hold in Australia. In the United States, though, it has yet to return.

Along with his Cleveland Daredevil coaching experience, Marion Motley's 1968 story centered on one highlight moment. In July 1968, Marion Motley was inducted into the Professional Football Hall of Fame, the second Black player, after Emlen Tunnell, to be so honored. That the Hall is in Motley's hometown of Canton made the honor even more special. It was an unprecedented, and still unequalled, career. 4720 yards rushing, 1107 yards receiving, 1122 yards returning kickoffs, two interceptions (one for a touchdown) and four fumble recoveries on defense, and a long list of tackles, blocks, and deflections, all culminating in five professional championships over a nine-year career.[29]

He went in with a luminous collection of peers, including Cliff Battles, Art Donovan, Elroy "Crazy Legs" Hirsch, Wayne Millner, Charlie Trippi, and Alex Wojciechowicz. The group had been culled from the list of hundreds of eligible players by a team of media members that included: Lew Atchison of the *Washington Evening Star*, Hugh Brown from the *Philadelphia Bulletin*, former player and St. Louis coach Jim Conzelman, television sportscaster Buddy Diliberto, Cleveland's Chuck Heaton, Bob Oates from the *Los Angeles Times*, George Puscas from the *Detroit Free Press*, Jack Sell of the *Pittsburgh Post-Gazette*, Blackie Sherrod of the *Dallas Times Herald*, John Steadman from the *Baltimore News Post*, the *Chicago Tribune*'s George Strickler, and Al Taomy and Roger Williams, Atlanta and San Francisco, respectively.

Despite football's resonance throughout the region, Motley was Canton's first son to be so honored. Despite the seeming inevitability of the election, given Motley's history, "The news kind of shook me up. I was surprised it really happened now because I thought if it ever did happen, it would be years from now. I feel proud but I feel kind of numb, too. I guess the only thing I can really say is that I am very thankful to all the people who have been my friends and fans."[30]

Motley spoke only briefly on his enshrinement day, and as one always looking to put team first and self a very distant second. Motley's Hall of Fame acceptance speech:

> Thank you, Bill [Willis, his presenter], and I'd like to thank the many friends that have come to pay tribute to seven of us today. I look out over this crowd, and I see many faces that I know that I've gone to school with. And it makes a person being from his hometown, of being presented into the Hall of Fame, in the hometown. It's a wonderful feeling. I've been asked many times in the last two or three days as to how you feel, or what will be your feeling. Well, trying to express or say how you feel about this, going into the Hall of Fame, it's rather hard. I'd like to thank the many teammates that I've played with that helped me to be the so-called player that I was at that particular time. Fellows like Bill Willis, Lin Houston, Cliff Lewis, Dante Lavelli, and many others that I could go on and name, but it would take quite a while. But I'd just like to say again, I'd like to thank everyone for coming and thank the people that inducted me into the Hall of Fame. Thank you very much.[31]

The most immediately obvious aspect of the speech is its brevity, especially when contrasted by the 20- or 30-minute orations that characterize induction acceptances in the baseball Hall of Fame. At 192 words, the majority focused on expressing gratitude, it is typical Motley.

10. Life After Football (1956–1998)

Even in the last days of his life, according to family and others who knew him, he never conflated his extraordinary football achievements with his personal dignity or worth. He absolutely knew how accomplished an athlete he'd been. Those he met who were unaware of his football stature, however, often walked away still unaware of the resume of the person with whom they'd just chatted. There is an old joke in military aviation: "Never ask a man if he is a fighter pilot. If he is, he'll let you know. If he isn't, don't embarrass him." Motley's genuinely humble ethos was the diametric opposite. It was not that he was shy about his football successes, but rather that he chose not to define himself, and measure his self-worth, by them.

At the time, he was also working in job placement for the Cleveland Neighborhood Youth Corps in 1968, counselling underprivileged youth in how to get, and keep, a job. Still playing basketball for fitness, he was not substantially heavier than he had been when he retired from the NFL in 1955. In 1974 he again considered entering the political arena and ran on the Democrat ticket for Stark County commissioner. He was defeated, and the experience may have dissuaded him from politics as he aged.

Motley's first political forays had actually occurred in 1956, when he filed as a candidate for state representative.[32] He did not receive the Democratic party nomination, and after an unsuccessful bid in 1960, had put politics on the back burner.[33]

In 1976, Motley was elected to the Black Sports Hall of Fame, sponsored by *Black Sports Magazine* (a periodical edited by Bryant Gumbel), and— locally—the Canton

Motley at his induction into the Pro Football Hall of Fame, 1967 (courtesy Pro Football Hall of Fame).

167

Negro Oldtimers Hall of Fame.[34] Motley spoke briefly at the latter ceremony, as was the norm for him, saying to the audience: "Being inducted in the two halls of fame was a great honor, of course. But when you are inducted in this, where you are with your lifelong friends, it means a great deal. This certainly is as great an honor to me as the others." Were it not so genuine, Motley's humility would have been suspicious and, possibly, patronizing. Yet, in his case, his public and private words were internally consistent and entirely organic.

In the late 1970s Motley accepted a job in public relations with the Ohio Lottery Commission, a spot he held for eight years. The Ohio Department of Youth Services then approached Motley about working for them, not as a mouthpiece or public relations asset, but as a front-line mentor and example to the disadvantaged youth in Canton. He remembered: "The Ohio Department of Youth services asked me to come work for them…. Today I'm working at the Indian River School, which is a maximum security boys' industrial school. We handle them up to eighteen years old, and sometimes we get them as young as twelve…. I'm involved with recreation…. Most of the kids stay about nine months, but we have a few felony-one and felony-two inmates who are here for quite a while longer. I enjoy working with them, and so far I've been very fortunate because I think I relate to them and they relate to me…. I tell them, 'You better be trying to get yourself some education and make something of yourself. Otherwise, you're going to be in these kinds of places for the rest of your life.'"[35]

After his enshrinement in 1968, Motley had enjoyed a bit of a popular resurgence, attending ceremonies, signing autographs, and working as an ambassador for football, the Hall of Fame, and the NFL. By the late 1980s, he was on the road almost continuously supporting NFL alumni events. Those events were usually golf tournaments, and Motley played a great deal of golf in his latter years. Almost every newspaper photo of Motley after 1980, or so it seems, is of a big, smiling man with the ubiquitous cigar on one side of his mouth, and either holding a golf club or sitting in a golf cart.

He also spent time talking to school assemblies about his story, and the lessons of persistence. "I tell the kids to treat people the way you want to be treated. Respect other and keep a humble attitude. My father was a disciplinarian. Although I was bigger than him, that didn't make no difference. He and I believe that people are basically good and I live my life with that thought in mind."[36]

Divorced from Eula for far longer than they were married, Marion enjoyed several relationships, even throughout his final years. Maddie, he said, "walks five miles every day, and she tries to get me out there with her. I just can't keep up. She gets that little old gait of hers going and walks away from me every time. Sometimes I go shopping with her, and when we go into the mall, I always find one of those benches. I sit down, light up my cigar, and don't even try to keep up with her."[37]

Motley's grandchildren have clear memories of their famous grandpa. He walked around with a gruff expression, but that certainly did not reflect his emotions. Stuart Leuthner, when collecting Motley's oral history in the late 1980s, described their first face-to-face meeting with a chuckle. "I flew into town, and he picked me up at the airport. He had a smaller car for such a large man, and one of the first things he said was, 'I don't trust the press.' Well, he warmed up as we drove around town, running errands like picking up dry cleaning and such, and everywhere we went, people lit up when they saw him. Everyone loved Marion Motley."[38]

He was reduced to walking with a limp late in life, his battered knees balking at old age, but he always had a cigar. From family gatherings to golf to a walk in town, "he led with a cigar," as Joe Dose laughingly remembers.[39] Wherever he went, he always signed autographs when asked. As the cancer worsened, he became a bit more reserved, even withdrawn, but that was as much about the physical pain he was suffering than it was irritation with fans. He was a decent, dignified man throughout his life, and carried that mantle until the day he died.

In 1989 he was admitted to the Cleveland Clinic for chest pain, but there was no formal report that he'd suffered a heart attack.[40] By 1993, fully retired from salaried work, Motley played a lot of golf, and spent time spreading goodwill for Cleveland football. When the Browns left in 1996, he was vocal in his disappointment (probably not surprised that Modell was the driving force behind gutting his community), but other than that his life remained placid. In 1998, Motley finally agreed to see a doctor in order to deal with some pain he'd been suffering, pain beyond the aches of a decade in professional football. He was diagnosed with prostate cancer, and he deteriorated quickly.

Doctors later told Motley's grandson Joe Dose that the man might have survived a few more years had he sought medical treatment when the symptoms, mostly the fatigue, first emerged. Even as his physical condition deteriorated, though, Motley never lost his dignity. Though his body failed, he was still able to have brief conversations with the array of family members who visited. Until the end of his life, those who knew him remember, he filled the room with his presence. To this day, he remains a great man in those memories.

⑾ **11** ⑾

Legacy (1999)

Marion Motley passed away on June 27, 1999, less than four weeks after his 79th birthday. His prostate cancer had left him bedridden for months, and he lived out his final weeks in private hospice care in the living room of son Raymond. His funeral was held on July 1 at the Mt. Sinai Baptist Church in Cleveland. The list of honorary pallbearers could have had their own wing in the Hall of Fame, and they included Lou Groza, Paul Warfield, John Henry Johnson, Ollie Matson, Bill Willis and Leroy Kelly.[1] Joe Perry, yet another Hall of Fame running back from the longtime AAFC and NFL rival San Francisco 49ers, travelled across the country to the funeral as well. "I had to come. Marion's my man. He was the greatest all-around football player there ever was."[2]

Son George Kennedy made it to the service, but for some reason he left his children at home, forcing them to miss the chance to say goodbye to the giant they called Grandpa. George passed away in 2017, and he never explained the slight, but Aldreeta and her brothers at least managed to watch the ceremony on local television.[3]

Motley is buried in a plot at the Evergreen Memorial Cemetery in Bedford Heights, Ohio. The town is roughly a 20-minute drive from downtown Cleveland, and the general absence of pageantry or decoration around his grave is, in itself, a relatively accurate reflection of the character of the man interred therein. He is closer to family—his mother, brother Clarence and sister Dorothy are also buried there—with no concern of fame. It would be hard to imagine, in the contemporary, celebrity-infused world, that such a notable athlete and person would be allowed to rest in that sort of peace. Motley played football in the years before television, and his exploits and accomplishments have been too often consigned to anonymity, but the benefit has been a much more private peace than some more celebrated athletes.

His legacy, as with each of us, is the echo of his life. What was

Marion Motley's legacy? There are two arenas in which his achievements, his presence, his performance, are still well worth acknowledging and appreciating: football, and his life beyond football. It is easier to start with the football aspects, in reviewing his contributions, as those give the life beyond football a foundation.

Football—Motley's History

Implicit in any discussion over where Marion Motley resides in the pantheon of football immortals is that there is no debate as to whether he belongs among the greatest players of all time. Bill Willis, himself a Hall of Famer, said this in introducing Motley for induction into the Pro Football Hall of Fame in 1968:

> The Cleveland Browns were organized in 1946. About a week after they were organized, Paul Brown realized that he did not have what it took to win the Championship, so he called Marion Motley—the rest is history. Every year that the Cleveland Browns participated in the All-American Conference they won the championship. Marion Motley was the leading rusher in the All-American Conference. Whenever you think of the Cleveland Browns, you must think of Paul Brown—really. Whenever you think of Paul Brown, you think of Marion and you think of Otto Graham. But you can neither think of Otto Graham the Paul Browns or the Cleveland Browns without thinking of Marion Motley. He was truly a complete football player, and for a team as the Cleveland Browns were in those days who were titled to be a passing club, Motley gained 4,712 yards and made 39 touchdowns. So, it gives me a distinct pleasure to present to the Hall of Fame the greatest full-back of all times, Marion Motley.

Such testament is invaluable in gauging Motley's place in the memories of his peers, of those who played with and against him, but those recollections are susceptible to the memory-eroding nature of time. As years pass, those deceased football players get faster, stronger, smarter, and generally better, at least in the collective memory. But were they as talented as aging recollections purport? In an era in which football games were not televised at anywhere near the volume that they have been since 1958, the only other path along which any sort of meaningful context regarding on-field performance emerges is the one illuminated by the numbers. Although Scottish historian and writer Andrew Lang once said that "most people use statistics like a drunk man uses a lamppost; more for support than illumination," what follows is an argument in support of Motley's abilities, not as a polemic contrast with the more broadly recognized immortals of the game.

A month after Motley passed away, *Sports Illustrated* magazine published a short letter to the editor from Elizabeth Gregory. She was referring to a photo of Motley from the July 5, 1999, issue in which a player, San Francisco 49er Gail Bruce, is trying to tackle the big fullback. Gregory writes: "After this picture was snapped, Motley dragged my father 30 more yards. My father did not let go, but he later said that he would have felt more comfortable tackling a freight train than Motley."[4]

There are many articles, contained in decades of newspaper and magazine stories, about Motley's level of football excellence. Throughout that slice of literature there has been a great deal of specific discussion, starting in Cleveland but quickly proliferating across the football world, about who was the better player, Marion Motley or Jim Brown. The argument about how Jim Brown compared with Marion Motley has provided journalistic fodder for unoccupied sports columnists for years, yet the discussion never seems to succumb to universal resolution.

Before charging once more into that breech, though, a stipulation: Jim Brown was, and perhaps still is, the greatest running back in the history of football. He was a nine-time Pro-Bowler, three-time NFL Most Valuable Player, eight-time league rushing leader and, by the end of his playing career, had rushed for an all-time professional football record 12,312 yards. It was not until 1984 that Walter Payton surpassed that mark, and as of 2021 Brown's total is still among the top 15 all-time. At first blush, a comparison with Motley seems almost unfair.

Marion Motley also played for Paul Brown, but in those earlier years, coach Brown was much more focused on exploiting Otto Graham's array of tools as the center of his offensive philosophy. While Jim Brown served as the primary weapon on Cleveland teams in the late '50s and 1960s, Motley was used as much as a blocker, and linebacker, by coach Brown a decade earlier. Still, a cursory look at the raw data does offer some space for comparison of the two.

Both players enjoyed professional careers of about ten years. While Jim Brown carried the ball 2359 times, though, Motley had only 828 rushing attempts. Simply put, over his entire career, Brown carried the ball 2.8 times more than Motley did over his. Brown rushed for 12,312 yards, and Motley only 4720, but the former's total was only 2.6 times that of the latter. In other words, Brown had 2.8 times the carries, and only 2.6 times the yards of Motley. Notably, Motley's career mark of 5.7 yards per carry exceeds Brown's mark of 5.2 by a full half yard.

As far as receiving, Brown amassed 2499 yards catching passes to Motley's 1107. Brown's yards came on 262 receptions, while Motley had only 85 catches. Again, Motley caught just fewer than one-third the number of passes as Brown but racked up 44 percent of Brown's yardage total. Motley's yards per reception mark of 13.0 also exceeded Brown's 9.5 yards per catch.

None of that is intended to minimize Jim Brown's well-deserved football immortality, but it does reveal a level of excellence in Motley's running that seems often overlooked. Motley deserves appreciation for not only his ball handling, but for all the various aspects of the game in which he not only excelled but dominated. Once again, the testimony of Hall of Famer Bill Willis:

> At Ohio State I had played against Marion when he was playing for the Great Lakes Navy team. Some might say he was so great a fullback as to be the equal of Jim Brown, who came after him in Cleveland, but there is really no fair way in which Motley can be compared with Brown. Jim Brown was perhaps the greatest running back in pro football. In my opinion, however, Motley was a better all-around ballplayer than Brown—a great runner, great blocker, and a threat as a pass receiver. Also, Motley was a great defensive ball player. Those famous goal-line stands we used to make were due to a very large degree to the effectiveness of Motley as a linebacker. He was not quite as fast as Brown, but he was fast. He wasn't as shifty as Brown, but, brother, he could shed those tacklers.[5]

Statistics, as Paul Zimmerman observed, are inadequate in describing Motley's capability as an all-around football player. Only some of the vast array of components of any particular game are measurable in terms of scoring. Yards, points, attempts and so on all have some degree of a mathematical correlation to the score. So many more actions, events that occur on every play of every game, events that are equally critical to a team's success, cannot be measured with the same, simple scaling. Blocks made, blocks missed, passes tipped but not intercepted, decision making, and execution, all are critical in determining a final score, yet they defy easy quantification. Motley's linebacking saved touchdowns or stopped many plays that might have led to opponent scoring. His blocking enabled, on almost every occasion, Otto Graham to not suffer an early sack, at least by the man Motley was blocking, or to pop free on a run.

11. Legacy (1999)

To think about Motley's football prowess, and how it can be fairly studied, it may be helpful to examine an analogy from a much better-known example in a different sport. Using the game of baseball as a model, there has long been similar sports columnist fodder, written and re-written, regarding the identity of the greatest baseball player of all time. The natural choice for most non-baseball scholars is Babe Ruth, but there are always voices who make substantive cases for Ty Cobb, or Ted Williams, or Mickey Mantle or Barry Bonds as better hitters. The numbers are what they are, and Ruth's were terrific in his time, but there is a case to be made that the Babe may not have been the greatest hitter in the game's history. That case, however, is irrelevant in terms of the framing question. While Ruth circulates near, or at, the top of any list of great hitters, it is his pitching achievements that put him in an entirely different class. Pick any of the aforementioned hitters, or any other slugger from the game, and it is a matter of record that none won a league Earned Run Average (ERA) title, tossed 17 career shutouts, or pitched 107 complete games, or had a career won-loss pitching record of 94–46. None of those hitters had a 3–0 record in 31 World Series innings, as well, or a post-season ERA of 0.87. To accurately judge a complete player, in any sport, it is necessary to include all facets of the game and then examine how well the subject performed in each. In the case of Babe Ruth, and his excellence in the two fundamental phases of baseball, there is no vocabulary or comprehensive statistical standard by which to describe him, much less cogently evaluate his career.

Such is the case with Marion Motley. Yes, he was a two-way player for four years due to the limits on substitutions, effectively forcing players to play "two-way," both offense and defense, but Motley not only played both sides of the ball, he starred at both. Paul Brown was convinced that Motley could have made it to the Hall of Fame strictly as a linebacker, and Blanton Collier (and, certainly, Otto Graham) swears that no fullback has ever blocked as well. Those alone would have made Motley a great all-around football player. Yet, when afforded the opportunities to carry or catch the ball, his performance was equal to, perhaps better than, that of the great Jim Brown. Just as with Babe Ruth, or even Shohei Otani in the 21st century, there is no accurate statistical tool with which to measure Motley's all-around excellence, and the lexicon is inadequate to accurately describing his value and his place in the game's lore.

Marion Motley's on-field performances absolutely contributed to enticing the NFL into a merger with the All-America Football Conference, but also helped pull the Cleveland Browns to a stretch of football domination, AAFC and NFL, akin to that of the Boston Celtics in the NBA of the early 1960s. Six straight professional titles, eight consecutive championship game appearances, and induction into the Professional Football Hall of Fame fill Motley's athletic resume. It was a football life that will, likely, never be equaled.

Marion Motley Lifetime Professional (Offensive) Football Statistics[6]

		Games		Rushing					Receiving					Total Yds	
Year	Age	G	GS	Rush	Yds	TD	Long	Y/A	Rec	Yds	Y/R	TD	Long	Touch	Y/Tch
1946	26	13	10	73	601	5	76	8.2	10	188	18.8	1	63	83	9.5
1947	27	14	12	146	889	8	50	6.1	7	73	10.4	1	0	153	6.3
1948	28	14	14	157	964	5	unk	6.1	13	192	14.8	2	78	170	6.8
1949	29	11	10	113	570	8	unk	5	15	191	12.7	0	0	128	5.9
1950	30	12	12	140	810	3	69	5.8	11	151	13.7	1	41	151	6.4
1951	31	11	10	61	273	1	26	4.5	10	52	5.2	0	34	71	4.6
1952	32	12	10	104	444	1	59	4.3	13	213	16.4	2	68	117	5.6
1953	33	12	0	32	161	0	34	5	6	47	7.8	0	23	38	5.5
1955	35	6	0	2	8	0	8	4						2	4
Career		105	78	828	4720	31	76	5.7	85	1107	13	7	78	913	6.4

Race—Motley's Memory

Baltimore Ravens executive Kevin Byrne, in a retrospective on baseball immortal Hank Aaron, after the slugger's death in 2020, related that Aaron was a zealous Cleveland Browns (and, after the franchise moved to Maryland in 1996, Baltimore Ravens) fan. He would, during the heyday of the old Dawg Pound section of the end zone at Cleveland's Municipal Stadium, often fly from Georgia on a Sunday morning, watch the game in either a disguise or a dog-face mask and Brown's gear from the Pound, and then fly back home to Georgia in the evening. Why was Aaron, who was born in Mobile, Alabama, and who lived in Atlanta, Georgia, such a passionate Cleveland football fan? Aaron explained that he first adopted the Browns "back in the days of Marion Motley. You'll find a lot of southern Blacks are Browns fans. You were the first

NFL team to have prominent Black players. We didn't see that on other teams. You were on TV and that's who we watched. That's why I root for the Browns."[7]

This is not insignificant. Hank Aaron's major league career started in Milwaukee, and when the Braves moved to Atlanta in the mid–1960s, he took his Browns allegiance with him. He was not the only fan of the Cleveland team who happened to live in the Deep South, but he was one of the most famous. Before 1968, when the NFL and AFL finally put franchises in the former college-exclusive football hotbeds of the Deep South, in New Orleans, Atlanta, and Miami, there was only one professional team whose radio broadcasts reached the that part of the country: The Washington (at the time) Redskins. The organization has since dropped the racially-questionable "Redskins" from the franchise identity, but throughout most of football's televised history, not only did they use the name, but they were the last NFL team to desegregate. Team owner George Preston Marshall was an acknowledged racist, a man who had once reputedly said, "We'll start signing Negroes when the Harlem Globetrotters start signing Whites," and it took a combination of public and private pressure in an evolving social world to compel him to hire running back Bobby Mitchell in 1962. This team, despite what was arguably a stronger Caucasian-centric ethos than the rest of the league, was the only team that fans in the South could reliably follow on Sunday afternoon radio or television.

The Cleveland Browns, though, gave Black fans in the South, and across the other football-deprived parts of the nation, a team with which they could more easily identify. Black fans could cheer Black stars like Motley, Willis and Gillom, and along with White fans could appreciate Paul Brown's drive to win without letting skin pigmentation interfere with his vision. The Browns sustained this momentum with players like Jim Brown, Ernie Davis, and John Wooten, and only once during Paul Brown's entire tenure as head coach did the team finish lower than third place in its division or league. The proof of Brown's plan was on the field.

Back in 1946, though, Marion Motley and Bill Willis may have had an even larger influence on civil rights progress in the United States than imagined. In one notable interview, Motley told a writer, "In [a] letter I saved, Branch Rickey [general manager of the Brooklyn Dodgers football and baseball teams in the mid–1940s] says, 'If Marion Motley and Bill Willis can break the color barrier in a contact sport, then Jackie

Robinson sure can do it in a non-contact sport.'"[8] Motley was never jealous of Robinson's acclaim in breaking the race barrier in baseball. "Getting credit wouldn't put anything in my pocket," he said.[9] So many years later, it is clear that he and Willis, along with Kenny Washington and Woody Strode and the executives that made the desegregation possible, should get more credit than they have for taking that social risk, and for the commensurate leap forward that it buttressed.

Hank Aaron encapsulated what Motley and Willis, and football, meant to the nation in the 1940s. "That man [Motley] is why I'm a Browns fan," Aaron told Terry Pluto. "He was a hero before blacks were allowed to be heroes."[10]

One of the generic questions that Motley was often asked, especially in his later years, was something to the effect of "Are you bitter?" When he'd say he was not, "Why?" quickly followed from interviewers. It is curious in that Motley had a trove of personal stories about racial inequity, before, during, and after football, but he refused to let those wrongs define him or frame his life. This psychological feat has analogs in other sports, especially baseball, as the time before, during and after Jackie Robinson's career affected a great number of Black athletes.

Bill Greason is a living example of that rationalization. Greason was a terrific pitcher for the 1948 Birmingham Black Barons, the last living teammate of Willie Mays from that Negro League World Series squad, and one of the first Black players to crack the big-league St. Louis Cardinals roster in 1954.

Greason grew up in a starkly segregated Atlanta, Georgia, on Auburn Avenue, across the street from a younger neighbor named Martin Luther King, Jr. He joined the United States Marine Corps in 1943, at the peak of World War II, and was assigned to Montford Point, North Carolina, for segregated basic training. He survived the assault on Iwo Jima in 1945, and after his discharge returned home to play baseball. The Birmingham Black Barons, a tremendously talented team, signed him, and Greason pitched well enough to earn a spot in the prestigious East-West All-Star Game, one of the annual highlights of the Negro League's seasons. After playing in slowly desegregating minor leagues in Texas for two years, he finally earned a cup of coffee with the St. Louis Cardinals. After baseball, Greason became a pastor and, in 1963, was preaching regularly at the Sixteenth Street Baptist Church in Birmingham.

11. Legacy (1999)

On September 15, 1963, Greason was away from the church putting together a youth baseball program in Tuscaloosa, and thus was not in the building when the Ku Klux Klan set off a bomb that killed four girls.[11] He has watched the progress of the Civil Rights movement in the United States his entire life. After decades of service to his country, his church, and his community, and of being forced to spend his best baseball years in a segregated, underappreciated league, bitterness would be an entirely defensible feeling.

Yet Greason will have none of it. He told a group of historians at a 2018 conference: "Why be bitter? What good would that do?"[12] Other Negro League stars, people like Art Pennington, have shared similar feelings toward their earlier lives. It is almost unthinkable that such strength and self-possession still exist in an increasing litigious world, a place where every slight demands retribution, but these men, Marion Motley included, continue to serve as examples of forgive but never forget, that critical step enabling real progress toward a better world.

In 1995, when asked his feelings about his contribution to de-segregating pro football, Motley summarized his thoughts: "I look at some of the players today and wonder if they could've done what we did. Most of 'em, 99 percent, have no idea who I am. They don't owe me anything. I've got this [Hall of Fame] ring, and the people who saw me play know what I did. I don't need any more than that."[13]

The Bottom Line

Marion Motley's life story is a chronicle of a unique journey through the 20th century. He was a Black man, born to a struggling family in the Deep South during a stretch of the most virulent racism displayed since the end of the Civil War. It is easy to judge the past as inhumane, but such assertion was irrelevant to Motley and his peers. The world was what the world was. Motley grew up in northeast Ohio, a minority in a community that was much more racially accepting than his birthplace, yet he was still a young member of a minority race. Over the course of his life, the United States moved from a culture that, at least in some regions, tolerated the oppression of lynching, of denial of due process, and of racial subjugation, to a nation that saw professional sports desegregated, a nation in which civil rights for all are the law of the land, and in which a poor, sharecroppers son could rise to athletic immortality in the eyes of White and Black alike. This is not to argue that the world is free of racial strife, or that it ever will be so, but rather that it is occasionally useful to figuratively pause and look back at the road already travelled, if only to marvel at the power of persistence in creating positive change.

Marion Motley developed his athletic gifts to a point that he was, perhaps, the greatest all-around football player in the history of the game. He loved, he laughed, he married, he fathered four children and raised three of them. He lived life mid-century not as an aging superstar, but as a middle-aged Black man scraping together a living through hard work, risk, and focus. He was shut out of the coaching and scouting fraternities, and could have abandoned football forever, but when he was finally enshrined with the other immortals of the game, he allowed football back into his life. He was a golfer, a community servant, and a friend to those he trusted. He was complete.

Yet he was, by no means, and by his own admission, perfect. His dalliances with women cost him his marriage, and half of his money, and kept him working for others for as long as he could. Only in his later years, it seems, did he find the peace accorded to those who leave it all on the field. In football, as well as in life, Marion Motley gave his all. He left nothing out there.

To those that both saw him play and knew him best, Motley was a walking dichotomy: a gracious and dignified man off the field, and a monster during a game. The football judgment is clear. Marion Motley was one of the greatest all-around football players to ever take the field. Mike Brown, son of coach Paul Brown and owner of the Cincinnati Bengals, has said on several occasions: "Jim Brown may have been a great runner, but Marion was a better runner. He could really run. He was a complete player. He was a great blocker. Marion was a great player ... my dad always felt Marion was the greatest back he ever had."[14]

The memories of the man remain alive in those who were closest to him. Both granddaughter Bianca Bloom and grandson Joe Dose, two of youngest son Raymond's children, remember a dignified man, ubiquitous cigar protruding from one side of his mouth, untethered from the fading memories of his distant football past, a man whose ethos carried not a hint of superiority derived from glory earned on distant fields decades earlier. At his funeral Bill Willis said: "He was a big, jovial, gentle individual. He would do anything for you that he possibly could. If you were his friend, then nothing was too good for you. If you needed anything that had, he'd let you have it. He was just a guy you would really, really enjoy being around."[15] Otto Graham took it a step further. "If every [one] in the world, whether black or white, lived with people like Marion did, there would be no racial problems. He was a great man."[16]

That is an epitaph worth chiseling in granite.

Appendix

United States Senate Resolution Honoring Motley and Bill Willis, 2006

109TH CONGRESS
2D SESSION
S. RES. 533

Commemorating the 60th anniversary of the permanent integration of professional football by 4 pioneering players.

IN THE SENATE OF THE UNITED STATES
JULY 17, 2006

Mr. VOINOVICH (for himself, Mr. DEWINE, and Mr. ALLEN) submitted the following resolution; which was considered and agreed to

---

RESOLUTION

Commemorating the 60th anniversary of the permanent integration of professional football by 4 pioneering players.

Whereas the integration of sports supported other ongoing efforts to permanently end racial segregation as an accepted practice in the United States;

Whereas, in 1946, 4 African American football players, William "Bill" K. Willis and Marion Motley, who played for the Cleveland Browns, and Kenny Washington and Woody Strode, who played for the Los Angeles Rams, all signed contracts to play professional football;

Whereas, on August 7, 1946, Bill Willis was the first of this pioneering foursome to sign a contract to play professional football for the Cleveland Browns forever ending the race barrier in professional football, 1 full year before Jackie Robinson broke the race barrier in professional baseball;

Appendix

Whereas, thanks to the significant contributions of Bill Willis and Marion Motley, the Cleveland Browns won the National Football League [NFL] Championship in 1950 which was the first year the Cleveland Browns played in the NFL;

Whereas, in addition to permanently ending the race barrier in professional football, Bill Willis and Marion Motley were recognized for their outstanding professional football careers by their election to the Pro Football Hall of Fame; and

Whereas 2006 marks the 60th anniversary of the permanent integration of professional football, and the NFL will commemorate this milestone during the 2006 Pro Football Hall of Fame Game: Now, therefore, be it

Resolved, That the Senate—

(1) recognizes the 60th anniversary of the permanent integration of professional football; and

(2) respectfully requests the Secretary of the Senate to transmit for appropriate display an enrolled copy of this resolution to—

(A) the Pro Football Hall of Fame in Canton, Ohio; and

(B) William K. Willis, the only surviving member of the pioneering foursome who permanently ended the race barrier in professional football.

The introduction of the "forgotten four," as they've come to be known in print and film, created a different dynamic for the nation and the press than would Jackie Robinson six months later. In the case of the latter, the diorama centered on one, lone heroic figure, playing for a media-dense New York City team no less, standing on a field that represented a slice of pure Americana. Jackie Robinson was a Black player at the apex of the hitherto segregated National Pastime. The baseball diamond itself isolates individual players by natural, positional spacing, and a linear, one-at-a-time approach to offense within the batting order. At its densest, with bases loaded and nine defenders, there can be no more than 13 players in the field of play. Football, in contrast, herds 11 players on each side, 22 in all, along a single line of scrimmage within a regular, rectangular arena. The players are hidden from spectators by helmets, their identities limited to their jersey numbers, their contributions made simultaneously on every snap.

It is understandable, then, that the appearance of Strode and Washington in California, and Willis and Motley in Ohio, as a single event did not lend itself to the same, unique moment, the poetic pause that can be captured and commemorated, as did Robinson's act of taking the field in Brooklyn. That stipulated, the "forgotten four" collectively made a critical step forward in the evolution of race relations in the United States. The sport they played had been segregated for 13 years, yet those four opted to stand and be recognized for their football excellence, regardless of race. That they gave Branch Rickey some reinforcing confidence in his plan to introduce Jackie Robinson the following year is likely. Together, the four, Robinson, Rickey, Bill Veeck, and the American people, not only sanctioned the desegregation but blessed the action. Such results come only from silent sacrifice, and the United States' Senate's resolution acknowledged the nation's shared admiration and gratitude.

This resolution, while not unique among political gestures past and present, is still a tangible reminder of the significance of the contribution to the nation, to progress toward reducing or even eliminating racial separation and attendant inequality, by Marion Motley and Bill Willis. The "Forgotten Four" of Washington, Strode, Willis and Motley, remain underserviced in the literature of football, of sport, and of the nation.

Notes

Introduction

1. Richard Hofstadter, *The Progressive Historians: Turner, Beard, Parrington* (New York: Alfred A. Knopf, 1968), 3.

2. Paul Zimmerman, "The Monster in My Memory," *Sports Illustrated*, July 5, 1999, accessed November 11, 2020, https://vault..si.com/vault/1999/07/05/THE-MONSTER-IN-MY-MEMORY.

3. Paul Brown, *PB: The Paul Brown Story* (New York: Atheneum, 1979), 132.

4. Paul Brown, *PB*, 131.

5. All statistical information, unless otherwise noted, is drawn from the website Pro-Football-Reference, online at https://www.pro-football-reference.com/players/M/MotlMa00.htm#all_defense.

6. "NFL 100: Official All-Time Roster," NFL.com, https://www.nfl.com/100/all-time-team/roster.

7. Sean Lahman, "Marion Motley," *The Pro Football Historical Abstract* (Guilford, CT: Lyons Press, 2008), 128–129.

8. Lahman, "Marion Motley," 128.

Chapter 1

1. 1910 United States Census (Ancestry.com—1910 United States Federal Census), and John Henry Motley's World War I draft registration card (Ancestry.com—U.S., World War I Draft Registration Cards, 1917–1918), accessed December 2, 2020.

2. Shakvol Motley military draft registration (P.M.G.O. Form No. 1), April 12, 1918. Of note: In some sources, such as family trees on sites like Ancestry.com, he is listed as Shakeful Motley, which was likely the proper pronunciation, but his given name was Shakvol.

3. Marion Motley military draft registration (D.S.S. Form 1, order number 2–1786), 1941, and signed by Motley while in college in Nevada, states the date of birth was June 10, 1920. The Social Security death index records available digitally state that he was born June 5. The latter date is most often found on sites like Pro-Football-Reference, but there is some doubt as to which date is accurate.

4. "The Great Migration," History.com, https://www.history.com/topics/black-history/great-migration.

5. George E. Haynes, "The Migration of Negroes into Northern Cities, 1917," presentation at the 44th Meeting of the National Conference of Social Welfare, Pittsburgh, PA, June 6–13, 1917, 494.

6. This is corroborated in scholarship by both Thomas J. Sugrue, in *Sweet Land of Liberty: The Forgotten Struggle for Civil Rights in the North* (New York: Random House, 2009), and Steve Luxenberg, in *Separate: The Story of Plessy v, Ferguson, and America's Journey from Slavery to Segregation*. Both argue that in the immediate post-war South, it was impossible to physically segregate White and Black, whereas in the Northern cities that sort of stove-piped separation was a by-product of ethnic neighborhoods in the larger cities.

7. "Mob Storms Jail; Takes Six Blacks," *Atlanta Constitution*, January 21, 1916, 1.

8. "Negro Is Taken at Jail and Lynched," *Little Rock Daily News*, August 1, 1922, 1.

9. Roosevelt Grier, *Rosey—The Gentle Giant* (Tulsa: Honor, 1986), 4.

10. Mark Craig, "Motley Broke Barriers and Tackles," *News-Journal* (Mansfield, OH), September 11, 1999, 20.

11. Bob Stilwell, "How the Great Depression and World War II Affected Ohio," *Parma Observer*, January 5, 2017, http://parmaobserver.com/read/2017/01/05/how-the-great-depression-and-world-war-ii-affected-ohio.

12. Stuart Leuthner, *Iron Men: Bucko, Crazylegs, and the Boys Recall the Golden Days of Professional Football* (New York: Doubleday, 1988), 229–230.

13. Leuthner, *Iron Men*, 230.

14. Leuthner, *Iron Men*, 229.

15. Leuthner, *Iron Men*, 229.

16. "Steubenville Drops First Game to Erie (East)," *Evening Independent* (Massillon, OH), October 11, 1937, 10.

17. "Canton Wins from Big Red; Magics Lose," *Evening Independent*, November 8, 1937, 13.

18. "Massillon vs. Canton McKinley," Massillon Tigers website, https://massillontigers.com/history/massillon-vs-canton-mckinley/history-of-the-rivalry/#:~:text=No%20high%20school%20football%20rivalry%20in%20the%20nation,fact%2C%20it%E-2%80%99s%20almost%20akin%20to%20going%20to%20war, accessed December 20, 2020.

19. *Timeless Rivals* plot summary, Internet Movie DataBase (IMDB), https://www.imdb.com/title/tt8200472/plotsummary?ref_=tt_ov_pl, accessed August 19, 2021.

20. Luther Emery, "Tigers and Bulldogs Will Battle on Wet Gridiron," *Evening Independent*, November 19, 1937, 20.

21. "Young Elected President of the Booster Club," *Evening Independent*, November 23, 1937, 12.

22. Leland Stein III, "Legendary Marion Motley: Football Jackie Robinson," *Black Voice News*, February 6, 1997, B1-B2.

23. Paul Brown, *PB: The Paul Brown Story* (New York: Atheneum, 1979), 132.

24. "Bulldogs Approved," *Evening Independent* (Massillon), August 3, 1938, 10.

25. "South Triumph Over Canton Not Impossible, Says Wargo," *Akron Beacon Journal*, September 21, 1938, 19.

26. "Stars for McKinley," *News-Journal* (Mansfield, OH), September 17, 1938, 28.

27. Bob Elliott, "Sellout Is Sure for Big Game," *Akron Beacon Journal*, November 13, 1938, 25.

28. Fritz Howell, "Carl Grate Top Scorer," *Akron Beacon Journal*, November 1, 1938, 24.

29. "Tigers Eye Canton McKinley in Practice This Week," *Evening Independent*, October 31, 1938, 8.

30. Fritz Howell, "Two of Ohio's Best Elevens Meet in Game," *Salem* (OH) *News*, November 13, 1938, 12.

31. Christian Malone, "Valdosta vs. Massillon a Possibility," *Valdosta* (GA) *Daily Times*, July 28, 2006, 8.

32. Luther Emery, "Tigers Beat Bulldogs 12–0 to Win State Championship," *Evening Independent* (Massillon), November 21, 1938, 10.

33. Emery, 10.

34. Emery, 10.

35. Megan Malone, "Houston Recalls '38 Battle with Motley," *Canton Repository*, November 3, 1994, E-17.

36. "Massillon-Canton Tilt Should Decide Honors," *Akron Beacon Journal*, November 15, 1938, 25.

37. Leuthner, *Iron Men*, 230.

38. Joe Santoro, "Marion Motley Changed Nevada Sports and Professional Football," *Nevada Appeal*, June 27, 2020, C6.

Chapter 2

1. "History of SC State University," https://www.scsu.edu/aboutscstate/historyofscstateuniversity.aspx.

2. "Knox Bulldogs to Scrimmage Today," *Knoxville Journal*, October 3, 1939, 8.

3. "Knox College Meets Tough Enemy Today," *Knoxville Journal*, October 7, 1939, 7.

4. "State Arrives for Clark Tilt," *Atlanta Constitution*, October 27, 1939, 25.

5. "Clark to Face Hard Runners," *Atlanta Constitution*, October 26, 1939, 21.

6. "Carolina Eleven Beats Clark, 7–6," *Atlanta Constitution*, October 29, 1939, 21.

7. "Hold Conference at State College," *Times and Democrat* (Knoxville, TN), December 12, 1939, 7.

8. "Knox College and S.C. Tie at 7–7," *Knoxville News-Sentinel*, October 8, 1939, 18.

9. South Carolina State Bulldogs website, South Carolina State University Athletics—Marion Motley#—South Carolina State Athletics University Hall of Fame—South Carolina State University (scsuathletics.com).

10. "100 Best HBCU Football Players of All Time," https://hbcubuzz.com/2019/11/100-best-hbcu-football-players-of-all-time/.

11. Leland Stein III, "Legendary Marion Motley: Football's Jackie Robinson," *Black Voice News*, February 6, 1997, B-2.

12. Stuart Leuthner, *Iron Men: Bucko, Crazylegs, and the Boys Recall the Golden Days of Professional Football* (New York: Doubleday, 1988), 230.

13. Canton McKinley high school archive, https://www.ohsaa.org/Portals/0/Sports/Football/history/OhioHighSchool-StateChampions1895-1946.pdf.

14. "Ex-Duck Grid Coach Jim Aiken Dies," *Eugene* (OR) *Register-Guard*, November 1, 1961, 5.

15. Santoro, "Motley Changed Nevada."

16. Herman Hill, "'Reno-ated' Nevada Team Has 'Second Kenny Washington' in New Star, Claim," *Pittsburgh Courier*, September 21, 1940, 16.

17. Green, "'Mississippi of the West,'" 71.

18. Roger Kahn, "Willie Mays, Yesterday and Today," *Thirty Years of Best Sports Stories* (New York: E.P. Dutton, 1975), 267–268.

19. Helen Blue interview for University of Nevada Oral History project and the university centennial celebration. Provided from the archival collection of Guy Clifton.

20. Blue interview.

21. Leland Stein III, "Legendary Marion Motley: Football Jackie Robinson," *Black Voice News*, February 6, 1997, B1-B2.

22. Green, "'Mississippi of the West,'" 57, 57–70.

23. "Grid Player Faces Charge of Homicide," *Sacramento Bee*, April 8, 1940, 8.

24. "Canton Man Dies in Elmore Crash," *News-Messenger* (Fremont, OH), August 31, 1940, 12.

25. "Grid Star Held in Auto Death," *Oakland Tribune*, April 7, 1940, 3.

26. "Friends Pay Gridder's Fine," *Oakland Tribune*, November 8, 1940, 36.

27. Joe Santoro, "Marion Motley Changed Nevada Sports and Professional Football," *Nevada Appeal*, June 27 2020, https://www.nevadaappeal.com/sports/marion-motley-changed-nevada-sports-and-professional-football/, accessed November 13, 2020.

28. "Berkeley Woman Sues Nevada Football Star," *Sacramento Bee*, February 13, 1941, 6.

29. Ty Cobb, "Inside Stuff," *Nevada State Journal*, October 28, 1940, 5.

30. Cobb, "Inside Stuff."

31. Blue interview.

32. "Idaho Edges Nevada Pack," *San Francisco Examiner*, November 17, 1940, 54.

33. Blue interview.

34. Francis Stann, "Win, Lose, or Draw," *Washington Evening Star*, August 31, 1950, 50.

35. *Reno Evening Gazette*, April 17, 1941.

36. "Reno Club Stops Dixie Baseballers," *Nevada State Journal*, June 24, 1940, 4.

37. Amy Essington, *The Integration of the Pacific Coast League: Race and Baseball on the West Coast* (Lincoln: University of Nebraska Press, 2018), 22.

38. Gordon Edes, "Opening a New Wide World," *Boston Globe*, March 28, 1997, 39.

39. Tom Hawthorn, "Jimmy Claxton," Society for American Baseball Research Biography Project, https://sabr.org/bioproj/person/jimmy-claxton/.

40. "Jimmy Claxton," Seamheads Negro League Database, https://www.seamheads.com/NegroLgs/player.php?playerID=claxt01jim.

41. "Larks Retrieve Monarch Game," *Nevada State Journal*, July 9, 1941, 8.

42. "1941 Kansas City Monarchs," Seamheads Negro Leagues Database, December 15, 2020.

43. "Nevada Coach Finds New Passing Pair," *Sacramento Bee*, October 2, 1941, 17.

44. "Grid Season's Longest Run 105 Yards," *St. Louis Post Dispatch*, December 5, 1941, 40.

45. Red McQueen, "All Major Athletic Events Are Cancelled," *Honolulu Advertiser*, December 9, 1941, 10.

46. Ernie Nevers to Harry Borba, "Side Lines," *San Francisco Examiner*, October 9, 1941, 28.

47. Blue interview.

48. Interview with Bianca Bloom (Motley's granddaughter), October 26, 2020.

49. Harry Borba, "Dons Rally to Trim Nevada Eleven, 27–7," *San Francisco Examiner*, October 5, 1942, 16.

50. Bob Brachman, "St. Mary's Crushes Nevada Through Air," *San Francisco Examiner*, October 12, 1942, 17.

51. "Nevada Plays 0–0 Tie with New Mexicans," *Nevada State Journal*, November 1, 1942, A1, S1.

52. Santoro, "Motley Changed Nevada."

53. John H. Woolsey, "Fond Memories of Mr. Motley," *Santa Rosa Press-Democrat*, November 27, 1994, 28.

54. Santoro, "Motley Changed Nevada."

55. Dave Reardon, "Nevada," *The ESPN College Football Encyclopedia* (New York: ESPN, 2005), 576–579.

56. Reardon, "Nevada," 579.

57. Motley acknowledged a fourth son in an interview with Helen Blue of the University of Nevada Oral History project in the late 1990s. Motley's granddaughter, Bianca Bloom, in an interview on October 26, 2020, noted that a man named George showed up at Motley's 1999 funeral, and identified himself as Motley's son. That was her only exposure to her half-uncle, the fourth Motley boy.

58. Inteview with Aldreeta Kennedy (Motley's granddaughter), telephone, August 8, 2021.

Chapter 3

1. Stuart Leuthner, *Iron Men: Bucko, Crazylegs, and the Boys Recall the Golden Days of Professional Football* (New York: Doubleday, 1988), 231.

2. "Motley Would Like to Return and Play Football at Nevada," *Reno Gazette-Journal*, January 21, 1943, 14.

3. "Motley Would Like to Return," 14.

4. Brenden Welper, "Like 2020, College Football Was Very Different During World War II," NCAA.com, https://www.ncaa.com/news/football/article/2020-09-21/2020-college-football-was-very-different-during-world-war-ii.

5. "Onward, 1943," *Street and Smith's Football Pictorial Year Book* (New York: Street and Smith Publications, 1943), inside cover.

6. Michael G. Smith, "The Aerial Game: How Football and Aviation Grew Up Together," *Smithsonian Air and Space* magazine, February 2, 2018, https://www.officedepot.com/a/products/801187/SanDisk-Cruzer-Glide-USB-Flash-Drive/?mediaplacementid=290605936&gclid=EAIaIQobChMIuNe78YPK8gIVy9fICh3mKgPPEAEYASACEgIH5fD_BwE&mediaplacementid=290605936&mediacreativeid=142916956.

7. Smith, "Aerial Game."

8. Charles Einstein, "When Football Went to War," *Sports Illustrated*, December 6, 1971, https://vault.si.com/vault/1971/12/06/when-football-went-to-war.

9. George Cantor, *Paul Brown: The Man That Invented Modern Football* (Chicago: Triumph, 2008), 15.

10. "Coach of the Year," *Pro Football Illustrated* (Mt. Morris, IL: Elbak,1948), 18.

11. David Dayen, "How Teddy Roosevelt Saved Football," *Politico Magazine*, September 20, 2014, https://www.politico.com/magazine/story/2014/09/teddy-roosevelt-saved-football-111146/.

12. Otto Graham, *Otto Graham: T Quarterback* (New York: Prentice Hall, 1953), 51.

13. Frank Leahy, *Notre Dame Football: The T Formation* (New York: Prentice Hall, 1949), 14.

14. "The Quarterback," *The Sporting News*, November 29, 1950, 6.

15. Leuthner, *Iron Men, 231.*

16. Paul Brown, *PB: The Paul Brown Story* (New York: Atheneum, 1979), 114.

17. Mark Craig, "Motley Powered Browns to '48 Title Win," *Zanesville Times-Recorder*, July 26, 1999, 1.

18. Terry Pluto, *When All the World Was Browns' Town* (New York: Simon & Schuster, 1997), 53.

19. Allen Dowlin, "Michigan Tips Great Lakes by Decisive 27–2 Score," *Daily Herald* (Provo, UT), September 16, 1945, 8.

20. Wilfrid Smith, "Teninga Stars in Michigan's 27–2 Victory Over Great Lakes," *Chicago Tribune*, September 16, 1945, 21.

21. Lyall Smith, "Wolverines Start, Finish with a Bang," *Detroit Free Press*, September 16, 1945, 11.

22. Jack Scott, "1945 Great Lakes: The Best for Last," *College Football Historical Society Newsletter*, 5–8.

23. Brown, *PB*, 117.

24. Michael Lerseth, "Grover Klemmer, Cal Track Star and Longtime CCSF Coach, Dies at 94," *San Francisco Chronicle*, August 26, 2015, https://www.sfgate.com/news/article/Grover-Klemmer-Cal-track-star-and-longtime-CCSF-6467587.php.

25. Wilfrid Smith, "Tar 'Cripples' Run Wild; 2d Irish Setback," *Chicago Tribune*, December 2, 1945, 36.

26. Smith, "Tar 'Cripples' Run Wild," 33.

27. Brown, *PB*, 117.

28. Frank McCulloch, "Nevada Sports," *Reno Evening Gazette*, December 4, 1945, 16.

29. McCulloch, "Nevada Sports."

Chapter 4

1. "War Was Never Like This!" *Cincinnati Enquirer*, January 1, 1946, 1.

2. Harold Classen, *The History of Professional Football* (New York: Prentice Hall, 1963), 93.

3. Stan Grosshandler, "All-America Football Conference," *The Coffin Corner* 2, no. 7 (1980), 1.

4. Edward Prell, "Rams Shift Franchise to Los Angeles," *Chicago Sunday Tribune*, January 13, 1946, 44.

5. "How the Browns Were Named," *Cleveland Browns Media Guide*, 2003, 284.

6. *Cleveland Browns Media Guide*, 284.

7. Joe Santoro, "Marion Motley Changed Nevada Sports and Professional Football," *The Nevada Appeal*, June 27, 2020, https://www.nevadaappeal.com/sports/marion-motley-changed-nevada-sports-and-professional-football/, accessed November 13, 2020.

8. Marion Motley oral history in clipping file at the Professional Football Hall of Fame, Canton, Ohio, undated.

9. Stuart Leuthner, *Iron Men* (New York: Doubleday, 1988), 232.

10. Paul Brown, *PB: The Paul Brown Story* (New York: Atheneum, 1979), 131.

11. Brown, *PB*, 131.

12. Brown, *PB*, 131.

13. Clement Willis World War I military draft registration card, https://www.ancestry.com/imageviewer/collections/6482/images/005146791_04073?treeid=&personid=&usePUB=true&_phsrc=gwK2&_phstart=successSource&pId=11856470.

14. Fourteenth Census of the United States: 1920—Population. Ancestry.com—1920 United States Federal Census, https://www.ancestry.com/imageviewer/collections/6061/images/4300157_00298?usePUB=true&_phsrc=gwK2&_phstart=successSource&usePUBJs=true&pId=4692365.

15. David Campbell, "Bill Willis Dies," https://www.cleveland.com/sports/2007/11/bill_willis_dies.html, November 28, 2007.

16. Kentucky Hall of Fame, https://ksuthorobreds.com/honors/hall-of-fame.

17. "Willis Recalls 'Pioneer' Days," *Evening Independent*, August 1, 1977, 19.

18. "Bill Willis," https://www.encyclopedia.com/education/news-wires-white-papers-and-books/willis-bill.

19. "Bill Willis," Professional Football Hall of Fame, https://www.profootballhof.com/players/bill-willis/.

20. "Bill Willis," Professional Football Hall of Fame, https://www.profootballhof.com/players/bill-willis/.

21. "Bill Willis," Professional Football Hall of Fame, https://www.profootballhof.com/players/bill-willis/.

22. "Bill Willis Obituary," http://www.legacy.com/ns/bill-willis-obituary/98753510.

23. "The 1946 Cleveland Browns," 1946 Browns Highlights—Bing video.

24. Al Dunmore, "Coach Paul Brown Okays Negro Stars," *Pittsburgh Courier*, August 17, 1946, 17.

25. Dunmore.

26. Tom Melody, "Motley Could Do It All," *Pro Football Digest*, November 1968, 28.

27. Frank Leahy, *The Notre Dame "T" Formation* (New York: Prentice Hall, 1949), 16–17.

28. Otto Graham, *Otto Graham: T Quarterback* (New York: Prentice Hall, 1953), 132–133.

29. "Otto Graham: Football, Basketball, and Baseball," *Northwestern Magazine*, Fall 2013, https://www.northwestern.edu/magazine/fall2013/feature/top-cats-sidebar/otto-graham-football,-basketball-and-baseball.html.

30. Greg Bedard, "Otto Graham's 14/60 Jersey," *Sports Illustrated*, June 17, 2014, https://www.si.com/nfl/2014/06/17/nfl-history-in-95-objects-otto-graham-jersey.

31. "Otto Graham," Find-A-Grave.com, https://www.findagrave.com/memorial/8191242/otto-graham.

32. Otto Graham, *Otto Graham: T Quarterback* (New York: Prentice Hall, 1953).

33. Graham, 14.

34. Graham, 49.

35. Graham, 54.

36. Tom Melody, "Motley Could Do It All," *Pro Football Digest*, November 1968, 28.

37. "Marion Motley Joins Browns," *News-Journal* (Mansfield, OH), August 10, 1946, 6.

38. Ray Didinger, "Color His Skin Thick," *Philadelphia Daily News*, October 18, 1995, 73.

39. Andy Piascik, *The Best Show in Football: The 1946–1955 Cleveland Browns* (Lanham, MD: Taylor Trade, 2007), Kindle edition.

40. James C. Sulecki, *The Cleveland Rams* (Jefferson, NC: McFarland, 2016), 188.

41. Sulecki, *Cleveland Rams*, 192.

42. Didinger, "Color His Skin Thick," 73.

43. Terry Pluto, "Marion Motley Was a Giant of Any Time," *Akron Beacon Journal*, June 28, 1999, 16.

44. Dunmore.

45. Didinger.

46. Chris Haft, "Motley, Willis Say Brown Helped Integrate Football," *Massachusetts Independent*, April 16, 1997, B5.

47. Fritz Howell, "Browns Crush Seahawks Before Record Crowd in First Conference Game," *Evening Independent* (Massillon, OH), September 7, 1946, 6.

48. Jim Schlemmer, "Browns Roll Over Hawks, 44–0, Before 60,135," *Akron Beacon Journal*, September 7, 1946, 10.

49. Schlemmer, 10.

50. Schlemmer, 10.

51. "Canton's Motley Stars as Browns Rip Rockets, 20–6, Before 51,962," *Akron Beacon Journal*, September 14, 1946, 10.

52. "Canton's Motley Stars as Browns Rip Rockets, 20–6, Before 51,962," *Akron Beacon Journal*, September 14, 1946, 10.

53. "Cleveland Browns Beat Rockets 20–6 Before 51,962 Fans," *Pittsburgh Courier*, September 21, 1946, 17.

54. "Cleveland Browns Beat Rockets 20–6 Before 51,962 Fans," 17.
55. "Motley Scores 2 Touchdowns as Cleveland Beats L.A. 11," *Pittsburgh Courier*, October 26, 1946, 12.
56. "Motley Stars, Browns Lose," *Pittsburgh Courier*, November 9, 1946, 13.
57. Bob Yonkers, "Browns Take the Air for Florida Tilt," *Dayton Herald*, November 30, 1946, 15.
58. "Browns' Motley, Willis Will Miss Seahawk Contest," *Newark Advocate*, November 9, 1946, 6.
59. "Without Willis and Motley," *The Chronicle-Telegram* (Elyria, OH), November 30, 1946, 12.
60. Bill Furlong, "A Negro Ballplayer's Life Today," *Sport Magazine*, May 1962, 91–94.
61. Furlong, 93.
62. Woody Strode, quoted by Alexander Wolff, "The NFL's Jackie Robinson," *Sports Illustrated*, October 12, 2009, https://vault.si.com/vault/2009/10/12/the-nfls-jackie-robinson.
63. Santoro, "Motley Changed Nevada."
64. "Browns Battle Rockets Sunday in Home Game," *Chronicle-Telegram* (Elyria), November 16, 1946, 6.
65. Dick Young, "Browns Edge Yankees for AAC Crown, 14–9," *New York Daily News*, December 23, 1946, 19.
66. Paul Zimmerman, *The New Thinking Man's Guide to Professional Football* (New York: Simon & Schuster, 1987), 394.

Chapter 5

1. Marion Motley, oral interview on file in the archives of the Professional Football Hall of Fame in Canton, Ohio.
2. Harold Claasen, *The History of Professional Football* (New York: Prentice Hall, 1964), 302.
3. "Cage Carnival Slated Feb. 6," *Akron Beacon Journal*, January 27, 1946, 24.
4. "Brown Gridder Hurt in Crash," *Evening Independent* (Massillon, OH), February 11, 1947, 2.

5. "Star Cleveland Back Injured in Accident," (Spokane, WA) *Spokesman Review*, February 17, 1947, 16.
6. Interview with Bianca Motley Bloom, October 26, 2020.
7. Narcolepsy—Symptoms and Causes—Mayo Clinic, https://www.mayoclinic.org/diseases-conditions/narcolepsy/symptoms-causes/syc-20375497.
8. Paul Brown, *PB: The Paul Brown Story* (New York: Atheneum, 1979), 132.
9. F.T. Kable, "Editorial," *Pro Football Illustrated* (Morris, IL: Elbak, 1947), 4.
10. Kable, 4.
11. Kable, 4.
12. Robert Peterson, *Pigskin: The Early Years of Pro Football* (New York: Oxford University Press, 1997), 154.
13. Peterson, 155.
14. "Horace Gillom, Ex-Nevada End, Signs with Cleveland," *Nevada State Journal*, January 3, 1947, 14.
15. John Trent, "Legacy of the Greats: How the Wolf Pack Teams of the 1940s Beat Jim Crow," *Nevada Today*, https://www.unr.edu/nevada-today/news/2018/legacy-of-the-greats.
16. *Nevada State Journal*, January 3, 1947, 14.
17. Larry Smith, "Gillom Makes Browns End Supply Plentiful," *The Times Recorder* (Zanesville, OH), October 10, 1947, 13.
18. Smith, 13.
19. Leo Suarez, "Tough at the Top," *Miami News*, January 3, 1985, 13.
20. Andy Piascik, *The Best Show in Football: The 1946–1955 Cleveland Browns* (Lanham, MD: Taylor Trade, 2007), 72.
21. Marion Motley oral history in clipping file at the Professional Football Hall of Fame, Canton, Ohio, undated.
22. Motley oral history.
23. *Cleveland Browns Media Guide*, 2003, 360.
24. "Browns Easily Defeat Baltimore 28–0," *Daily Times* (Philadelphia, OH), September 22, 1947, 6.
25. "Browns Late Rally Ties Yankees 28–28," *Daily Times*, November 24, 1947, 6.

26. *Daily Times*, November 24, 1947, 6.

27. "Yanks-Browns in Tie," *Cincinnati Enquirer*, November 24, 1947, 20.

28. John Unitas and Harold Rosenthal. *Playing Pro Football to Win* (New York: Signet, 1968), 33.

29. Unitas, 35.

30. Jim Schlemmer, "Browns Retain A-A Pro Football Crown," *Akron Beacon Journal*, December 15, 1947, 26.

31. Tom Wancho, "Cleveland Municipal Stadium," *Society of American Baseball Research Biography Project*, https://sabr.org/bioproj/park/cleveland-stadium/, accessed August 11, 2021.

32. National Weather Service, "What Is Lake Effect Snow?" https://www.weather.gov/safety/winter-lake-effect-snow,

33. The game film is available on YouTube: 1947–12–14 AAFC Championship Game New York Yankees vs Cleveland Browns—Bing video.

34. Paul Zimmerman, "Gridiron Heroes" source unmarked and undated, from the Marion Motley clippings archive in the Professional Football Hall of Fame.

35. An outstanding summary of the game exists on the website for the Golden Football Magazine, https://goldenrankings.com/AAFCchampionshipGame1947.htm.

36. Schlemmer, December 15, 1947, 26.

37. Paul Brown, *PB: The Paul Brown Story* (New York: Atheneum, 1979), 131.

38. "Cleveland Browns Ended Pro Grid Ban," *Pittsburgh Courier*, October 22, 1960, 35.

Chapter 6

1. Jim Schlemmer, "Buttons Lip," *Akron Beacon Journal*, January 1, 1948, 27.

2. Frank Litsky, "Marion Motley, Bruising Back for Storied Browns, Dies at 79," *New York Times*, June 28, 1999, B-7.

3. "Marion Motley," Professional Football Hall of Fame website, Marion

Motley | Pro Football Hall of Fame Official Site (profootballhof.com).

4. Sam DeLuca, *The Football Playbook* (New York: Jonathan David, 1972), 19.

5. Dave Christensen and James Peterson, *Coaching Offensive Linemen* (Monterey, CA: Coaches Choice, 2003), 46.

6. Paul Zimmerman, "Yesterday's Heroes: Marion Motley," *Gridiron*, date unknown, from Motley's clipping file in the Ralph Wilson Research Center at the Professional Football Hall of Fame.

7. Otto Graham, *Otto Graham: T Quarterback*. (New York: Prentice Hall, 1953), 54–55.

8. Charlie Powel to author Andy Piascik, *Gridiron Gauntlet: The Story of the Men Who Integrated Pro Football in Their Own Words* (Lanham, MD: Taylor Trade, 2009).

9. DeLuca, 23.

10. Extract from the game program on September 18, 1977, *New England Patriots Versus the Kansas City Chiefs*, "Big Play: The Draw Play—Marion Motley and the Cleveland Browns," from the Motley clippings file at the Ralph Wilson Research Center at the Professional Football Hall of Fame.

11. Paul Brown, *PB: The Paul Brown Story* (New York: Atheneum, 1979), 132.

12. Leonard Lyons, "The Lyons Den," *The Pittsburgh Press*, January 11, 1955, 12.

13. DeLuca, 22.

14. "Brown Satisfied with Showing of Pro Gridders," *Circleville* (OH) *Herald*, August 4, 1948, 9.

15. "Groza Shifted to Working Tackle for Browns This Season," *Sandusky Register*, September 1, 1948, 11.

16. Bob Yonkers, "Gillom Gets Nod to Show Grid Ability," *Dayton Herald*, September 1, 1948, 21.

17. Jim Schlemmer, "Score Only Thing Close as Grid Browns Top Dons, 19–14," *Akron Beacon Journal*, September 4, 1948, 10.

18. "Brownies Hoist Warning After Blasting Buffalo," *Circleville Herald*, September 13, 1948, 11.

19. Prescott Sullivan, "82,769 See Browns Beat 49ers, 14 to 7," *San Francisco Examiner*, November 15, 1948, 25.

20. Paul Brown, *PB: The Paul Brown Story*, 132.

21. Frank Eck "Browns, Cards Each Place Three on 1948 All-Pro Eleven by AP," *Sandusky Register*, December 17, 1948, 14.

22. Stan Opotowsky, "Mac Speedie Again Rates AAC All-Star Selection," *Salt Lake City Tribune*, December 15, 1948, 28.

23. "Eagles and Browns Win Pro Grid Titles," *Cincinnati Enquirer*, December 20, 1948, 22.

24. "Pro Grid Peace Near? Rival Loops to Meet to Discuss Problems," *Cincinnati Enquirer*, December 20, 1948, 22.

25. "Pro Grid Peace Near? Rival Loops to Meet to Discuss Problems," *Cincinnati Enquirer*, December 20, 1948, 22.

26. "Pro Grid Peace Near? Rival Loops to Meet to Discuss Problems," *Cincinnati Enquirer*, December 20, 1948, 22.

Chapter 7

1. "Cleveland Brown Gridders Not Loafing During 'Vacation,'" *News Messenger* (Fremont, OH), March 11, 1949, 13.

2. "Browns' Stars Booking Games," *Marysville Journal-Tribune* (OH), January 19, 1949, 6.

3. Tom Carroll, "Local Scene," *Dayton Daily News*, January 14, 1949, 36.

4. Carroll, 36.

5. "Marino Motley Says He Isn't Missing," *Times Recorder* (Zanesville, OH), January 22, 1949, 2.

6. "Motley Is Safe in Big Town," *Akron Beacon Journal*, January 22, 1949, 2.

7. "Motley 'Missing' Report Unfounded," *Dayton Journal Herald*, January 22, 1949, 36.

8. "Erring Browns in Tie with Frisco Eleven," *Akron Beacon Journal*, August 20, 1949, 11.

9. "Adamle Gets Defensive Position," *Daily Times* (New Philadelphia, OH), August 10, 1949, 8.

10. "'New' New York Gridders Ready for Brownie Test," *Circleville* (OH) *Herald*, August 26, 1949, 8.

11. Jim Schlemmer, "Injuries Mar 21–0 Grid Win," *Akron Beacon Journal*, September 12, 1949, 23.

12. "Mashin' Motley Leads Browns to 42–7 Victory," *Circleville Herald*, October 3, 1949, 7.

13. "Mashin' Motley Leads Browns to 42–7 Victory," *Circleville Herald*, October 3, 1949, 7.

14. "Mashin' Motley Leads Browns to 42–7 Victory," *Circleville Herald*, October 3, 1949, 7.

15. Frankie Albert and Dave Payne, "The Game I'll Never Forget," *Football Digest* 9, no. 3 (November 1949): 78.

16. Albert and Payne, 82.

17. Tom Melody, "Motley Could Do It All!" *Pro Football Digest*, November 1968, 28.

18. From Motley's clipping file at the Pro Football Hall of Fame, Canton, Ohio.

19. Melody, 29.

20. Linda Elsen, "Marion Motley: He Never Said No," *Black Sports Magazine* (May 1973), from Motley's clipping file at the Pro Football Hall of Fame, Canton, Ohio.

21. Marion Motley audio interview, from the files of the Pro Football Hall of Fame.

22. Marion Motley audio interview.

23. Stuart Leuthner, *Iron Men: Bucko, Crazylegs, and the Boys Recall the Golden Days of Professional Football* (New York: Doubleday, 1988), 239.

24. Paul Brown, *PB: The Paul Brown Story* (New York: Atheneum, 1979), 131.

25. Kenneth Crippen and Matt Reaser, *The All-America Football Conference* (Jefferson, NC: McFarland, 2010), 16.

26. Crippen and Reaser, 16.

27. Milton Richman, "Nobody Ever Kidded About 'Marion'—or 'Motley,'" *Dispatch* (Moline), March 31, 1976, 52.

28. Herb Altschull, "NFL and AAFC Merge to Form 13-Team League," Associated Press feed to the *Hawaii Tribune-Herald*, December 10, 1949, 9.

29. Altschull, 9.

30. Stan Baumgartner, "Grid Pros

Blow Whistle on Red Ink Battle," *The Sporting News*, December 21, 1949, 35.

31. Altschull, 9.

32. Harry Borba, "Cleveland Favored by 7½ Points Today," *San Francisco Examiner*, December 11, 1949, 33.

33. Hal Lebovitz, "Champions Close Out AAC to Strains of Taps," *The Sporting News*, December 21, 1949, 39.

34. Lebovitz, 39.

35. Lebovitz, 39.

36. David Barron, "Sixty Years Later, Shamrock Bowl One to Remember," *The Houston Chronicle*, December 17, 2009, https://www.chron.com/sports/texans/article/Sixty-years-later-Shamrock-Bowl-one-to-remember-1617617.php,

37. Ray Didinger, "Color His Skin Thick," *Philadelphia Daily News*, October 18, 1995, 73.

38. Barron.

39. Jim Brown, *Out of Bounds* (New York: Citadel, 1989), 7.

40. Pro Football Hall of Fame web page on the Cleveland Browns, https://www.profootballhof.com/teams/cleveland-browns/team-history/.

41. Andrew Harner, "Cleveland Browns All-Time Best Team," *Sports Illustrated*, November 11, 2020, https://www.si.com/nfl/Cleveland-Browns-All-Time-Best-Team.

Chapter 8

1. Joe Cootter, "Sport-o-grams," *The News* (Paterson, NJ), January 3, 1950, 26.

2. Cootter, 26.

3. "16 Brownies Will Take Up Basketball," *The Greenville Daily Advocate*, January 4, 1950, 6.

4. "Crowd Mark," *Cincinnati Enquirer*, February 22, 1950, 18.

5. Bill Ford, "Globetrotters Win; 12,020 at the Gardens," *Cincinnati Enquirer*, February 28, 1950, 19.

6. Howard Babcock, "Brownies, Bears to Clash in Cleveland," *Daily Times* (New Philadelphia, OH), September 1, 1950, 12.

7. Babcock, 12.

8. "National Clubs No Problem to Browns," *Sandusky Register*, September 2, 1950, 6.

9. Mort Berry, "Motley's Theory: Run Over Foes," *Philadelphia Enquirer*, September 13, 1950, 48.

10. Berry, 48.

11. Berry, 48.

12. Greasy Neale career statistics, https://www.baseball-reference.com/players/n/nealegr01.shtml.

13. "We Will Win, If…—Greasy Neale," (Pottstown) *Mercury*, September 14, 1950, 22.

14. "Pro Grid Elevens to Clash Tonight," *Philadelphia Enquirer*, September 16, 1950, 8.

15. "Otto Graham Puts on Great Show as Browns Trim Eagles," *Wilkes Barre Times Leader*, September 18, 1950, 14.

16. Stuart Leuthner, *Iron Men: Bucko, Crazylegs, and the Boys Recall the Golden Days of Professional Football* (New York: Doubleday, 1988), 234–235.

17. Harold Sauerbrei, "Browns Held Scoreless First Time in 62 Games as Giants Win 6–0," *Cleveland Plain Dealer*, October 1, 1950, 18.

18. Jim Schlemmer, "Browns Throttle Over-the-Hill Charges," *Akron Beacon Journal*, October 30, 1950, 17.

19. An abridged version of the game film is available on YouTube, at 1950 Steelers at Browns Game 7—Bing video.

20. Schlemmer, 17.

21. Harold Sauerbrei, "Browns Crush Steelers, 45–7, with Spectacular 338-Yard Ground Attack," *Cleveland Plain Dealer*, October 29, 1950, https://www.webcitation.org/6KSfW0oXd?url=http://www.cleveland.com/brownshistory/plaindealer/index.ssf?%2Fbrowns%2Fmore%2Fhistory%2F19501029BROWNS.html.

22. Leuthner, *Iron Men*, 235.

23. "Weather Factor? Stydahar Says No," *Akron Beacon Journal*, December 25, 1950, 36.

24. Jim Schlemmer, "Storybook Finish Provided by Groza," *Akron Beacon Journal*, December 25, 1950, 36.

25. Leuthner, *Iron Men*, 235.

26. Tom Melody, "Motley Could Do It All!" *Pro Football Digest* 1, no. 6 (November 1968,): 29.

Chapter 9

1. "Motley Sues for $50,000 Damages," United Press feed to the (Coshocton, OH) *Times*, February 6, 1952, 12.

2. Tom Melody, "Marion Could Do It All," *Pro Football Digest*, November 1968, 30.

3. Marion Motley audio interview, from the files of the Pro Football Hall of Fame.

4. Stuart Leuthner, *Iron Men: Bucko, Crazy Legs, and the Boys Recall the Golden Days of Professional Football* (New York: Doubleday, 1988), 237.

5. Marion Motley audio interview, from the files of the Pro Football Hall of Fame.

6. "Motley's Future in the Balance," *Akron Beacon Journal*, September 18, 1951, 38.

7. "Big Marion Goes on Trial in California," *Akron Beacon Journal*, September 26, 1951, 29.

8. Harold Sauerbrei, "Browns Lose Title to Rams, 24–17," *Cleveland Plain Dealer*, December 23, 1951, 23.

9. "Rams Collect $2,108 Each," *Milwaukee Journal*, December 24, 1951, 2.

10. Jack McCallum, "By the Numbers" *Sports Illustrated*, February 24, 1986, https://vault.si.com/vault/1986/02/24/by-the-numbers.

11. "Browns Hope Nine Old Men Will Hold Up," *Charlotte Observer*, December 24, 1952, 17.

12. "Lions Conquer Browns, 17–7, for NFL Title," (Dayton) *Journal Herald*, December 29, 1952, 6.

13. Bill Nunn, "Record Number of Negro Players Trying Out for NFL Berths," *Pittsburgh Courier*, August 1, 1953, 14.

14. "Brownies Set Back 58–45 by All-Stars," *Evening Independent* (Massillon, OH), January 23, 1954, 11.

15. "Motley's Housing," *Akron Beacon Journal*, February 12, 1954, 5.

16. "Motley Likes Terms; Signs Ninth Contract," *Cincinnati Enquirer*, March 27, 1954, 17.

17. "Browns' Jones Quits Football for Lumber," (Dayton) *Journal Herald*, June 3, 1954, 10.

18. "Chick Jagade to Quit Browns for Industry," *Daily Times* (New Philadelphia), June 24, 1954, 13.

19. Fritz Howell, "Paul Brown Needs Goes Fishing, Forgets Portable Radio; Fish Fail to Bite," *The Newark Advocate*, June 24, 1954, 14.

20. "Motley's Ailing Knee Is Recovering Slowly," *Sandusky Register*, September 1, 1954, 14.

21. "Browns May Drop Motley; Prepare to Meet Bears," (Bucyrus) *Telegraph-Forum*, September 16, 1954, 5.

22. "Marion Motley Quits," *Akron Beacon Journal*, September 20, 1954, 22.

23. Morrison Takes Over for Motley," *Akron Beacon Journal*, September 21, 1954, 39.

24. "Tiff in Marion Motley's Tavern Leads to Shooting," *The Chillicothe Gazette*, December 11, 1954, 11. Additional details are contained in "Motley's Café Is Scene of Shooting," (Coshocton) *Tribune*, December 12, 1954, 19.

25. "Paramount Nips Browns," *News-Messenger* (Fremont, OH), February 4, 1955, 14.

26. "Motley Considering Pro Grid Comeback," *The Akron Beacon Journal*, March 3, 1955, 40.

27. "Landlords Cited," *Marion Star*, March 29, 1955, 11.

28. "Motley Pulls Another Trap," *Evening Independent*, June 15, 1955, 19.

29. "All-Time AFL Team—Offense," Pro Football Hall of Fame, January 1, 2005, https://www.profootballhof.com/news/all-time-afl-team-offense1/.

30. Cookie Gilchrist and Chris Garbarino, *The Cookie That Did Not Crumble* (Staten Island, NY, 2011), 22.

31. Gilchrist and Garabino, 22.

32. "Motley Tries Comeback as Linebacker," *Dayton Daily News*, May 17, 1955, 18.

33. *Dayton Daily News*, May 17, 1955, 18.

34. "Marion Motley May Regain Brown Fullback Berth," *Daily Times* (New Philadelphia), July 26, 1955, 11.

35. Ritter Collett, "Journal of Sports," *Dayton Journal Herald*, August 15, 1955, 6.

36. "Steelers Get Marion Motley," *Salem News*, September 8, 1955, 12.

37. Paul Brown, *PB: The Paul Brown Story* (New York: Atheneum, 1979), 239.

38. Leuthner, *Iron Men*, 237.

39. Milton Richman, "Nobody Ever Kidded About 'Marion'—or 'Motley,'" (Moline, IL) *Dispatch*, March 31, 1976, 52.

40. "Marshall Pins Browns' Lead on 'Nothing Trade' of Steelers," *Pittsburgh Press*, November 28, 1955, 30.

41. Pat Livingston, "Training Camp Brings a Motley of Memories" *Pittsburgh Press*, July 7, 1976, 28.

42. "Steelers Release Marion Motley; Career Ended?" *Daily Republican* (Monongahela, PA), November 1, 1955, 2.

43. Vince Quatrini, "Sport Prints," *Latrobe Bulletin*, November 8, 1955, 11.

44. Wendell Smith, "Wendell Smith's Sports Beat," *Pittsburgh Courier*, November 19, 1955, 28.

Chapter 10

1. Marion Motley to Stuart Leuthner, *Iron Men: Bucko, Crazylegs, and the Boys Recall the Golden Days of Professional Football* (New York: Doubleday, 1988), 237.

2. Eric W. Rise, "Race, Rape, and Radicalism: The Case of the Martinsville Seven, 1949–1951," *The Journal of Southern History* 58, no. 3 (1992): 461–490.

3. Chris Tomasson, "Motley Remains Greatest All-Around Player," *Canton Repository*, July 20, 1988, C-3.

4. Jim Grant, in Edward Kiersh, *Where Have You Gone Vince DiMaggio* (New York: Bantam, 1983), 217.

5. Jim "Mudcat" Grant, Tom Sabellico, and Pat O'Brien, *The Black Aces: Baseball's Only African American 20-Game Winners*, 2d ed. (New York: Aventine Press, 2007).

6. Tom Fitzpatrick, "Motley Stays in Football—As Coach of Sandlot Team," *Lima News*, October 12, 1958, 37.

7. Marion Motley audio interview, from the files of the Pro Football Hall of Fame.

8. "Court Grants Mrs. Motley a Separation," *Cleveland Call and Post*, June 30, 1962, 2A.

9. Marion Motley audio interview, from the files of the Pro Football Hall of Fame.

10. Motley audio interview, from the files of the Pro Football Hall of Fame.

11. Motley audio interview, from the files of the Pro Football Hall of Fame.

12. Motley's letter, published by Bill Nunn, Jr., in "Change of Pace," *The Pittsburgh Courier*, February 20, 1965, 15.

13. Motley audio interview, from the files of the Pro Football Hall of Fame.

14. Jim Brown, *Out of Bounds* (New York: Citadel, 1989), 57.

15. Harry Edwards, "Jim Brown," *A Football Life*, broadcast on the NFL Network, season 6, episode 8, originally aired November 10, 2016.

16. "Rap: John Carlos, Willie Davis and Allan Barron Discuss After-Glory-business, Endorsements, and Discrimination," *Black Sports Magazine*, April 1971, 15, 16.

17. "Csonka's Footwork Styled After Motley's," *The Cleveland Plain Dealer*, May 16, 1978, 33.

18. Marion Motley clipping file Professional Football Hall of Fame.

19. "Gals Football Idea Grows," *Akron Beacon Journal*, January 31, 1968, E-18.

20. Stuart Kantor, "The History of Women's Professional Football," *The Coffin Corner* 22, no. 1 (2000).

21. Untitled note, *Akron Beacon Journal*, January 31, 1968, E-18.

22. Hal Lebovitz, "Want to Coach Girls' Team?" *Cleveland Plain Dealer*, November 12, 1967, E-4.

23. Marion Motley clipping file Professional Football Hall of Fame.

24. Lebovitz, "Want to Coach," E-4.

25. Lebovitz, "Want to Coach," E-4.

26. Lebovitz, "Want to Coach," E-4.

27. "With 'OOFs,' 'AARGHS' Girl Gridders Tangle," *The Cleveland Plain Dealer*, November 13, 1967, 42.

28. "Angels in the Backfield," aired January 25, 1978, https://www.imdb.com/title/tt0539180/.

29. Bill Willis, Introduction of Marion Motley at the Professional Football Hall of Fame Enshrinement in 1968.

30. Charlie Powell, "Motley Really 'Shook' by HOF Recognition," *Canton Repository*, February 20, 1968, 21.

31. Professional Football Hall of Fame website, https://www.profootballhof.com/players/marion-motley/.

32. List of candidacy filings for Ohio House of Representatives, *Cleveland Plain Dealer*, February 9, 1956, 8.

33. "Citizens League Evaluates Candidates," *Cleveland Plain Dealer*, April 19, 1960, 10.

34. Bob Stewart, "Motley Leads the Way for 5 in Black HOF," *Canton Repository*, April 26, 1976, 20.

35. Leuthner, *Iron Men*, 238–239.

36. Stein III, "Legendary Marion Motley: Football Jackie Robinson," *The Black Voice News* February 6, 1997, B1-B2.

37. Leuthner, *Iron Men*, 239.

38. Interview with Stuart Leuthner, July 15, 2021.

39. Interview with Joe Dose, November 19, 2020.

40. "Motley Hospitalized," *Canton Repository*, October 3, 1989, page unknown, from the Motley clipping file at the Professional Football Hall of Fame.

Chapter 11

1. "Marion Motley's Funeral Set for Today," *The Dayton Daily News*, July 1, 1999, 35.

2. Andy Piascik, *The Best Show in Football: The 1946–1955 Cleveland Browns* (Lanham, MD: Taylor Trade, 2010), 290.

3. Interview with Aldreeta Kennedy, August 8, 2021.

4. Elizabeth Gregory, letter to *Sports Illustrated*, August 9, 1999, Letters—Sports Illustrated Vault | SI.com.

5. Bill Willis to Myron Cope, *The Game That Was: The Early Days of Pro Football* (New York: World, 1970), 253.

6. https://www.pro-football-reference.com/players/M/MotlMa00.htm.

7. Kevin Byrne, "Byrne Identity: Hammerin' Hank Loved the Ravens," https://www.baltimoreravens.com/news/byrne-identity-hammerin-hank-loved-the-ravens.

8. Mark Craig, "Motley Broke Barriers and Tackles," *Mansfield News-Journal*, September 11, 1999, 21.

9. Craig, 15.

10. Pluto, 18.

11. David J. Krajicek, "Justice Story: Birmingham Church Bombing Kills 4 Innocent Girls in Racially Motivated Attack," *New York Daily News*, September 1, 2013.

12. Bill Greason remarks at the 2018 Southern Negro League Baseball Conference, Birmingham, Alabama, October 6, 2018.

13. Didinger, "Color His Skin Thick," *Philadelphia Daily News*, October 18, 1995, 73.

14. "Marion Motley," *Zanesville Times Recorder* (obituary), June 28, 1999, 5.

15. Chris Beaven, "Canton, Football Lose a True Hero," *Canton Repository*, June 28, 1999, A-6.

16. Beaven, A-6.

Bibliography

Except where otherwise noted, all football statistics come from Pro-Football-Reference.com. Baseball statistics from the Seamheads Negro Leagues Database are available at https://www.seamheads.com/NegroLgs/.

Interviews

Bloom, Bianca, online, October 26, 2020.
Dose, Joe, online, November 19, 2020.
Kennedy, Aldreeta, telephone, August 8, 2021.
Leuthner, Stuart, telephone, July 15, 2021.
Washington, Candice, telephone, May 7, 2021.

Archival Sources

Census of U.S., 1910. Washington: U.S. G.P.O., 1910.
"DSS Form 1" (U.S. Military Draft Registration), Digital image. Accessed June 20, 2021.
Haynes, George. "The Migration of Negroes Into Northern Cities." Proceedings of 44th Meeting of the National Conference on Social Welfare, Pittsburgh, PA, 1917.

Books

Brown, Jim, and Myron Cope. *Off My Chest.* Garden City, NY: Doubleday, 1964.
Brown, Jim, and Steve Delsohn. *Out of Bounds.* New York: Citadel 2018.
Brown, Paul, and Jack T. Clary. *PB: The Paul Brown Story.* New York: Atheneum, 1980.
Cantor, George. *Paul Brown: The Man Who Invented Modern Football.* Chicago: Triumph, 2008.
Classen, Harold. *The History of Professional Football.* New York: Prentice-Hall, 1963.
Cope, Myron. *The Game That Was: The Early Days of Pro Football.* New York: World, 1970.
Crippen, Kenneth R., and Matt Reaser. *The All-America Football Conference: Players, Coaches, Records, Games and Awards, 1946–1949.* Jefferson, NC: McFarland, 2018.
Essington, Amy. *The Integration of the Pacific Coast League: Race and Baseball on the West Coast.* Lincoln: University of Nebraska Press, 2018.

Graham, Otto. *Otto Graham: T Quarterback*. New York: Prentice Hall, 1953.
Grier, Rosey, and Dennis Baker. *Rosey—the Gentle Giant*. Tulsa: Honor, 1986.
Hofstadter, Richard. *The Progressive Historians: Turner, Beard, Parrington*. New York: Alfred A. Knopf, 1968.
Leahy, Frank. *Notre Dame Football: The T Formation*. New York: Prentice Hall, 1950.
Leuthner, Stuart. *Iron Men: Bucko, Crazylegs, and the Boys Recall the Golden Days of Professional Football*. New York: Doubleday, 1988.
Levy, Alan Howard. *Tackling Jim Crow: Racial Segregation in Professional Football*. Jefferson, NC: McFarland, 2003.
MacCambridge, Michael, and Dan Jenkins. *ESPN College Football Encyclopedia: The Complete History of the Game*. New York: ESPN, 2005.
Marsh, Irving T., and Roger Kahn. *Thirty Years of Best Sports Stories*. New York: Dutton, 1975.
Peterson, Robert W. *Pigskin: The Early Years of Pro Football*. New York: Oxford University Press, 1998.
Piascik, Andy. *Best Show in Football: The 1946–1955 Cleveland Browns, Pro Football's Greatest Dynasty*. Lanham, MD: Taylor Trade, 2010.
Pluto, Terry. *When All the World Was Browns Town: Cleveland's Browns and the Championship Season of 64*. New York: Simon & Schuster, 1997.
Sulecki, James C. *The Cleveland Rams: The NFL Champs Who Left Too Soon, 1936–1945*. Jefferson, NC: McFarland, 2016.

Articles

Dayen, David. "How Teddy Roosevelt Saved Football." *Politico Magazine*, September 20, 2014 .https://www.politico.com/magazine/story/2014/09/teddy-roosevelt-saved-football-111146/, accessed July 26, 2021.
Einstein, Charles. "When Football Went to War." *Sports Illustrated*, December 6, 1971. https://vault.si.com/vault/1971/12/06/when-football-went-to-war, accessed December 18, 2020.
Furlong, Bill. "A Negro Ballplayer's Life Today." *Sport Magazine*, May 1962.
Green, Michael. "The Mississippi of the West." *Nevada Law Journal*, 1st ser., 5, no. 57 (2004): 71.
Grosshandler, Stan. "All-America Football Conference" *Coffin Corner* 2, no. 7 (1980): 1–13.
Hawthorn, Tom. "Jimmy Claxton." SABR Biography Project, https://sabr.org/bioproj/person/jimmy-claxton/, accessed June 25, 2021.
"History of the Rivalry." MassillonTigers.com, May 28, 2021. https://massillontigers.com/history/massillon-vs-canton-mckinley/history-of-the-rivalry/#:~:text=No, accessed June 24, 2021.
Kable, F.T. "Coach of the Year." *Pro Football Illustrated*, 1948, 18.
_____. "Editorial." *Pro Football Illustrated*. Morris, IL: Elbak, 1947.
"Legacy of the Greats: How the Wolf Pack Teams of the 1940s Beat Jim Crow." University of Nevada, Reno. https://www.unr.edu/nevada-today/news/2018/legacy-of-the-greats, accessed June 26, 2021.
Melody, Tom. "Motley Could Do It All." *Pro Football Digest*, November 1968.
"100 Best HBCU Football Players of All Time." HBCU Buzz, November 23, 2019, hbcu-buzz.com/2019/11/100-best-hbcu-football-players-of-all-time/.
"1,254 Football Games History, 1894–2021 'Through the Years'—1930–1939." CantonMcKinley.com, https://www.cantonmckinley.com/just-the-facts/jtf-football/163-football-season-results-1894-2019?start=5.
"Onward, 1943." *Street and Smith's Football Pictorial Year Book*, 1943.
Schwartz, Larry. "'Automatic Otto' Defined Versatility." ESPN.com, https://web.archive.

Bibliography

org/web/20120523153641/http:/espn.go.com/sportscentury/features/00014210. html, accessed June 26, 2021.

Scott, Jack. "1945 Great Lakes: The Best for Last." *College Football Historical Society Newsletter* 13, no. 1 (November 1999): 5–8. https://digital.la84.org/digital/collection/p17103coll10/id/8246, accessed June 26, 2021.

Smith, Michael G. "The Aerial Game: How Football and Aviation Grew Up Together." *Air and Space Magazine,* February 2, 2018. https://www.airspacemag.com/daily-planet/aerial-game-how-football-and-aviation-grew-together-180968029/, accessed December 18, 2020.

Stein, Leland, III. "Legendary Marion Motley: Football Jackie Robinson." *Black Voice News,* February 6, 1997, B1-B2.

Stilwell, Bob. "How the Great Depression and World War II Affected Ohio." ParmaObserver.com, January 5, 2017. http://parmaobserver.com/read/2017/01/05/how-the-great-depression-and-world-war-ii-affected-ohio, accessed June 24, 2021.

Welper, Brenden. "Like 2020, College Football Was Very Different During World War II." NCAA.com, October 7, 2020. https://www.ncaa.com/news/football/article/2020-09-21/2020-college-football-was-very-different-during-world-war-ii, accessed June 25, 2021.

Wolff, Alexander, and Woody Strode. "The NFL's Jackie Robinson." *Sports Illustrated,* October 12, 2009. https://vault.si.com/vault/2009/10/12/the-nfls-jackie-robinson, accessed May 12, 2021.

Zimmerman, Paul. "The Monster in My Memory." *Sports Illustrated,* July 5, 1999. https://vault..si.com/vault/1999/07/05/THE-MONSTER-IN-MY-MEMORY, accessed November 11, 2020.

Multimedia/Online

Jingo, Dave, dir. Timeless Rivals. Documentary. IMDb. N.p.: Timeless Rivals Film, LLC. https://www.imdb.com/title/tt8200472/plotsummary?ref_=tt_ov_pl, accessed June 24, 2021.

"1946 Browns Highlights." YouTube. Posted November 22, 2016. https://www.youtube.com/watch?v=bHbF_P3mLNg&t=5s, accessed June 26, 2021.

Newspapers

Akron Beacon Journal
Arizona Daily Star (Tucson)
Atlanta Constitution
Boston Globe
Canton Repository (Canton, OH)
Chicago Tribune
Chronicle-Telegram (Elyria, OH)
Cincinnati Enquirer
Cleveland Call and Post
Cleveland News
Cleveland Plain Dealer
Daily Herald (Provo, UT)
Daily Times (Philadelphia, OH)
Dayton Daily News
Dayton Herald
Detroit Free Press
Eugene Register-Guard (OR)

Evening Independent (Massillon, OH)
Honolulu Advertiser
Knoxville Journal (TN)
Knoxville News-Sentinel (TN)
Lima News (OH)
Massachusetts Independent
Nevada Appeal (NV)
Nevada State Journal (NV)
New York Daily News
Newark Advocate
News-Journal (Mansfield, OH)
News-Messenger (Fremont, OH)
Oakland Tribune
Philadelphia Daily News
Pittsburgh Courier
Press-Democrat (Santa Rosa, CA)
Reno Gazette-Journal

Bibliography

Sacramento Bee
Saint Louis Post-Dispatch
Salem News (OH)
San Francisco Chronicle
San Francisco Examiner
Spokesman Review (Spokane, WA)

Sporting News
Times and Democrat (Knoxville, TN)
Valdosta Daily Times (GA)
Washington Evening Star
Zanesville Times-Recorder (OH)

Index

INDEX

Index

Motley, Blanche (mother, née Jones) 10, 14, 16, 31
Motley, Candice (Washington, niece) 16, 31
Motley, Clarence (brother) 11, 16, 31, 171
Motley, Dorothy (sister) 11, 31, 171
Motley, Eula (wife, née Coleman) 38, 40, 43, 98, 112–114, 141, 150, 159, 169
Motley, John Henry (grandfather) 10
Motley, Phillip (son) 40, 43
Motley, Raymond (son) 40, 43, 171
Motley, Ronald (son) 40
Motley, Shakvol (father) 10, 14, 31, 158
Motley, William Countee (brother) 11
Municipal Stadium, Cleveland 94–95, 106, 122
Mutryn, Chet 123

narcolepsy, Motley's affliction with 84
National Basketball Association 70
National Basketball League 70
National Football League (NFL) 6, 58–59
Navy enlistment 51
Neal, Bob 137
Neale, Greasy 28, 130–132, 135
Nevers, Ernie 38
New York Giants 65
NFL All-Decade Team(s) 66
Nobori, Thomas 31
Nobori, Violet 32
Northwestern University 69
Novick, Peter: *That Noble Dream: The "Objectivity Question" and the American Historical Profession* 2
Nussbaumer, Bill 160

Oakland Oaks baseball team 35
Ohio High School Athletic Association (OHSAA) 20
Ohio State University 46–47, 49, 57, 64, 67
Orange Bowl 54
Owen, Steve 133
Owens, Jesse 162

Pacific Coast League 35
Paige, Satchel 105–106
Palmer, Derrell 149
Palmer House Stars (baseball) 36
Parker, Buddy 148
Parseghian, Ara 107, 121, 124
Payton, Walter 26, 173
Pennington, Art 179

Perry, Joe 107–108, 115, 122–123, 171
Peters, Gus 19
Plessy v. Ferguson (1896 U.S. Supreme Court decision) 13
Pollard, Fritz 7
Pollock's Cuban Stars (baseball) 35
Powell, Charlie 101–102
Pro Bowl 140, 146
Pro Football Historical Abstract 6
Professional Football Hall of Fame, Canton, Ohio 3, 65–66, 70, 75, 155, 159, 165–166, 176
Purdue University 54

Ratterman, George 55, 90
Reaser, Matt 118
Redskins (football team name) Boston/Washington 7
Reed, John 20
Reeves, Daniel 60, 73
Reno Larks (baseball) 36
Rice, Jerry 26
Rickey, Branch 63, 73, 89, 114, 177
Riggs, Bobby 164
Riley, Susan 164
Roberts, Gene 65
Robertson, Oscar 127
Robinson, Jackie 6, 11, 63, 72–73, 89, 98, 105, 113, 178
Robinson, John 29
Robustelli, Andy 145
Rockefeller, John D. 59
Rooney, Art 153
Roosevelt, Theodore, and saving college football 48
Rose Bowl 44
Ryan, Ellis 147
Rymkus, Lou 80, 87, 103, 106, 108

Saban, Lou 81, 104, 108, 124
St. Mary's college (California) 38
San Francisco 49ers 60, 77–78, 102, 106–108, 114–115, 122, 173
Sanborn, Marcella 164
Sanders, Orban "Spec" 92
screen pass 103
Sensabraugher, Dean 105
Shamrock Bowl (Houston) 122
Shaughnessy, Clark 48, 50
Shaw, Buck 122
Shula, Don 88, 110
Slater, Duke 7
Snead, Sylvester 37
South Carolina State College 24–27

Index